CONTRACTING YOUR SERVICES

CONTRACTING YOUR SERVICES

Robert L. Davidson, III

John Wiley & Sons, Inc.

New York • Chichester • Brisbane • Toronto • Singapore

Permission to reproduce materials in this book was granted by the following individuals/organizations: Figure 11–1 courtesy of Harry S. Dixon; Figure 11–2 courtesy of George J. Levosinski; Figure 11–3 courtesy of Bobby L. Newman, President, ACTA Investigations, Inc.; Figure 11–4 courtesy of Elizabeth Devine-Hall; Figure 11–5 courtesy of Douglas A. Stolk, Metallurgical Engineering Services, Inc.; Figure 11–6 courtesy of John H. Kelleher, President, Kelleher & Company; Figure 11–8 courtesy of John E. Hempstead, President, Hempstead & Co.; Figure 11–9 courtesy of Dr. Steven E. Lerner; Figure 11–11 courtesy of the Stelter Company.

Library of Congress Cataloging-in-Publication Data

Davidson, Robert L., III.
    Contracting Your Services
  by Robert L. Davidson, III.
      p.   cm.
    Includes bibliographical references (p.   ).
    ISBN 0-471-50694-X
    1. Independent contractors. 2. Self-employed. 3. New business enterprises—Management.   I. Title.
    HD2365.D38   1990
    658'.041—dc20   89-28507
                                                        CIP

Printed in the United States of America

90 91 10 9 8 7 6 5 4 3 2 1

Contents

PART II
Planning Ahead for Success
17

PART IV
What You Need to Know about Law
and Contracts
145

PART V
Putting It Together and Making It Work
199

Preface

Have you ever wanted to be your own boss? Have you ever dreamed of running your own business? Maybe you can. Thousands of professional men and women do it as independent contractors. I have been doing it successfully for a decade, and many of my friends are independent contractors.

What is an independent contractor? It is a person or firm providing a service under contract, rather than as an employee. Doctors, dentists, and lawyers are usually independent contractors, as are real estate brokers and insurance agents. Consultants can be independent contractors; also computer programmers, certified public accountants, accountants and auditors, engineers of all types, financial advisors and planners, builders, artists, writers, and editors. Advertising and public relations agencies normally operate as independent contractors. There is virtually no limit to the professional skills that can be provided under contract as services by independent contractors.

How does one get started as an independent contractor? The rules are simple. You will need:

- The skill and experience to provide a needed service
- Sensible business, financial, and marketing plans
- The self-discipline and determination to make it work

Consider what you do now as an employee. Instead of doing it for wages, provide it as a service under contract. Instead of doing it for one company or person only, offer your service under contract to many companies or persons. Become a businessperson; become an independent contractor.

This book will show you how to create viable business, financial, and marketing plans, but it is you who must provide a marketable service and the stubborn determination to succeed. Analyze yourself, your personal characteristics, your goals, your motivations. If you are a self-starter, if you get along with people, if you have determination and can face, survive, and overcome obstacles, and if you have an important and marketable service to provide, then you are a prime candidate to be an independent contractor.

Robert L. Davidson, III

PART I

Do You Really Want to Be an Independent Contractor?

CHAPTER 1

What (Who) Is an Independent Contractor?

What Is Independent Contracting?

Independent contracting is a personal or business service to an individual or firm provided by another individual or firm for pay under contract. The services provided may be legal, medical, architectural, in real estate, design, construction, accounting/auditing, engineering, advertising, public relations, writing/editing, or any other area.

The independent contractor must be free to offer services on the open market, not just to one person or firm. And the independent contractor must not be *controlled* in the manner in which the work is accomplished. The legal and tax aspects of holding your status as an independent contractor are discussed in Chapter 15.

Who Can Be an Independent Contractor?

Anyone who has the experience and training or ability to provide a service for which others will pay can be an independent contractor. You can provide that service as a company or as an individual.

To be independent, you cannot provide your service as an employee. You can, however, own and operate an independent contractor firm that provides services to others under contract. Your firm then will be an

3

independent contractor. Your employees, if you have any, will provide services to your clients or customers under your direction as your employees, not as independent contractors.

What Do Independent Contractors Do?

A number of professional areas can be the basis for independent contractor services, so do not let yourself be limited by the following listing. Put your own imagination and creativity to work.

Independent contracting can be limited to the giving of advice, as for management or finance. Or it can go a step further and provide design services, as for architects or computer programmers. The next step for independent contracting is to provide installation or erection services, as in construction or manufacturing. While it may be necessary to create, form, or shape physical items for installation or erection, the independent contractor is not a manufacturer of products for mass or retail distribution.

When you do select the service you intend to offer as an independent contractor, do not try to be all things to all persons, at least not in the beginning. Specialize in what you offer so that you can be very good at it and earn a favorable word-of-mouth reputation for the quality of your services. Target the geographical area you will serve. Limit your service offerings to identifiable customer groupings, such as individuals, small-, medium-, or large-sized companies, partnerships, proprietorships, or local or area governmental or educational bodies and agencies.

Select a service that is compatible with your interests, abilities, and financial resources. Consider where you will do the work, what equipment or supplies you will need, what services you will need.

Accountancy

Accountant services can be as simple as keeping daily ledgers for client customers or as complex as financial advice and planning. Consider preparation of tax returns for firms, partnerships, and individuals; preparation of business plans for new business start-ups; handling of payroll tax and tax-shelter records; estate planning; auditing; financial management consulting; computerizing accounting systems; analyzing tax and profit/loss implications of purchases and sales; venture capital evaluation and consultation; fraud detection; Internal Revenue Service representation; managing employee pension, profit sharing, bonus, Employee Stock Ownership Plan, and other benefit plans.

Advertising

Advertising services cover a broad range. Consider the design, preparation, and distribution or placement of advertising messages via space advertisements in publications, time messages on radio or television, brochures, mailing pieces, annual reports, trade-show exhibits, slide and video programs, logo design and corporate image programs, outdoor advertising, sales promotion packages, package design, business-form design, business signs, direct-mail list building and maintenance, bulk-mail preparation, posters and point-of-sale displays, advertising premiums and awards, fund-raising programs, company safety programs, bumper stickers.

Architecture

This is an excellent field for the independent contractor. If you now are employed by a general services architectural firm and you are developing a specialty and your employer's business does not take full advantage of this specialty, you can consider becoming an independent contractor to offer your personal services under contract back to your old firm, as well as to other firms. Consider, for example, solar-design residences, interior design, office layout and design, structures rehabilitation, space planning, retail shop design and layout, single-structure residence planning, yard and landscape planning, model making, kitchen remodeling.

Art Services

There is more to art than fine art or the creation of so-called commercial art. Business art is an independent contracting opportunity for the professional artist. Consider interior decorating for homes, business offices, and public areas, such as restaurants, retail shops, convention halls, motels and hotels; design of company logos, stationery, and business signs; design of advertisements, brochures, sales packages, direct mail packages, point-of-sale displays, outdoor advertising; slide presentations for meetings, sales calls, conventions; design of annual reports; typography and cover designs for books; cartoons; product packaging; graphic designs.

Engineering

Virtually any area of engineering specialization can be the basis for an independent contractor service. Consider the engineering, design, and installation aspects of acoustics; air cleaning and purification; heating, ventilation, refrigeration, and air-conditioning; energy conservation; humidity and air-quality controls; water treatment; solar energy; air-pollution control; appliance repair; drafting and blueprints; safety programs; fire and burglar alarm and protection systems; sound and public address systems; automation; laboratory and pilot-plant design; instrument calibration; chemical cleaning; industrial wastes treatment; communications systems; computer systems, training, and programming; building and construction; environmental and ecology protection; nondestructive inspection; cost control; data processing; business and industrial lighting; hazardous and toxic waste treatment and management; machinery design; process automation and controls.

Legal and Law

A licensed attorney can work for a company or in a law firm and can practice general law or specialize. Activities for which a legal background can be the building block for an independent contractor business also include arbitration and mediation; labor relations; patent searches, drafting, applications, and defense.

Personal/Personnel Services

There are many opportunities for professionals with training and experience in working with people. Included are psychologists, psychiatrists, clinical psychologists and psychology majors, and human resources specialists. Many smaller firms unable to afford full-time staffing for personal/personnel services are candidates for independent contractor services. Consider hiring and reference checking, firing and outplacement, company morale and training programs, alcoholism and drug-abuse rehabilitation, learning disabilities, lie detection, marriage and family counseling, nursing care, occupational therapy, career counseling, phobia treatment, sex and pregnancy counseling, self-defense instruction, speech and hearing therapy, teaching (all types).

Scientific Services

Testing and analytical services, both industrial and medical, are lucrative areas of activity for the "independent" laboratory providing contract services. Consider chemical analysis of air and water pollutants, radon detection and remedy, analysis of hazardous and toxic materials, X-ray and ultrasonic testing, identification of allergy-causing materials, such special medical tests as those for blood sugar and cholesterol, instrument calibration.

Writing/Editing Services

Professional writers and editors with experience in newspaper, news-letter, magazine, book, or advertising and public relations firms have many opportunities to offer their services as independent contractors. Consider nonpublishers with occasional or important needs for quality writing and editing for internal and external newsletters, advertising and public relations copy, special reports, project proposals, meeting papers, executive speeches, sales presentations; resumé writing; copy editing and proofreading.

Don't stop with this list. Develop your own. Look around you at work and at play. What services are offered by others? What services are needed but unsatisfied? Compare these observations with your own background and resources. Somewhere there is the exactly right service opportunity that can convert you into an independent contractor.

CHAPTER 2

Life as an Independent Contractor

Isaac E. was in a panic. He was to retire from his job as a computer programmer in six months. Reviewing his pension benefits, he realized that he and his wife would have to sacrifice the house that had been their home for the past 27 years.

George S., a direct-mail marketing specialist, fell victim to company consolidation and the erasure of his department at a major publishing house. With longevity pay, he would receive his salary for another six months, then nothing. He was too young to qualify for pension payments.

What did Isaac and George have in common? They were the fortunate ones. Both had spent many productive years learning and practicing marketable professional specializations. Both were prime candidates to become independent contractors.

Why Make the Move?

As an independent contractor, you will be a businessperson. At the start, your service will be a small business. You will have total personal authority over the way your business operates. You will gain the profits, you will enjoy the successes. But you will also have total personal responsibility and, unless you seek legal advice, you may have total personal financial liability. You will suffer the losses, and you will agonize over the defeats.

8

So, why would anyone wish to leave the nest? Why leave the security of a regular paycheck and scheduled work hours? There are many reasons, varying widely from person to person. Which of the following fit you?

- ☐ Desire for independence
- ☐ Desire to do the work you like
- ☐ Freedom to plan and grow
- ☐ Chance to bring out latent skills and powers
- ☐ Desire for recognition
- ☐ Boredom or frustration on the job
- ☐ Lack of opportunity for advancement
- ☐ Insufficient income

Or, job security may be the most important issue. Is your job at risk because of a business downturn, loss of competitiveness by your firm, merger or acquisition and consolidation, or the facility's move to another part of the country? Are you about to retire or be laid off or fired? Is there a shortage of jobs in your area, or are the jobs that are available not the right kind?

Which are the right reasons to start your own independent contractor business? Any, or all, or none. Only you can determine how strongly you feel, how important it is to you to own and manage your own show. If your desires for independence and personal control are lukewarm, or the idea of being on your own is frightening, life as an independent contractor may be wrong for you.

What Will You Gain?

If you choose a business that is good for you and for which you are good, you will have a new feeling of satisfaction and accomplishment. Life will be richer, more satisfying. You will wonder why you waited so long.

You can make your own working conditions. You can do the work you know and like in the way you prefer. You can see and act on challenges and opportunities. You can work without bureaucratic red tape, memorandums, committee meetings, reports, and other nonproductive interruptions. And you can work from your home, your garage, or a nearby office or shop, and in virtually any town or state you wish.

Is There a Downside?

Do not expect to gain your business independence without paying a price. Consider that you will have no one to make excuses to. There will be no more paid vacations or holidays. No one will be there to set your schedules or priorities.

Consider also the demands you must face when running your own business. Most likely, you will find yourself working from dawn to dusk, as well as weekends and holidays, at least at the beginning. Without a staff and secretary, there will be mountains of day-to-day details and decisions you must handle.

Your income will be irregular, feast or famine. You must deal on one hand with unreliable suppliers and fickle customers, and on the other hand with family, financial, and leisure-time frustrations. In short, you must be everything to everybody, at work and at home.

Skills You Will Need

If your business is to succeed, and you are not to flounder then founder under seemingly never-ending stress, you will have to develop skills that the professional person seldom needs when working on the company team. In addition to actually providing the services for which you are to be paid, you will be responsible for all of the supporting administrative business needs, such as:

- Cost and tax accounting
- Financial management
- Marketing and sales
- Contract negotiation
- Purchasing and expediting
- Personnel relations
- Customer relations and records
- Correspondence, filing, and telephoning

What Are You Looking For?

If you are still in doubt, here is an exercise that can help. Ask yourself the following questions, then write down your answers. You will be surprised to see what you will reveal to yourself when you study your answers.

1. How does an entrepreneur think? Do I think like one?
2. What are my income goals? Are they reasonable?
3. What am I good at that people will pay for?
4. What are my special skills and experiences?
5. What are my strengths? What are my weaknesses?
6. What is unique about the service I will offer?

7. Am I self-disciplined? Am I a self-starter?
8. Am I ready to work hard for long hours?
9. What are my start-up financial resources?
10. Do I have family support?
11. Do I have good health and a high energy level?
12. Can I sell myself and my ideas to others?
13. What business skills will I need? Which do I have now?

CHAPTER 3

Is Independent Contracting Right for You?

Roger S. was voted "Boy Most Likely to Succeed" in his senior year of high school. He then earned a degree in chemical engineering and was honored by membership in Tau Beta Pi, the engineers' Phi Beta Kappa. In his senior year at college, he was president of the Engineers Club. After graduation, he was hired by a major chemical company as a shift-work engineer for new process development. It was not long before his sunny disposition and superior ability to get along with people earned him a transfer to the firm's customer-service department. He covered a large portion of Texas, Oklahoma, and New Mexico as a customer-service representative.

After five years on the road, Roger was bored. He chafed at the company imposed restrictions and the lack of upward mobility of a field job. At age 25, he was confident that he now had the experience and the knowledge to start his own business as a chemical-industry trouble-shooter. Business started with a boom, based on orders from many of the people he had contacted before as a customer-service representative. At the end of two years, Roger was bankrupt and looking desperately for a new job.

Why did Roger fail? He did not take the time to understand himself, his motivations, his strengths, and his weaknesses before he took the plunge. There was no question that he was knowledgeable, experienced, and personable. But his concept of management was erratic. At decision time, which is most of the time when one operates one's own business, he was overcome by waves of debilitating doubt. Delays followed by alibis alienated his customers. Simply stated, Roger was a stellar performer when his schedule was laid out for him by others, but he was uncomfortable and inadequate as a manager of himself.

Be Honest with Yourself

Before you walk away from a good job and a regular paycheck, be sure you are temperamentally and dispositionally suited to make a success as an entrepreneur. Get in touch with your inner self. Try the following test on yourself. As in the last chapter, put your answers in writing. As your words pour out, you will see yourself as never before.

Do I Work Well with Others?

Do you find it easy to work in a team atmosphere? Or are you a loner? Do you accept instruction, or do you try to take over leadership? Do your fellow workers like you? Resent you? Follow you?

One is never completely independent of others. If you prefer working alone, you may make a great research scientist or poet, but not a businessperson. As a self-employed entrepreneur, you must be able to work with others and work alone with equal ease. You must listen to and respect the desires of customers and clients, and you must take charge of how you do your work.

Am I a Good Listener?

Hearing and listening are not the same. You can hear people talking, but to comprehend the meaning of what they say, you must listen. The ability to listen meaningfully is essential to customer relations.

Most of us who have the physical ability to hear assume that we are good listeners. But most of us listen selectively. We hear what we want to hear, or we interpret what we hear in light of our own desires and biases. To succeed in listening, one must be aware of the true meanings and desires expressed by the other person. Such awareness is not always simple, particularly when you and the other person use the same words with meanings based on divergent experiences. It takes practice and patience.

Do I Have Initiative?

If you are to be boss of your own business operation, you must set your own standards and your own schedules. You must be your own Simon Legree with your very own cat-o'-nine-tails.

Initiative is often difficult to distinguish from other traits. What may be considered initiative by one person may be obnoxiousness or over-aggressiveness to another person. Taking initiative is not to assume carte blanche to do whatever one wishes. Rather, it is to take action when action is needed, while being willing to follow routine or take instructions. If you see something that needs to be done, or if there is a safety hazard in your work area, do you speak out with proper suggestions or warnings? Or do you wait for someone else to speak out? Do you generate opportunities and take positive action, or do you wait for opportunity to come to you?

Am I Resourceful?

You will not be alone when you start your new business. You will have the partner we all have, Murphy. Whatever can go wrong will go wrong. When it does, how resourceful are you?

If you deal with outdoor construction, rain or snow will delay you. If you need special materials for a job, there will be a truckers' strike or a warehouse will burn down. If you are putting in a foundation, you will suddenly hit solid rock. If you are developing a new computer program, there will be a power outage. When disaster strikes, how do you react? Do you wait for a normal resolution to the problem, or do you search for alternative approaches?

Am I an Energetic Person?

You can learn to work with others, you can learn to listen, and you can develop the mental attitude needed for initiative and resourcefulness. But you cannot invent an energy level you do not have. Or can you?

True, your potential for energy is genetic. The question is, do you perform to the maximum of your genetic potential, and is this enough to handle the burdens of an entrepreneurial enterprise? If you answer is negative, do not despair—not yet. It is truly amazing how excitement or incentive can pump energy into our bodies. And it is truly depressing how boredom and despair can rob our bodies of energy. Judge your energy level at those times you are doing something that excites you. Plan your new business. See if excitement surges through you.

Am I Perseverant?

Once you start a project, do you stick with it? Do you persevere to the end? Do you have the common sense to know when further effort is of no avail, then move on to the next challenge?

If you begin projects eagerly, but despair quickly, this may be a signal that you lack the determination needed for self-employment. On the other hand, it may mean that you do not exercise good judgment in your selection of projects. Success in life requires a streak of stubbornness, a will to survive and succeed. The more you must rely on yourself, the broader this streak of stubbornness must be. But do not be ridiculous and, as the saying goes, "flog a dead horse."

Am I a Good Organizer?

Business requires the ability to organize. The more complicated the business, the greater the necessity for procedures and organization. One must recognize the orderly sequence and interrelation of activities.

How well can you juggle details and schedules for overlapping activities? Do you plan ahead so that services or materials that will be needed next week are arranged for this week? Or do you wait until the need arises to react? If you are putting in forms for a foundation, have you already made arrangements for the delivery of ready-mix cement? If you have a dozen deadlines coming in a short period of time, have you established priorities to accommodate them all? If summertime is a slow season for your business, have you established a bank credit line well in advance to tide you over until the fall when business will pick up?

How Well Did You Do?

Read and reread you answers. How do you feel about yourself now? Where do you feel the need for improvement? Where do you feel that you already have the requisite strengths?

But do not stop there. We all harbor some degree of delusion about ourselves. Seldom do we see ourselves as others see us. The indecisive person argues the need for caution. The rash person argues the need for action. And so on.

Take these questions to someone who knows you, but is not emotionally involved with you. Ask them to rate you on the same points. Where the two of you disagree, analyze the reasons for the differences. Discuss them with the other person. Find out why their perception differs from yours. You will learn much about yourself from this exercise.

PART II

Planning Ahead for Success

CHAPTER 4

What to Do Ahead of Time

Never Burn a Bridge

Someday you may need to cross that bridge again. You may dream of telling off your stupid boss as you toss your letter of resignation into his or her face. Do not do it. You will have made an enemy. It is far better to keep that person as a friend, or at least neutral. You may need your former boss to say kind words for you, to recommend you to future customers, to confirm your skills and experience. Better yet, your former boss may become your future customer. Here are suggestions to keep in mind as you make the transition from employee to independent contractor:

- Lean over backward to be fair to your employer.
- Do not steal business time being paid for by your employer to develop your own business.
- Give your employer reasonable (more than the minimum two weeks) notice.
- Do not leave your employer in the lurch, even if it means staying on the job a while longer.
- If you can, help your employer find your replacement. That way you will have another friend.

It Is Decision Time

There are a number of important decisions and plans you can make and actions you can take while you can still rely on a regular paycheck, things you can and should do before you actually commit yourself to a life as an independent contractor entrepreneur. By making these decisions and plans in advance, not only will you create a sound basis for your future business operations, but you will have a chance to carefully consider what will be involved and if such involvement is to your liking. Here are some of the advance considerations:

- Your business name
- Your business plan (see Chapter 8)
- Your marketing plan (see Chapter 7)
- Your business form (see Chapter 5)
- Your financial backing (see Chapter 6)
- Your working facilities
- Your office furniture
- Your office equipment
- Your professional equipment
- Your office supplies
- Your business associates

Your Business Name

The name that you select for your business may be one of your most important business planning decisions. It is the name of your service that will identify it to the world. If the name you select does not work for you, it is working against you.

Following are things to keep in mind as you decide how your service is to be identified.

The name should stand out. Pick a name that people will notice and remember. Many people use their own names, such as James Jones & Associates, or Roger Smith, Computer Programming. Jones and Smith are perfectly acceptable names, but they hardly stand out in a crowd of names, nor do they glue themselves onto the memories of potential customers.

Attention through a play on words. An excellent example of a name that both indicates the type of service and sticks in the memory is that used by the Roto-Rooter national franchise. If you were to establish a similar service, you might want to call it Sewercide to identify the area served and to stick in the memory.

Avoid the grandiose. Too often, small businesses dress up with fancy, fanciful names. Note the simplicity of names for some of our largest corporations: General Motors, Ford Motor, Chrysler Motors, AT&T, FMC, AMF, Coca-Cola, Xerox. Resist the temptation to append the word "International" onto your business name unless your operation is truly international in scope and operation.

Identify your activity. Since your own name may never appear on the cover of *Time Magazine* or reach the status of a household word, you may wish to identify your service in the name you select. Service identification stands out in your advertising, promotion, and listing in the telephone company yellow pages.

Assume that you offer computer programming services for business users of microcomputers. Roger Smith, Computer Programming, would be an example of a service identification name—as would PC-Programmers, or DeskTop Programmers.

Do not worry about a narrow identity. Many newcomers to the business world worry that too narrow or too specific a name will limit future expansion and diversification of services. They select some vague name, such as Service Enterprises. This can be a mistake for a newly launched independent contractor business with a service that is aimed at a specific niche. One wants to be identified with that niche.

Too narrow a niche identity is something you can worry about when your operation suddenly blossoms into a megamillion-dollar giant. Here are three examples of very large firms that shed their narrow names when their activities broadened greatly or changed character: AMF Corporation was previously known as American Machinery & Foundry; FMC Corporation was previously known as Food Machinery Corporation; 3M Company was previously known as Minnesota Mining & Minerals Company.

Avoid naming no-nos. There are few set rules for naming your business. A profanity or vulgarity will be prohibited, as will a name that either duplicates or is similar to a name already registered in your state. Unfortunately, there is no national registration of company names, frequently resulting in several firms, each in a different state, with the same or similar name.

If a name is the same as or very similar to an existing business name, court action, not statutory law, may prevent its use because of the danger

of confusing the source. You might, for example, be able to use the name
Cadillac for a toothpaste, but you can be sure that General Motors will
not sit still if you are making an automobile named Cadillac.

Register your name. Once you have selected a name for your service,
you must register it according to the laws of your county and state. In
many jurisdictions, an unincorporated name is registered with the
county clerk as a DBA (Doing Business As) if you use your own name, or
with a "Fictitious Name Statement" if you chose a name that is not your
own. You may also be required to advertise the fact that you are going
into business, and you may be required to renew your business name
registration periodically to keep it active.

Your lawyer can help you register and protect your business name,
regardless of the legal form you choose for your business. See Chapter 14
for how to select a lawyer. If you decide to incorporate, your lawyer may
ask you to submit several names, in order of preference. If the first name
is not available, you can go to the second, or third. Your lawyer can then
reserve this name for you during the period of time required to complete
the papers of incorporation.

Your Working Facilities

Where will you work, or work out of, as an independent contractor? Your
home? Your basement or garage? Rental space? Two factors will help you
in this decision: cost and suitability. Your facilities must, of course, meet
your present needs. Ideally, present facilities should accommodate your
need to expand as your business grows, but this may have to wait.

Your basic needs will be working space, office space, storage space,
bathroom facilities, and a place to park your car. In most cases, "image"
quarters, while great for the ego, can wait for future prosperity. If your
service does not require extensive equipment or storage room for supplies and materials, you may wish to work out of your home. Otherwise,
the search for quarters is on.

Following are the basic decisions you must make when deciding on a
home for your business:

- How much space will I need for office, work, and storage?
- Will I have special utility or service needs?
- How important is location, and why?
- How important is image, and why?
- Should I work at home, buy, or lease?
- Will I need room for expansion?
- How much can I afford?

How much space? If you are a writer, a room for a desk, a chair, and a couple of file cabinets may suffice. If you are rebuilding electric motors, you will need a workshop area, storage area, work-in-progress and back-logged projects area, room for tools and supplies, loading/unloading facilities, parking space, and an office area for bookkeeping, correspondence, phone calls, and miscellaneous reports and paper work.

Make a list of every activity that will be involved in your service, and designate required space for each. Make a sketch to scale showing the necessary space elements. Do not forget meetings and conferences with customers. If in doubt, visit other service firms to see how they allocate space.

Accommodate special needs. Special types of activity may limit your search for facilities. If you work with explosives, flammable chemicals, or toxic materials, you will need special facilities that meet requirements of the law. If you provide machine-shop services, you will need to locate in an area where noise is permitted. Consider the following:

- □ *Parking.* Space for prospects, customers, suppliers, staff, and yourself.
- □ *Outside storage.* Space to store equipment and large items, both mobile and stationary.
- □ *Internal storage.* Space with provisions for stacks, shelves, and bins; ventilation, temperature, and humidity control, if needed.
- □ *Delivery provisions.* Roadway, driveway, railroad spur; other means to receive or deliver goods and materials.
- □ *Utility needs.* Availability of needed amounts of electrical power, water, sewage disposal, private-line telephone; other special services essential to your work.
- □ *Legal occupancy.* Certificate of occupancy for the structure and zoning permission for the area that will allow your type of operation to take place.

How important is location? Will you rely on walk-in/walk-out business, or will you carry your services to your customers' facilities? Walk-in/walk-out business is more typical of a retail store than of a service, with exceptions such as tailoring and radio-television repairs. If you do need walk-in/walk-out customers, the worst mistake you can make is to locate on some seldom-traveled side street or on a remote country road merely to save money. Be sure there is steady pedestrian traffic and parking space for your customers.

If walk-in/walk-out business is not important for the service you offer, you will have greater flexibility of choice. You would be foolish to pay a high shopping-mall rental when a side street or country road would serve you just as well. Keep in mind that you must be able to reach your facility in all kinds of weather, you must be able to receive and deliver items, you must have all needed utilities available, and, as your business prospers, you must provide convenient accessibility for full- and part-time staff.

How important is image? Answer: Image is always important (see Chapters 7, 10, 11, and 12). If your service is mechanical, a machine-shop image would be appropriate. If you are a computer programmer, you had better be ready to display at least two types of computers and a laser printer. If you are an interior decorator, the decor of your office and waiting area must favorably mirror the quality and taste of your service.

While you may not encourage visits from your customers, you must always be prepared for the sudden appearance of a key customer. If the image produced by your facility is severely discordant with what you have projected for your service, you may be in trouble. You would not locate a pail of lubricating grease in the reception area of an advertising agency specializing in cosmetics.

Home? Buy or lease? Some communities allow dual residential-commercial activities. In others, you will be limited to the type of business allowed. If you live in Houston, Texas, however, there are absolutely no zoning regulations. In Chicago, it is illegal to use the home as a primary business location.

Home businesses are illegal in Los Angeles, but this may change soon. Wichita, Kansas, allows one to make and sell arts and crafts in home businesses, but it is illegal to manufacture or process anything, or to conduct a business in a garage or display a business sign. In other words, check with your local authorities before planning to run a business out of your home. If you still have questions, ask your attorney to check it out for you.

If it is impractical to have your business in your home, then you must consider buying or leasing facilities. If you lease, you do not encumber yourself with debt, but neither do you build an equity. Which is better for the start of your business? There are advantages either way. Let your financial advisor assist you in this decision.

If you lease, your start-up expenses are lower than if you buy. Your banker will appreciate your caution and your desire to shepherd your limited finances at the beginning of your business venture. But beware of long-term leases that hold you financially responsible, or short-term leases whereby you can be evicted on short notice. If you lease, your lease payments are tax deductible, but you cannot take a deduction for depreciation, and you cannot use leased property as collateral for a loan. It may be more difficult to modify or rearrange a leased facility than one you own.

The financial benefits of leasing are felt most in the early stages of business start-up. Often at the five-year mark, however, the lease option and the purchase option have about the same benefit. A certified public accountant (CPA) can show you how to calculate the arrival of the equal-benefit time.

There are variations to the lease-or-buy scenario. In a lease-purchase arrangement, lease payments apply in part toward eventual purchase of the property. Some cities have space- or time-sharing of office facilities. Other cities have office buildings that rent space in combination with secretarial services, reception areas and receptionists, telephone answering, conference rooms, libraries, computer networks, and more.

Allow the opportunity for expansion. As you prosper, there is the risk of outgrowing the facilities that met your space needs satisfactorily at the time you launched your business. What then? What if you are tied down by a long-term lease? Much of the answer depends on how well you planned at the start.

If you chose a storefront in a row of storefronts, you may be squeezed in a vise. If, however, you leased from a person or firm with a number of commercial properties, you may request a space upgrading provision in your lease contract.

If you lease an office in a building of offices, you may face the same squeeze problem. In this case, however, there is greater opportunity for availability of adjacent office space, or greater space on another floor. Be sure that your lease gives you a first-refusal agreement with the leasing agent, or some other space-upgrade provision.

If you lease in a stand-alone structure with unused adjacent land, your landlord may agree to expand your facilities. It will not be free. The owner will want to amortize the investment over the allowable period of time, meanwhile earning a respectable return on the money invested in the expansion. Some basis of agreement in advance in your lease contract is desirable.

What can you afford? A hard question? Yes. Do not expect to answer yet. First, you must complete your Business Plan (Chapter 8). In it your budget will have an allowance for facilities. Then you must make arrangements for start-up funds (Chapter 6). If what you need, what you plan to spend, and what financial support you can arrange mesh, you have your answer. If not, you will need to reassess your needs to lower the cost.

Your Office Furniture

Space is fine, but not empty space. The furnishings you will need will be related to the way you intend to do business. Will you meet with your prospects and customers at your office? Or will your office be strictly a place for administrative chores, such as answering the phone, making calls, handling correspondence, and bookkeeping?

It would be foolish to squander your money on fancy new office furniture at the launch of your business. See what you have at home that you can use. Check with relatives and friends. What they cannot lend to you, look for in garage or lawn sales. Keep your eye on the local classified advertisements for items on sale. There are many reasons people sell used furniture in public garage/lawn sales or classified ads. They may be moving. They may have bought new furniture and do not want to throw or give the old furniture away. The furniture may require repairs with which they do not want to bother. Regardless of the reason, there are bargains to be found.

Presidential desk and chair. This is for you, the founder, CEO, COO, and more of your service. If you are short of start-up money, and plan to be out of the office providing your service to customers most of the time, you may wish to let this desk and chair serve triple duty: executive, secretarial, and receptionist.

Conference/work table and chairs. Will you hold planning and negotiation sessions at your office? If so, you will need a large table and seating for participants. The table can be an old dining room table; the chairs can be easily storable folding types.

Secretarial desk and chair. Will you have a secretary? Most likely not at first, although a friend or family member may support you by serving as a part-time secretary—but only if they have a place to sit and work.

Receptionist's desk and chair. This may be an unnecessary luxury in the early days of your business. But sooner or later you may need to have someone to meet and greet business visitors, particularly at those times when you are away from the office providing your service.

Shelving. Every office needs shelving on which items and supplies can be stored. New shelving is very expensive, as is raw wood. But used shelving can be quite a bargain, particularly if it needs refinishing or there are minor defects and scars on its visible surfaces.

Your Office Equipment

There are even more good bargains in used equipment than in furniture. Unlike furniture, items such as typewriters, computers, telephone systems, and copy machines are outdated by fast-moving technology and the introduction of new models. Here are items to consider when you are making plans for equipping your office:

Typewriter. At the very least, you will need a typewriter, preferably electric. While there are some very fine electronic models now on the market, a good strictly mechanical electric IBM will work quite well.

Desktop computer. Every business can benefit from a computer. The more you use it, the more uses you will find for it. It can serve multiple duty for correspondence, memos, reports, invoices, purchase orders, and the like. With a mail-merge program and a database management program, you can keep a file of prospect's names and prepare personalized mass mailings with flexible form letters. You can create and update your budget and tax records with a spreadsheet program. With a modem, you can communicate with other computers via telephone. An important factor to remember when buying a computer, other than proof that it is in working order, is whether you can arrange for a maintenance contract for that particular computer.

File facilities. You will need a way to file and store records. Start with a four-drawer file cabinet sized for regular paper. Only attorneys need the extra-wide drawers designed for legal papers.

Telephone system. Start modestly with a single line and a simple phone from a discount store. Avoid the trap that caught Michelle W. She received a large advance payment from a customer, and invested $5,000 in a state-of-the-art computerized telephone-intercom-transcription system. The following week the customer cancelled the payment. Michelle had to return the system, now used, at a significant loss of money.

Copy machine. A copy machine is more necessity than luxury. Modern desk models are available at reasonable prices or rental terms. Be sure a maintenance contract is included. If you are adjacent to another office, you might work out a way to share a machine. Do not waste your valuable working time running across town to make photocopies.

Calculator. Regardless of who keeps your books, you will need a desk calculator. Small calculators with paper printout are available at very low costs.

Fan and/or air conditioner. If air-conditioning is not provided with your office quarters, it will be difficult to work during hot, humid summer days, with papers sticking to your arms and perspiration soiling your correspondence.

FAX. This is the age of the FAX. Do you need one? Yes, if a significant number of your customers use their FAX machines for communication. But you do not need to purchase a FAX. More and more FAX receiving/ transmitting services are coming into being at photocopy centers, stationery stores, and more.

Your Professional Equipment

You may already have the specialized equipment you need to provide your service, or it may have been your employer's equipment, and now you must start from ground zero. What you need will be so intimately connected with whatever your service is to be that it is impossible to anticipate everything in a simple list.

The suggestions for acquiring furniture and office equipment, however, also apply here. If you can find good used equipment, do so. If you can lease the equipment you need, you will reduce your initial dollar outlay. Check with dealers for trade-ins. Watch newspaper ads. Visit independent contractors providing your type of service in nearby cities. If you must settle for new equipment, consider leasing or a lease-purchase agreement.

Your Office Supplies

Paper is the lifeblood of modern-day business. Even in this age of computers, word processors, databases, and FAX machines, most communications are created, transmitted, received, or stored on paper as hard copy. As a business person, you will need your own paper-based supplies.

The design and printing of these materials should not be taken lightly. They will be visual images of your service, the only image many people may ever see. You can pay a layout artist to design the style and typography for your office supplies, but you will save a great deal of time and expense if you can find something in one of the sample books most local printers have on hand for business cards, stationery, envelopes, and such.

Business cards. Too many people are overly casual about business cards, until they meet a person with no business card to give in return for theirs. The business card reminds us of a person's name and often goes into a Rolodex file. In short, a business card identifies us, categorizes us, legitimizes us.

Letterhead stationery. Most printers have sample books showing letterhead options with various layouts, typography, and, if the mood strikes you, clever little bits of business (illustrations). Or you may have designed a business logo that you wish to use.

Envelopes. Your envelopes should match your stationery. If you have a business, it should be on your envelopes, too. Get several sizes of envelopes. A No. 10 is normally used for correspondence. Get No. 9 envelopes to enclose as return reply envelopes. For flat materials, you will want a supply of mailers to handle 8.5 × 11 and 9 × 12 inch materials.

Other forms. You will also need memo pads, invoice forms, receipt books, and purchase orders, all imprinted with the name, address, and logo of your firm.

Record-keeping books. You will need a journal book into which your daily transactions are entered, both income and expenditures. You will need several, up to six, ledger books into which you will transfer figures from your journal book (see Chapter 20 for record-keeping details).

Other supplies. You will need pens, pencils, erasers, white-out, computer paper, paper clips, rubber bands, cellophane tape, packaging tape, staples and stapler, and whatever else in the way of special drawing or graphing papers are needed for your service.

Your Business Associates

By associate, we mean anyone working with you under any type of arrangement, such as employee, independent contractor, service, or whatever. You may think that you can do everything by yourself, but this would be a major error. Who, for example, tends to your office needs when you are out providing your service? And when you are in the office, are you going to spend your time answering the phone, opening the mail, sealing envelopes and licking stamps, typing, delivering packages, and keeping the ledger books and journals up to date? You are? When, then, will you have time to work at your service?

If your business is a family affair, you may be able to rely on a family member to help you with the day-to-day office administration tasks. There are times, however, when you will need special assistance, as with contracts or tax accounting.

For business and tax records, there are trained persons who will provide a service to you at a nominal rate. Ask around. Talk to owners and managers of other small businesses. To handle incoming telephone calls when there is no one in the office, you can use an answering machine. But many people resent answering machines. An answering service with a live voice is better.

You will need financial advice regarding tax matters and basic business financial decisions, the sort that requires the background of a CPA (certified public accountant), not a mere bookkeeper. You will need legal advice for contracts, both those others present for you to sign, and those you present others to sign (see Chapter 14). You will need an insurance consultant to help you establish your insurance program (see Chapter 9).

Both the accountant and the lawyer can help you when your business grows to the extent that you must hire employees. There are state and federal laws you must observe, and there is always the Internal Revenue Service waiting to pounce. You will need help with the Fair Labor Standards Act, the Social Security Act, Federal Income Tax Legislation, Equal Pay Act, Workers Compensation, Unemployment Insurance, and more. As an employer, your life will become suddenly much more complicated.

CHAPTER 5

What Form for Your Business?

One of your earliest decisions is to select the form under which your business is to operate. You have three basic choices, each of which has its particular advantages and disadvantages.

1. Sole proprietorship
2. Partnership (general and limited)
3. Corporation (normal and Subchapter S)

The Sole Proprietorship

Harold A., a mechanical engineer, is a "can-do" person in a hurry to get started. After ten years employed in the maintenance department of a major manufacturing firm, he has decided to strike out on his own. In selecting the legal form for his business, his primary interests were direct control over his personal destiny and a minimum of required forms, record keeping, and reporting to local, state, and federal government agencies. Harold has chosen the sole proprietorship form of business as the fastest, easiest, and least costly way to get started in business.

He has selected a name, Trouble-Shooters Unlimited, registered it as a DBA with both county and state, and started prospecting for customers.

What he particularly likes about the sole proprietorship is that he does not have to share ownership or decision-making with anyone else. He is well aware that if his business expanded beyond his personal ability to handle the work, he could either hire employees or contract with others as independent contractors.

Proprietorship: Advantages and Disadvantages

Keeping tax records for a sole proprietorship is particularly simple. Harold A.'s allowable expenses of business are deducted from his recorded revenues. If there is a positive income, it is taxed to him as personal income; if there is a negative income, he takes a personal tax loss.

While Harold does not regret his decision, he and his wife are a touch nervous when seasonal cash flow sags and bills and debts bulge. Before he made his decision, Harold discussed his options with his attorney, who described in detail both the advantages and the disadvantages of the sole proprietorship. For instance:

1. When Harold dies, Trouble-Shooters Unlimited dies. Without the sole proprietor, either Harold or someone to whom he has sold his rights, the business becomes void. Where a corporation is considered impersonal and *immortal*, a sole proprietorship is quite personal and very *mortal*.

2. Harold's last will and testament must be very clear and specific. If Harold should die, his will must have clear provisions if his wife and children are to have clear title and unencumbered legal claims to the assets, accounts receivable, and potential revenues of Trouble-Shooters Unlimited.

3. Harold must bear all of the decision-making burden. Regardless of who works with him—friend, family member, or hired help—the sole proprietor is fully responsible for making or delegating all decisions bearing on bookkeeping, bill paying, debt collections, advertising, business development, contract negotiations and drafting, and more. In addition, he must provide or arrange for the services that are to be the source of his income.

4. There is nothing to limit Harold's business liability. True, he has insurance. But what if he is involved in a major calamity? What if he is on his way to see a customer, and he rams into the rear of a school bus? The liability could easily run into the millions of dollars, far more than the insurance coverage he can afford. He must cover what the insurance does not cover. His creditors will attach his personal assets. He may have to declare bankruptcy to protect the very roof over his head.

Aware of the potential hazards of a sole proprietorship, but also aware of the advantages in personal control and in simpler business and tax record keeping, Harold has taken several precautions. He has a carefully planned program of insurance coverage, both for liability to others and losses to his business. He has formally arranged for his wife to have full authority to continue his business should he suffer prolonged illness or die. He has taken the further precaution of naming a trusted employee as manager should his wife be unable or unwilling to take over the management. In his will, the ownership of Harold's business is carefully described so that his wife will have proper title to sell the business assets, should she so desire.

The Partnership

Robert S., Homer Z., and Anne W. formed the Accountants Today partnership. Their reasoning was typical. Each of the partners has something to offer that is not available from the others. Robert is a top-notch CPA and auditor with experience working in a major accounting firm. Homer has extensive experience as an office and business manager in both large and small businesses. Anne has a track record as an exceptionally effective business development and sales person for a number of different types of business. By combining their capabilities and assets, they have a business strength far exceeding what any of them alone would have.

A partnership is a contract between the partners to carry out the business activity for the purpose of making a profit. In many ways, the partnership is like a multiheaded sole proprietorship, with many of the same advantages and disadvantages, plus a few of its own.

There are two kinds of partners and partnerships: *general*, or *managing*, and *limited*. General partners have full authority and full liability. The limited partner buys into the operation for a specified investment only, has no voice in the management of the partnership, and is liable only for the amount invested at buy-in time. The limited partner to the partnership is much like the nonmanagement stockholder to the corporation, except that the term for the limited partnership is usually limited, normally to eight to ten years.

Partnership Advantages

There are a number of attractive aspects to the partnership arrangement. It is easy to form a partnership contract, either orally, by implication, or by a written document, but it is always best to have any financial understanding described and memorialized in writing (see Chapter 16 on contracts).

As is true for the sole proprietorship, the partnership is not taxable. Profits or losses are shared by the partners. All tax payments for profits are made by partnership members as personal income; all tax losses accrue to partnership members as personal credits against other or future income.

An advantage of the partnership is that it allows the combination of a number of talents or resources, as in the case of Accountants Today. Less government regulation exists for a partnership than for a corporation. It is easier for a partnership to operate legally in more than one state of the union. When compared to a sole proprietorship, it is usually easier for a partnership to raise money because there will be more than one person to guarantee repayment.

The limited partner has the best of several worlds. Liability is limited to the amount of investment. There is no obligation to work within or provide services for the partnership. If the partnership loses money at first, the limited partner has a tax loss to apply against other income. When the partnership is eventually successful, the limited partner investor receives a share of annual profits, and when the limited partnership term expires, a buyout sum based on the value of the partnership.

Partnership Disadvantages

As is true for the sole proprietorship, a partnership is mortal. If one of the partners dies or otherwise leaves the partnership, or sells his or her share in the partnership, the partnership dies. The remaining partners can establish a new partnership, but the old one no longer exists, except for any accrued liabilities which must be paid by one or more of the original partners.

Therein lie two of the major problems of a partnership. There is no limit on the personal liability of the partners for partnership debts or liabilities. One partner can amass huge debts in the name of the partnership, or can through negligence create a costly liability. If this partner then disappears or is otherwise unable or unwilling to make good on a proportionate share of the debt or liability, the total burden falls on the remaining partners.

If those who seek recompense from the partnership choose to mount suit against only one of the remaining partners, one perceived by the plaintiffs as "deep pocket," it is that unfortunate partner who must pay the entire judgment awarded by the court. In law, this is called *jointly and severally liable*—that is, everyone or anyone in the partnership is liable for the total amount. True, this unfortunate partner can in turn sue the remaining partners for pro rata contribution to the judgment, but such action is costly, time consuming, and not always successful.

Forming the Partnership

If you select the partnership form for your business, be sure you start out with good legal advice. Find a lawyer who is familiar with the specific peculiarities of partnership law. You will need your own personal lawyer. The lawyer who provides legal services and advice for the partnership will owe loyalty to the entire partnership, not to any single partner. If you want someone to watch out for your rights within the partnership, you will need your own personal lawyer.

Your lawyer can help you protect your role and rights within the partnership; can help you assure that your role in the partnership agreement is in harmony with the laws of your state; and can help you be sure that the agreement contains provisions for a fair and equitable passage of your ownership rights when you or one of the other partners sells, dies, or resigns.

But most important of all in a partnership is the personal relationship that exists between the individual partners. If you find that you cannot trust a partner, if each of your partners will not assume a rightful share of the work and responsibility, if any of your partners lack the experience or knowledge necessary to make a meaningful contribution to the profitability of the partnership, or if the partners clash personally or disagree as to business methods and objectives, the partnership may fail.

Here is some important advice for those who plan on forming a partnership:

Do it in writing. Insist on a written partnership agreement. True, an oral agreement is legally acceptable in many states, but without a written document for reference, there is a great chance of misunderstanding or forgetting, even of chicanery.

Share methods and objectives. Make sure in advance that you and your partners-to-be share the same or compatible business methods and objectives. Make sure that each partner understands what these methods and objectives are, and what they will mean to the operation of the partnership's business.

Know your partners. Would you marry an utter stranger? A partnership is a type of business marriage. Make sure of your partners' qualifications, financial standings, reputations for honesty. Be particularly sure that their ethical standards are compatible with yours.

Decide how the business is to operate. Before the partnership contract is signed is the time to agree on facilities and equipment, capitalization, staffing, advertising and promotion, and, most of all, who has what management role and what authority.

The Corporation

Charles D., a business management consultant with a variety of industrial management experiences, had an idea for a specialized information search service via personal computers and online telecommunications. Robert L. was an experienced user of online services. They needed an executive with the know-how to produce and package such a service, and a backer who could provide or otherwise obtain start-up capitalization. Charles and Robert created a corporation so that, with stock, they could negotiate ownership shares for the business with the prospective executive and backer or backers.

A corporation is an artificial *immortal person* created by law. It outlives its founders, barring prior bankruptcy or dissolution. As an artificial person, a corporation can sue and be sued. It can buy, own, lease, and sell property. It can enter into contract agreements with individuals, other corporations, partnerships, or government bodies. Control of the corporation is by the executives who receive their authority through the voting power of stock ownership.

All corporations are state-created and state-controlled entities. There is no federal corporation law, except for the special tax provisions for normal and Subchapter S corporations. Unfortunately, corporation laws vary widely between states. This means that you will need legal advice to understand the powers, obligations, and liabilities of incorporation specific to your state.

Corporations can be open (public), closed, closely held, or Subchapter S. Shares of stock for the open corporation are sold to the general public. In a closed or closely held corporation, all or most of the stock is held by a small number of persons, often a family group, who exercise control over the corporation.

Profits for the normal corporation are taxed before they are distributed to shareholders. The Subchapter S form of corporation has most of the characteristics of a normal corporation, except that, like a sole proprietorship or a partnership, it is taxed on profits and credited for losses in the same manner as an individual. Taxation aspects are discussed later.

Regular Corporation Advantages

A major advantage of incorporation is what some call the *corporate shield*. Your personal assets, except for what you have invested directly in the corporation itself, are normally protected from liabilities or losses by the business. You will not, however, be shielded from liability for illegal acts or gross personal or managerial negligence that results in damage, injury, or loss to others.

The second advantage is the ease with which ownership can be transferred. All that is needed is the simple act of buying, selling, or trading shares of stock. This contrasts to the partnership, where the sale of a partner's share dissolves the partnership, or the sole proprietorship, where a sale involves the transfer of personal business assets.

If your income is high and you are in line for large sums of income from your business, the corporation has certain legal tax advantages. Your accountant or tax advisor can explain these benefits to you. Being incorporated also can simplify income and estate taxation for gifts of stock to your children.

Subchapter S Corporation Advantages

The Subchapter S corporation is a hybrid of the corporation and a limited partnership. It has the general characteristics of a normal corporation, as discussed above, except that taxes for its profits and losses are handled as though the profits or losses were personal income or personal losses. This avoids the corporate curse of double taxation on business profits (that is, corporation profits are taxed, then when the remainder is distributed as dividends, the dividends are taxed).

The Subchapter S corporation is of greatest interest to small businesses, particularly those in their early days of operation before there is a bottom-line profit.

Not every business is eligible to be a Subchapter S corporation. For example, the corporation must be organized in the United States under federal or state law. It can have only one class of stock, each share with equal rights. It can have no more than 35 shareholders. Only individuals or estates can be shareholders, and they must be citizens or residents of the United States.

You can elect Subchapter S when you form the corporation, or you can elect S status at a later time. You can revoke or lose this election. Your accountant and lawyer can help you with the details of this type of corporation. If you want to become more familiar with the S corporation in advance, write to the Internal Revenue Service for Publication 589, *Tax Information on S Corporations*. The address of the IRS office for your area is on the back of your most recent Form 1040 tax instruction booklet.

Making Your Choice

Which form is best for your independent contractor business? Unfortunately, there is no universal truth. The decision you make will depend on what you are doing now, what you intend to do, and what things are of primary importance to you. Here are some questions, the answers to which will help you in making your decision:

☐ Do you want to maintain exclusive control over your business operations? Then consider the sole proprietorship.

☐ Do you need to team up with others who have assets or capabilities that will supplement your own resources and talents? Then consider the partnership or corporation.

☐ Is it your goal to build a business you can sell to a person or firm? Then consider the sole proprietorship or a closed or closely held corporation shared by family members.

☐ Do you want to build a business to pass on to your children or other family members? Then consider the sole proprietorship or a closed or closely held corporation shared by family members.

☐ Will your business have a high liability risk character, as for many types of construction where heavy machinery and explosives are used? Then consider the protective shield of the corporation.

☐ Will it take a measurable period of time before your business shows a positive net income? If you have other income, then consider the S corporation, which will allow you to allocate business losses against that other income at tax time.

☐ Is your personal income (or will your personal income be) higher than the corporation tax rate? Then consider the corporation as a way to shelter business income.

☐ Will you need to raise capital to finance facilities and equipment to get your business started? Then consider a partnership, perhaps with limited-partner investors, or a shareholder corporation with stock to allocate.

There is more, of course, and it all relates to your personal business objectives and needs. Discuss your plans with your lawyer and your financial advisor. Talk to your local banker. Talk to owners and managers of other small businesses in your area. Check with your local or area Chamber of Commerce for suggestions about whom to contact.

But first, do your own research. Check with your local library, your accountant, or your lawyer, or write to the IRS for a copy of Internal Revenue Service Publication 334, *Tax Guide for Small Businesses*.

In this publication, you will find nearly 200 pages that discuss income, excise, and employment taxes for individuals, sole proprietorships, partnerships, and normal and S corporations. It also includes information that is helpful when selecting the type of business to form, as well as required and recommended records and accounting methods, how to figure gross profit and net income (or loss), what can or cannot be deducted as business expenses, and more.

CHAPTER 6

Where to Find Financial Backing

A great many newly started business efforts are doomed to failure before they even begin. The expectant independent contractor, intent on his or her skills and experience to provide a specific service, often neglects the most basic element of successful enterprise: financial planning. Making the move away from a regular salary, the new independent contractor often has the unfounded optimism that skill, experience, and hard work will prevail. Not so, not by themselves.

Every business needs money to get started, and money to support one's self and family until the time when business revenues exceed expenses in great enough volume to ensure personal as well as commercial survival. The presence or lack of financial backing can be the deciding factor if one has family responsibilities, even for the most simple of services where one works out of one's own home and there is little or no need to invest in equipment or supplies.

This was the situation faced by Frank W. He was a direct-mail advertising specialist with eleven years of commercial experience. He had a business plan and a marketing plan, and he had a good idea of where to look for customers. What he lacked was money. He was too young to benefit from pension payments or Social Security. Married and with two children, a son aged twelve and a daughter aged nine, home mortgage, and car payments to make, he knew that his savings were inadequate to support his family while the volume of his business was being built. His wife, an experienced executive secretary, had been out of the job market for five years, making it unlikely that she could earn enough to support them during the business start-up years.

The question: Should Frank give up his dream? How long would it take to save enough money to finance his business plan? How would the use of this money affect college plans for his son and daughter? The answer: There are other ways.

Money to Get Started

There are five kinds of money needed to start and continue your service business as an independent contractor. You will need money to cover initial expenses for facilities, equipment, and supplies. You will need money to cover early ongoing business expenses. You will need money for living expenses. You will need money to expand or to finance a large project. And you will need money to supplement inevitable cyclic dips in cash flow.

Here is the list of potential start-up money sources considered by Frank.

- Personal savings. Valuable, but inadequate by themselves.
- Loans from family members. Possible, but Frank was reluctant to go to his parents, his two brothers, or his in-laws with hat in hand.
- Bank loan for start-up expenses, bank credit line for ongoing support. This most common and practical source will be discussed in detail below.
- Selling "stock" to investors. Sharing ownership in a business is the American way of business, but is usually easier if one contemplates a large-scale business rather than a personal service business.
- Credit from suppliers, called trade credit, could help sustain Frank after his business was in actual operation.
- Factoring (selling) accounts receivable would be a source of immediate cash if Frank found that customer payments were consistently delayed.
- Small Business Administration (SBA) or Small Business Investment Company (SBIC) loan. Frank was unable to meet the special requirements for a direct or guaranteed federal government loan, where others might succeed. These requirements are discussed later in this chapter.

Working with Savings

Frank wisely considered his savings to be his safety net. Here was the money he held in reserve for those bleak days when all else fails. And he knew that there will be bleak days and weeks when expenses would exceed income.

Frank was correct. Using one's savings should be the last resort, but they should be there, available if needed. If, like Frank, you are a look-to-the-future kind of person, you have been building your savings nest egg systematically while on salary.

Working through Banks

Bank loans can be useful to help you get started in your business. Equally important, a bank credit line (pre-approved ongoing loan limit) can provide cash flow to keep your business going. The credit line is your insurance to meet future, often unanticipated, operating expenses. If you wait until the cash is needed before you apply for a credit line, you may be nearly insolvent before it is approved. Worse yet, the bank may see evidence that you lack foresight by failing to arrange for a credit line in advance. Such lack of foresight will speak poorly of your business acumen. You may never need to draw on the credit line, but you will sleep better knowing that it is there, waiting for you.

Banks, like people, dogs, and cars, come in many sizes and shapes. Some banks cater to small businesses, aware that from tiny acorns mighty businesses may grow. Others prefer to wait for the business to become mighty. Long before you give up a regular salary and start business operations, you should lay the groundwork for a solid banking relationship.

Bankers respond most favorably to money requests that are based on sound financial principles. They will want to be sure that you have good Business and Marketing Plans. They will want to be sure that your business has a better than average chance of success, both because of the nature of the business, and because of the type of person you are.

Your first step is a survey of local banks. You will want to find a bank that provides the services you need and where the executives understand and are friendly to small businesses. When you find such a bank and a banker with whom you can communicate, let them know that you intend to make that bank your bank for all of your business.

Finding the Right Bank

As mentioned, not every bank will be right for you. Likewise, not every bank will be interested in your business. Your job is to find the bank most suited to your needs. Start out by talking to local small businesses about their banking experiences. Ask each of them if their bank is helpful and easy to deal with. Does their bank understand the specific needs of a small business? Does their bank stand by them when needed? Ask for the names of particularly helpful and knowledgeable managers and loan officers at recommended banks. Find out what special services these banks offer to small businesses.

Then, from your list of banks, select the one that appears most suited to your purposes. Visit the bank. Introduce yourself to the manager. Try to meet key loan officers, particularly those specializing in small-business loans. Tell the manager and loan officer of your plans to start a business. Tell them something of your background, experience, and other qualifications to start and operate a successful business.

Ask questions. The banker you talk to will be impressed with your business savvy if you ask such questions as the following:

- [ ] Does the bank have a small-business specialist?
- [ ] Does the bank serve businesses similar to yours?
- [ ] What is the bank's experience with new business start-ups?
- [ ] What banking and informational services does the bank offer?
- [ ] Is the bank autonomous, or a branch of a larger bank?
- [ ] Are the bank's decisions made locally? Elsewhere?
- [ ] What types of loans does the bank make?
- [ ] What are the loan terms?
- [ ] What types of collateral does the bank require or accept?
- [ ] What is required to establish a credit line?
- [ ] What type of information does the bank need from you?

The important thing is to establish a good working relationship as soon as possible. If the people you talk to are vague and only mildly attentive, try another bank. In fact, before you make your final selection, talk to more than one bank. Keep looking and talking until you find a bank and bankers interested in you and your business.

Establishing a Banking Relationship

Once you have found the bank you wish to do business with, be ready to devote all of your business, checking, savings, CDs, and loan applications to that bank. As your initial assets will be limited, you will want to concentrate them to maximize your clout, such as it is. Then set out to create an ongoing rapport with that bank.

- Establish a business banking account.
- Prove your reliability. Start with a small loan, even though you have no immediate need for money. Establish your image of reliability with prompt payments until the loan is paid off.
- Share your Business Plan with your banker (see Chapter 8). If you have done your homework well, your banker will be impressed with your ability to plan and manage a business.
- Communicate with your banker. Maintain regular contact. Keep your banker up-to-date on new developments with your business, both positive and negative. Yes, negative. Never lie to your banker, either with outright dishonesty or by hiding important facts. Once one loses credibility with a bank, trust never fully returns. Equally important, your banker may have constructive ideas that will help you through bad periods.

Your Grand Plan

Any careful banker will want specific information, such as you will have in your Business and Marketing Plans. Be prepared to discuss the prospects you see for your business, and on what you base these prospects. As most small businesses are poorly conceived and poorly planned, well-designed Business and Marketing Plans will be impressive.

Give your predictions for the growth of your business, and tell how you arrived at these predictions. Be ready to discuss markets and marketing, customer prospects and selling. Give your best estimate for the size of the market now, and whether or not it is decreasing, stabilizing, or growing overall. Describe the competition you will face, the share of market you intend to take away from the competition, and how you plan to accomplish this.

Show the banker that you have the ability and know-how to obtain necessary materials and supplies. Show that you have provided for secondary sources should primary sources be unable to meet your needs or schedules. Show that you know how to price your services competitively, yet profitably, including direct and indirect charges.

Proof for the Bank

Once you have covered your plan on a grand scale, be ready to share specific dollars-and-cents information with your banker. This too will be in your Business Plan. Your balance sheet will be expected to show business assets and liabilities, and anticipated income over three- or five-year growth periods. If you will have inventories, how will they be valued?

Your banker will want to know how you plan to finance your business. It is no surprise that banks are much more comfortable when they are not the sole source of your start-up and operations funding.

Will you have personal assets to be invested? Will there be investments by family members or friends? Do you intend to sell equity shares of your business? To whom? How much control will you sell, and for how much?

Although specific banks and loan officers within banks may differ in loan-making procedures, it is fair to say that your request for a loan will not be viewed with enthusiasm if you are unable to present a convincing demonstration of present or potential profitability.

For the financing you will request from the bank, be ready to show:

☐ How much up-front money you will need.

☐ How large a credit line you will need.

☐ How you plan to use the bank's financing: capital equipment, facilities, supplies, staffing, day-to-day operations.

☐ How you will meet and handle unexpected expenses.

☐ What kind of credit history and rating you have. The bank, of course, will confirm this through a credit bureau. You will be wise to obtain a copy of your personal credit rating in advance, rather than be hit by unpleasant surprises. Look for Credit Bureau Associates in your local phone book. In New Jersey, for instance, one sends a request and a $15.00 check to the Consumer Relations Department, Credit Bureau Associates, Box 203, Camden, NJ 08101.

☐ That you have sufficient backing of your own to warrant the bank taking a reasonable risk in advancing a portion of your financing needs.

☐ That your training and background qualify you to manage and operate your proposed business.

☐ That, with your Business and Marketing Plans and balance sheet, you are likely to produce sufficient income to repay the bank loan, as well as your other creditors or investors.

The loan officer may also wish to see that you have up-to-date books and records, particularly if you have been in business for a period of time. If you are not experienced in accounting, and most of us are not, get help from an accountant to establish your system for keeping business and tax records.

Accounts receivable and how they are handled provide another way for the loan officer to evaluate your business operation. If you are not yet operating and do not yet have accounts receivable, show how you plan to track payments, and what you intend to do about delinquent accounts.

Salaries for yourself and other key persons will be included in your

Business Plan. These should be high enough to be believed, low enough to be reasonable.

Other items that will be of interest are your provisions for handling tax payments, both withholding and estimated, for yourself and employees, as well as business income taxes. You can report fixed assets as those you already have, or as those you intend to acquire, possibly with the loan money under discussion with the bank.

Even if your business is new or not even yet started, a well-organized set of financial records will, in the eyes of the banker, signal your ability to manage, and your potential for success. Typically, lenders, creditors, or investors will want to see your cash budget and sales forecasts. Then, after you have been in business for several years, they will want to compare your past budgets and projections with actual operations. This is how they will judge your ability to forecast.

What Type of Loan?

Your discussion of loans will go more smoothly if you have a general idea of what various types of loans are called, and how one type differs from other types.

Character loans. Short-term unsecured loans for which no collateral is required. Character loans are usually reserved for bank customers with the highest credit ratings.

Lines of credit. This is the type of loan you will want to keep your business going. A credit line is an advance commitment by the bank to lend you money up to a specified maximum amount, and under specified conditions. Credit lines require credit investigations. This means you should work well in advance to be sure that the credit line is established and ready when you need it. Loans within the structure of the credit line are usually granted on a revolving basis. That is, more than one such loan can be outstanding at any one time.

Term loans. Term loans for a specific duration of time, such as a thirty-year home purchase mortgage loan, or a five-year car purchase loan. Short-term loans are usually granted for periods of less than a year. Intermediate-term loans will be for one to five years. Long-term loans may be from five to fifteen years, and longer. Longer term loans for businesses often require financial statements that have been certified by a certified public accountant.

Collateral loans. A collateral loan is any loan where the bank requires security to protect its loan. For short-term loans, collateral could be business inventory. For longer-term loans, collateral could be a chattel mortgage (mortgage on your non-land or non-building business property). Other forms of collateral include real estate, stocks, bonds, life-insurance cash value, and more.

Cosigner loans. If you lack suitable collateral, the bank may require that the loan papers be signed also (cosigned) by a responsible person in a position to guarantee repayment of the loan should you default. In most cases, the cosigner is someone close to the borrower, such as a parent, husband, wife, relative, or close friend or associate.

Warehouse/Field-warehouse loans. This type of loan is not typical for a service business, as it is based on the receipt of goods or materials at a warehouse. Collateral for the loan is a warehouse receipt delivered directly to the lender (the bank), not to the business. Normal procedure is for a warehouse operating company to take over the responsibility for the warehoused goods, placing a bonded employee in control.

Equipment loans. If your business involves equipment, such as in the construction industry, you may pledge that equipment as collateral for a loan. However, most banks are reluctant to issue equipment loans. If you default, they are now the owners of equipment that often has very little resale value when compared to its cost when new.

Accounts-receivable loans. After your business is in operation, and if your customers are slow to pay, but otherwise reliable, you can seek a loan using your accounts receivable as collateral.

Trade/Supplier Credit

When you purchase equipment, supplies, materials, or services and do not have to pay for them immediately upon delivery, credit has been extended to you. More precisely, trade credit or supplier credit has been extended to you.

Normally, you will earn a small discount if you pay within some specified period, such as 30 days. But you can, if you wish, wait until the last minute to pay, sacrifice the discount, and meanwhile use the money elsewhere in your business. A warning: Do not extend the time for payment so long that you damage your credit rating.

Factored Accounts Receivable

There are financial firms, called factors, that purchase accounts receivable from other firms. When accounts receivable are sold to a factor, the factor earns the right to collect from the customers.

The advantage of factoring one's accounts receivable is immediate receipt of money, rather than waiting. But there are disadvantages. You will sell your accounts receivable at a discount to allow a profit to the factor, as well as to allow for bad debts and collection expenses. If the factor is blunt or unpleasant in its methods of collection, your image will be tarnished in the eyes of your customer.

Selling Shares in Your Business

There is more than one way to raise money by selling shares in the ownership of your company. The simplest approach is to persuade friends and family members to invest in your dream. Or you can offer shares to strangers through brokers. Local accountants and lawyers often have clients interested in tax shelters, which are investments that initially will show a loss for tax purposes, followed by a buildup and eventual sale at a profit.

Either way, consult first with a lawyer. Find out what the statutory restrictions and requirements are for your state. Do you have to register with a state agency? Do you have to incorporate? Each of the 50 states has its own laws and regulations concerning the incorporation of businesses and the selling of ownership shares in a business.

A variation on the sale of shares is the sale of an equity position (partial ownership exceeding normal stock ownership) to venture capital companies. However, unless your business proposal is one that will excite Wall Street, most venture capitalists will not bother with you.

If you have opted for the partnership organization, you can sell limited partnerships to raise capital. Again, consult first with your lawyer.

SBA/SBIC Loans

The Small Business Administration (SBA) is authorized to make direct loans, or loans in conjunction with banks. It can guarantee bank loans, or it can authorize a Small Business Investment Company (SBIC) to make loans.

SBA business loans can be used to assist in the financing of construction, conversion, or expansion. They can be used to purchase equipment, facilities, machinery, supplies, or materials. Or they can be used for working capital.

To a large extent, SBA loans are "economic opportunity" loans to support the business aspirations of those persons with marginal or submarginal incomes, or minorities and women who have been denied equal opportunity. SBA loans are also available as economic injury loans for small companies that have suffered economic injury from some disaster, or for federally aided urban renewal or highway programs.

Once you qualify as a small company, mostly having fewer than 50 employees, you must avoid prohibited categories, namely newspapers, magazines, television and radio stations, gambling, the sale of alcoholic beverages, and several others. Then you must show that you cannot raise necessary funds elsewhere.

The SBA will then examine your character, business prospects, management ability, credit record, debt/net-worth ratio, collateral value, and personal finances. The biggest complaint about SBA loans is governmental red tape and extensive delays in getting approval.

If nothing else works for you, however, the SBA may be your answer. You can get information by writing to the SBA at 1441 L Street NW, Washington, DC 20416.

SBICs are licensed by the SBA, but are privately owned, profit-making financial organizations chartered under state law. Some are bank related. The type of information required for an SBIC loan is quite similar to that required by banks. A list of SBICs is available from the SBA.

Other Government Funds

A number of federal departments and agencies have special needs, and they can be sources of funding. In 1978 Congress enacted P.L. 95-507, mandating that agencies of the United States Government create offices to encourage the making of contracts with small and disadvantaged businesses, and for the allocation of government-contract business to areas with labor surpluses. Under Sections 8 and 15 of the Small Business Act, along with various presidential executive orders, each federal agency has established an Office of Small and Disadvantaged Business Utilization (OSDBU), or its equivalent. The direct result is a number of business opportunities, some providing limited start-up funding, for small firms.

To be eligible, a business must be independently owned, cannot be dominant in the area of business involved, and must be small by SBA definition, normally fewer than 50 employees. A business is considered to be owned and controlled by socially and economically disadvantaged individuals if one or more such persons must be involved in the daily management and operation of the business, and they must either own and control the business or own at least 51 percent of the business stock. Socially and economically disadvantaged persons include Black, Hispanic, Asian-Pacific, and Native Americans. Businesses run by women are also helped, though women are not formally classified as "socially and economically disadvantaged." A business is "female-controlled" if at least 51 percent of the ownership is by one or more women who control and operate the business.

Federal departments and agencies that might be of interest to you include:

- Department of Agriculture
- Department of Commerce
- Department of Defense
- Department of Education
- Department of Energy
- Department of Health and Human Services
- Department of Housing and Urban Development
- Department of Interior
- Department of Transportation
- Department of Treasury
- Environmental Protection Agency
- National Aeronautics and Space Administration
- Tennessee Valley Authority
- Veterans Administration

You can learn more about opportunities available from these federal bodies and how to contact them from the *Handbook for Small Business, A Survey of Business Programs of the Federal Government*, listed as a reference in the Appendix.

CHAPTER 7

Your Marketing Strategy

Do not be misled by the term *marketing*. It is no more than the tactic of selling reinforced with planning strategy. And do not be misled by the term *selling*. It is no more than bringing in the business that is needed to make your business prosper. Here is another area where many professionals who aspire to be self-employed entrepreneurs fail. A long, long time ago, there was a saying that "if you invent a better mouse trap, the world will beat a path to your door." Forget it.

There are a great many very talented people in the world, many of whom can do what you do and do it equally well. Marketing is a way to elevate yourself above the general noise level, a way to be seen, heard, and called upon. Marketing is also a way to present your service where the demand and opportunities are greatest.

Developing a successful business can be compared to fighting a war. If you rely on tactics alone, you may win battles (close sales), but you may lose the war (fail to overcome the opposition). To start, you develop an overall strategy—that is, you define your purpose, policies, and sense of direction. Then you undertake a series of tactical maneuvers to find and reach the prospects defined in your strategy and convert them into customers for the service defined in your Business Plan. The combination of marketing strategy and selling tactics is your Marketing Plan.

Marketing Plan Objectives

There are four basic objectives to a Marketing Plan:

- to attract new customers
- to create repeat business
- to create a positive image
- to outmaneuver competition

Attract New Customers

Of course you will need customers if you are to thrive as an independent contractor. You will need a constant inflow of new customers if your business is to grow. You will need a constant inflow of new customers to replace those that stray away from your service.

Create Repeat Business

Your best prospect for future business is a past customer who was satisfied with the service you provided. It is a form of marketing when you treat a customer in the best manner possible so that when future needs arise, the customer will think of you.

However, you cannot assume that you will be remembered. You cannot take the customer-prospect for granted, waiting for a call. Human nature being what it is, your customer-prospect may be lured away by your competition who made a more recent or more persuasive contact. You must find ways to keep prospects aware of the services you provide and your availability to provide them.

Create a Positive Image

How do your customers perceive you and your service? Are they pleased? Displeased? Or do they bother to think about you at all? Their perception of you as a person, or of your helpfulness and cooperation, may have as much influence on them, maybe more, as the way you did your work.

What is image? It is a perception. Perception is something you can control and build through interpersonal contacts, with advertising, and with promotion.

Outmaneuver Competition

If there ever was a single business truth, it is that no matter what you do, how well you do it, or where you do it, there are competitors lurking out there waiting to steal your customers. They will promise better, faster, or less costly services. They may even whisper negative rumors about you.

A major secret of success as an independent contractor is to know who your competitors are and what kind of work they do, then outmaneuver them. When they try to outflank you, have your counteroffensive ready to launch.

Marketing versus Sales

Speak to five people, ask them what the difference is between marketing and sales, and very likely you will find yourself with five answers. For the purposes of this book, the following definitions are used.

Marketing refers to those selling-related activities not directly involved in customer contacts for purposes of "closing the sale." Marketing includes image building, advertising, and promotion. Direct-mail programs designed to familiarize prospective customers with you and your services are marketing, even though a few actual sales may result.

In brief, marketing is a strategy designed to make your sales universe, customers and prospects, favorably aware of your business and its services.

Selling refers to the tactics you use for direct contact with prospective customers combined with direct efforts to "close the sale." The contact can be by mail, by phone, or in person.

In brief, selling is the effort to "close the sale."

Closing the sale refers to the final phase of the selling contact in which you try for a commitment from the prospect. The closing can be as definite as a signed purchase order or letter of intent, or it may be an intermediate commitment where seller and prospect part in apparent harmony, agreeing to meet again with additional facts, presentations, or negotiations.

In brief, closing the sale is a satisfactory response to a selling effort which has created an actual sale or a favorable intermediate step toward a sale.

In large firms, marketing and sales are often separate functions, with sales being a subset of marketing. Such a distinction normally does not exist in a small firm. But for purposes of explanation and discussion, marketing and sales will be treated separately.

The Marketing Approach

There are two basic marketing approaches: Ford versus Lincoln, or, if you prefer, Chevrolet versus Cadillac or Volkswagen versus Audi. In the Ford approach, you offer a low-cost, mass-appeal service to anyone and everyone. The objective is business volume. In the Lincoln approach, you offer a high-priced, premium service limited to a carefully selected list of prospective customers. Both approaches are viable, both are used, both have been proven successful.

The Ford approach is best used to sell a commodity for which there is a large, hard-to-define universe of prospective buyers, such as users of toothpaste, cosmetics, laundry detergents, or bathroom tissue. The Lincoln approach is more appropriate when selling a premium product or personal service to a small, definable universe of prospective customers, such as purchasers of construction, computer programming, or engineering maintenance.

The Lincoln approach is most appropriate for most service businesses, especially if the service is to be offered by one or a few independent contractors. For one thing, service businesses are people intensive. To handle more business, you need more people. To handle twice the volume of business, you need twice the number of people. In contrast, product-oriented businesses often can double output by the purchase of new machinery, with a marginal increase in the number of employees needed.

The Name of the Game

Frank W. knew that the service he wanted to offer was direct-mail advertising, but when he tried to create a marketing plan he ran into trouble. Working from telephone company yellow pages and local Chamber of Commerce business directories for Pennsylvania, New Jersey, Maryland, and Delaware, he had a list of more than three thousand prospects. With his experience in mail promotion programs, he knew instinctively that the cost of a top-quality mailing program comprising no fewer than three mailings to each prospect would amount to more than he was willing to spend at the outset.

What was wrong? Frank had not defined the service he was prepared to offer as an independent contractor. During his professional career, he had specialized in magazine subscription programs. His extended list of prospects included car repair shops, caterers, bakeries, real estate brokers, and more. He pruned the list to fewer than a hundred names by aiming his attention at the area he was best qualified to serve at start-up time. He could worry about spreading his wings to other areas at some future date.

What Is Your Business?

Frank W.'s next problem was why anyone would contract for his service when they already had the service, either from in-house staff or by outside contract. He would not be the only one ready to provide a direct-mail subscription program to publishers. And although he knew he was good at what he did, he also knew that there were others just as good already in the market.

What Frank had to realize was that the heart of his business would be service—not what he could and would do as much as how he did it—and how customers and prospects would view him as a provider of service. If he wanted to thrust his way into an area already being served by others, he would have to convince prospects that he could provide benefits, detect and solve problems, and define and meet needs.

In brief, your business is service. Design the service you offer so that it will promise new and desirable benefits for your customers. Position your service as better, faster, more effective, less expensive, or whatever it takes within reason to lift yourself above the hoi polloi.

Why Is Your Service Needed?

The magic word is *need*. If you are not needed, you will not get customers. So what is need? It is part factual and part fictional. Both, however, are real in the business world. The factual answer to need is what you can provide in the way of service, and how it is provided. The fictional answer to need is the perception that you offer positive benefits not provided by others offering your type of service, and who are equally skilled and equally dedicated.

Whatever you can offer in the way of benefits may be technically attractive, but may be commercially worthless if the marketplace you hope to serve fails to perceive the beneficial values of your offer. It is not important that the concerns of those in the marketplace be based on fact. There is only one universal truth in marketing, the customer's truth.

Start by answering these questions:

- What is needed in general by my prospects?
- What is needed by specific types of prospects?
- Are these needs real or fictional perceptions?
- What values are placed on these needs?
- Can my service provide for these needs?

What positive benefits will you provide? Better, more effective work? Faster turnaround? Lower cost? Creative solutions? When you can answer these questions, you are well along the road to defining your service, an essential step toward creating your Business Plan, as well as your Marketing Plan. Chapter 11, "Promoting Your Service," delves more deeply into the subject of service benefits.

How to Analyze the Marketplace

There will be different levels of interest in your service. There will be those primary markets within which the demand for your type of service is frequent and essential; there will be those secondary markets within which the need for your type of service is occasional, but real; and there will be those tertiary markets within which the need for your type of service is desirable, but optional.

Your Primary Markets

Your Marketing Plan will be most effective if it concentrates on your primary market prospects. If you find that this market is too small to provide the business you need, or in some manner is closed to you as an outsider and an independent contractor, try redefining your service.

Your first step is to identify the specific categories that comprise your primary market. For example, if you are a computer programmer, you will need to seek out those businesses and professions needing or otherwise most likely to benefit by using programs modified or tailored to their specific technical or business needs.

Your second step is to examine the individual component categories of your primary markets. In which of these is the need for your type of service growing? Stable? Decreasing? Again, the computer programming example: The sale of minicomputers is declining as new chips provide near-minicomputer capabilities for microcomputers. Where would you concentrate your attention? On minicomputer users, or on microcomputer users? The answer may not be as simple as one might assume. If increasing numbers of computer programmers desert the minicomputer in favor of microcomputers, there could be an increasing number of opportunities to work with those firms and organizations still using minicomputers.

Your third step is to determine which of these specific categories will be reached most easily and effectively by your sales-promotion efforts. The world may have a million, or a million-million people who can benefit from your service, but if you cannot find a cost-effective way to communicate with them, they will never learn of or pay for your service. In Chapter 11 promotion is discussed in detail.

How to Identify Market Categories

Numerous avenues are open to you in your efforts to identify the market categories of greatest interest to you for your service. You may find one or a combination of these sources helpful, or you may open up your own avenues.

Observe your competition. If other businesses in your area offer services similar or competitive to your intended service, analyze how and where they find their customers. Then organize these customers into identifiable groupings or categories.

Talk to users of the service. When you learn specific names of users of such services, talk to them. Ask about the service they use, why they use it, why they need it, what their perceived benefit from it is, what they like and dislike about it, what they would like to see in such a service. Not only will you learn a great deal, but you will be establishing yourself with a future customer. Such contacts will help determine which types of business or commercial operations will fit within your primary market definition.

Study your local newspaper. Read the business section articles and commercial announcements. Read the personals, as well as the display and classified advertisements. You will not only learn who else is offering your type of service, but you will get ideas of how such services are presented, of what benefits are claimed, and toward what categories the services are aimed. Talk to the newspaper's business editors and those in the market research department. Let them know that they can view you as a future advertiser.

Study regional publications. There is a great deal of market category information available in newspapers from nearby areas, as well as in local and regional business magazines and newsletters. Your local public library is a good source for such publications. Do not stop at local publications. You may learn a great deal from articles about what others are doing, not only those who are offering services similar to yours, but from purveyors of services of all kinds.

Talk to suppliers. If you will be using special equipment, supplies, or equipment as you provide your service, those firms that produce or distribute such items will be good sources of information about the types of customers the users of their product lines have. Do not hesitate to let the suppliers you contact know that you are potentially a customer for what they sell. Solidify this idea by also talking about prices, models, deliveries, discounts, and such.

Talk to businesses similar to yours. Locate businesses that will not compete with your service, but that offer services either similar to yours or the same service in another geographic location, or the same service in your area but to a specialized clientele that you are not targeting. Discuss users of the service, where and how they can be found, what benefits are looked for, and more.

Check with state agencies. Most states have some form of commerce department, and most are actively interested in the formation and prosperity of new businesses. Many have special offices that can and will provide information and assistance to small businesses.

Check with your chamber of commerce. Most cities and towns of any size have a local or regional chamber of commerce. Some states and some counties have chambers of commerce. These can be excellent sources of information about names and addresses of both small and large businesses in the area. The Princeton (NJ) Regional Chamber of Commerce, for example, publishes a directory that lists more than 1,200 local businesses by category and by name.

Finger through the yellow pages. Your local public library may have telephone directories from all over the country. If so, select several of the larger metropolitan areas, such as New York City, Los Angeles, Chicago, Houston, or Denver, and examine the alphabetical index of service categories they list. Then go to the actual yellow-page advertisements for services similar to yours and analyze the types and categories of customers to which they are offering their services.

Study industry/business directories. There seemingly is an endless supply of business and industry directories on virtually every subject of interest to you. Such directories range from religion to drama to specific businesses, industries, services, and products. Your local or regional library will have many such directories. Some will be local or regional, others, such as *Thomas' Register*, will be national.

Analyze Your Competition

You already have a distinct advantage over your competition. You can learn what your competitors are doing, how well or poorly they are doing it, and how they are viewed by their customers. Until you become an active independent contractor, there is very little that they can learn about your service and the benefits you intend to offer. Take advantage of your position while it remains an advantage. Analyze your competition.

- With whom will I compete directly?
- How many competitors are there?

- Do they compete directly or indirectly?
- Is the service exclusive or one of many that they offer?
- Are their other services allied to the primary one?
- Is the market open for my service, or is it saturated?
- Where is my competition located? Are areas uncovered?
- How and in what media does my competition advertise?
- How is their service priced?
- What kind of facilities do my competitors have?
- How do local businesspersons view my competitors?
- How do specific customers view my competitors?
- What are my competitors' strengths? Their weaknesses?
- Have any gone out of business recently?
- Have new ones entered the market recently?

How can you find answers to these questions? Local business directories, newspapers, and yellow pages will provide names and addresses. A few drive-bys will show you what they have for facilities and business vehicles. A couple of hours at the coffee shop across the street will allow you to estimate the volume of business.

As you make these observations, ask yourself how much of this total market you will need to be profitable. Will you need 10 percent? Or will 5 percent suffice? Or can you generate new users for the service? These observations can be used for your budget projections to be used in your Business Plan (see Chapter 8).

How Are Service Firms Selected?

Before you can sell your service to prospective customers, it will help if you understand the normal way independent contractors are selected. Selection can be on the basis of satisfaction with past work by specific contractors, or it can be through a careful competitive bidding approach. For the latter, a typical sequence of actions might be:

1. A listing is made of several firms known to be in the business.
2. Advertisements are placed to solicit additional proposals.
3. Firms with the more promising proposals are interviewed.
4. Firm's qualifications are reviewed (experience, understanding of problem and objectives, reputation for competence and integrity, adequacy of facilities, equipment, and staff).
5. The choice is narrowed to one or two top firms.
6. An agreement is negotiated, and a contract signed.

What Can You Offer?

Since you will be new in the field, you will not be selected on the basis of satisfaction with past work. And, unless the project is advertised, you will not even be on an approved bidders list. This means that you will have to introduce yourself and your service to potential customers, making them aware of you and the benefits you can provide. How you make the introduction is covered in Chapters 11, 12, and 13. Meanwhile, for the purposes of your marketing strategy, you need to decide just what it is that will make your service more desirable than the identical service from an existing firm.

Step back from yourself, place yourself in the position of a user of your service. With as much objectivity as possible, answer the following questions:

- How is the service better than that of the competition?
- How is the service weaker than that of the competition?
- Where and how can the service be modified or improved?
- What is unique and beneficial about the service?

Does your service still make sense? Will you need certain pre-inauguration bolstering or training? Should you modify your service to make it more competitive? Can you operate so as to exploit your strengths and avoid your weaknesses? Or should you chuck it all, and go "back to the drawing board" to map out a new marketing strategy or business definition?

Position Yourself to Win

To succeed in business, you must situate your business in an optimum position vis-à-vis the direct competition, prospective customers, alternative services, allied services, and yourself, with your strengths and weaknesses.

Finding a Niche

If you were introducing a new model of automobile, would you compete directly with General Motors by producing cars that emulated those available from GM? No. You would produce a model not available from GM, one that would appeal to a specific customer interest overlooked or ignored by GM.

When you introduce your independent contractor service, will you try to match and overmatch everyone else offering a similar service, regardless of how big and where located? No. You will look for a niche. If your service is very specialized, of interest only to a small universe of potential users, such as the famous oil-well-fire control services of Red Adair, you might see the need to offer your services on a national or international basis. More likely, you will concentrate your efforts locally or regionally, aiming at a geographic area easily reached from your business headquarters.

Returning to the computer programming example, or perhaps office equipment maintenance, or office design, any of the following or all of the following could be niche markets:

- Accounting/auditing/bookkeeping firms
- Advertising/public relations firms
- Engineering/construction firms
- Banking/finance/brokerage firms
- Manufacturing firms
- Air/rail/highway/waterway transportation firms
- Retail/wholesale/warehousing firms
- Oil/minerals/coal mining/production firms
- Medical/health/extended-care service firms
- Law firms/law enforcement agencies
- Insurance/real estate sales firms

Your Winning Marketing Strategy

You are now ready to design a winning marketing strategy as the first step toward your Marketing Plan. The steps you have taken, and which now must be consolidated into a single marketing strategy include:

- [ ] Your proposed business defined
- [ ] Your business objectives defined
- [ ] Your marketing approach selected
- [ ] Your market defined, identified, and analyzed
- [ ] Your competition identified and analyzed
- [ ] Your relative strengths and weaknesses evaluated
- [ ] Your unique benefits identified and explained
- [ ] Your market niche determined

What you have now created will be your guide in the preparation of the remainder of your Marketing Plan—namely, prospecting for specific customers, promoting your services, selling face to face, and selling with proposals (see Chapters 10 through 13).

CHAPTER 8

Mapping Your Business Plan

Few of us would start on a cross-country trip without a map, yet it is amazing how many people will commit their future economic welfare to an unmapped, undirected business effort. The illusion exists that if a person has a skill or talent to offer, success inevitably must follow. Not true. Much if not most of the high failure rate of newly launched businesses during the first year of operation can be attributed to poor planning, poor management, and failure to anticipate money needs in the face of cyclic income.

If you plan to offer your independent contractor services as a hobby, or by moonlighting in your spare time, a plan for your business will not be essential. You can stop reading this chapter right here. But if you are seriously planning to invest your time and effort toward financial self-sufficiency, you had better know where you are going, how you will get there, and what obstacles you will meet and need to surmount along the way.

Roger S., the chemical engineer who started his independent contractor business like a ball of fire, but then failed, did not believe that he needed a Business Plan. When problems arose, he had no vision of what should be done. He developed customers he was not able to serve adequately. Then, when he ran short of cash, he gave up and started a desperate search for another job.

Business Plan Benefits

A Business Plan can be simple or complex. What is most important is that you end up with a reasonably complete picture of your overall objectives, and specific estimates for your sales potential and revenues, your costs of doing business—namely, direct and indirect costs, overhead for your business, and your personal or family living costs.

Here are a few of the benefits you can expect to gain as you create your Business Plan:

- Your Business Plan will give you a sense of direction. It will describe a path for you to follow. It will contain clear statements of what you intend to do, your goals and targets, benchmarks along the way, strategies and tactics, programs, schedules, and policies.
- Your Business Plan will be a picture window to give a panoramic view of your business to bankers, suppliers, creditors, investors, customers, and, if your business prospers and grows, to your employees. It will allow them to see, appreciate, and value your business, even before you start actual business operations.
- Your Business Plan is an intellectual exercise. Creating it will sharpen your planning and managerial skills. Creating it enhances your ability to look ahead, to see potential good and potential bad, and to anticipate how to react to events of all kinds that you will be facing.

Elements of a Business Plan

Your Business Plan, when completed, will be a combination of policy with facts and figures. It starts with a definition of your business, its objectives and policies. You will decide on the operating form of your business and how you will handle the administrative support for your operations.

From there, you will consider such items as the naming of your business, facilities, equipment and supplies, staffing and/or services you will require, the financing of your business, and your financial and tax recordkeeping. When you are through, you will have a budget, a balance sheet, and a cash flow projection. You will have a profit plan and a basis for lease-or-buy decisions.

As you prepare your Business Plan, you will need to refer to the following chapters in this book:

- Naming your business (Chapter 4)
- Legal form for your business (Chapter 5)
- Administrative operations support (Chapter 4)

- Financing your start-up (Chapter 6)
- Financial and tax records (Chapter 20)
- Marketing strategy (Chapter 7)
- Sales tactics (Chapters 10 through 13)
- Facilities, equipment, supplies, services (Chapter 4)

What Is Your Business?

As noted earlier, your skill, talent, experiences, or a combination of the three may be the basis for becoming an independent contractor, but these in and of themselves are not your business *per se*. Your business, then, is not your capabilities; rather, it is to provide benefits to others in return for payment. Start by answering the following questions. Do it in writing so that you can review, analyze, modify, add, or delete as needed.

1. WHO am I? Professionally, what is it that makes me believe that I can become a successful independent contractor? Personally, what is it that makes me believe that the life of an independent contractor is right for me?
2. WHY am I going into business? Do I plan to be an independent contractor through choice? Is the move voluntary, or have I been a victim of Reduction in Forces (RIF)? Do I plan a career as an independent contractor, or is this merely a money-generating hobby?
3. WHAT is my service? What is it that I intend to provide that is useful to and of value to those with the resources to pay for my services? What benefits can I provide that are not already easily obtained from my competitors?
4. WHERE will I find my customers? Who needs my service? Who will pay for my service? Where are they?
5. WHEN should I launch my operation? What is my start-up schedule? Do I have a choice of timing?

Business Plan Checklist

With your answers to these questions in mind, it is time to outline the details of the key elements of your Business Plan. Taken together, statements of these details will create an overall picture of your service, your objectives, and your plans to make your service financially successful. The end result will be your road map toward success, a document you can use to keep you from straying off track, as well as a document that you can use to impress and convince a banker or investor that you know what you are doing and where you are going.

Your Business Plan is also a document that can be, and should be, reassessed and modified at regular intervals as your business progresses and you become more clearly aware of the obstacles and opportunities of real life.

One part of the Business Plan that may appear beyond your abilities is the financial records section. These various types of reports and projections (discussed in Chapter 20) are specializations practiced by accountants, either PA (public accountant) or CPA.

If you have done your homework in anticipating the number of customer prospects available and your ability to sell to them, and have analyzed your income and your expenses carefully, your accountant can work with you to prepare the various financial reporting forms that are so dearly loved by bankers and investors, but also essential as guideposts for you as you launch and develop your business.

Chapters 7 and 10 will help you put numbers to your business prospects. Chapter 20 will put you in touch with IRS tax-record requirements, expenses (direct and indirect), deductions, and financial reports.

Do not be self-conscious about your writing style. If you express your thoughts clearly and simply, and if the material is typed to be attractive and neat, with headings and paragraphs, your Business Plan should serve you well.

Introductory summary section. Start with a concise description of the key elements of your Business Plan. Not all of the listed points will apply to your service. You should add other points that are important, but do not appear in the following list:

- ☐ Name of business
- ☐ Location of business
- ☐ Description of facility; floor plan, if relevant
- ☐ Description of my service, its market, my competition
- ☐ My qualifications to provide the service
- ☐ Summary of financial projections (see Chapter 20)
- ☐ Financial resources available and/or needed
- ☐ Plans for use of financial resources
- ☐ Overall business goals

Description of service. This section picks up where the Summary Section left off, presenting the details of your proposed service. Items to include:

- ☐ Description of my service; purpose; where applicable
- ☐ Comparison to competitor's services; advantages I offer
- ☐ Factors that will influence demand for my service

☐ Overall market projections for my service
☐ My projected market penetration and sales

Financing objectives. You will need this section only if you are requesting an investment, a loan, or a credit line for a specific application. Here you would describe the purpose for the financial backing, what it will cost, and specifically how the financial backing will be used.

Management of your business. You need to map your management strategy ahead of time—specifically, who is to do what and how. In this section, show how you plan to cope with growth and its management, particularly as your business expands to an extent requiring a person or persons to share management chores and responsibilities.

☐ Organization chart
☐ Key individual responsibilities, resumés, salaries
☐ Other staffing, either employee or contract service
☐ Duties, compensation

Ownership. This section will be quite simple if you or you and your family have sole ownership of the business. If, however, you have incorporated or have a partnership and are sharing ownership and control with one or more other persons, you will need to answer the following:

☐ Names, addresses, business affiliations of principal holders of ownership (stock or equity) or partnership roles
☐ Management involvement of the principal holders
☐ Principal nonmanagement holders; names, addresses, etc.
☐ Board of directors; names, areas of expertise, roles
☐ Stock currently authorized and issued

The market for your service. Using the material you developed during your analysis of the market and your competition (Chapter 7), your next step is to extract details from analysis that describe the market you will serve, your marketing strategy for developing business within that market, and your sales tactics. This section will concentrate on the market to be served, major customer prospects within that market, description of your competition, and your proposed marketing and sales activities.

☐ The target market for my services:

• Description of market; basis for demand for my service
• Overall size of market; predicted growth, or decline
• Technological, social, economic effects on market

- Purchasing habits of current users of similar services
☐ The target customers for my service:

  - Types of activities/businesses needing my service
  - Customer requirements of my service or similar ones
  - Where target customers are located relative to me
  - Number of target customers that exist for my service
  - Percentage of targets I plan to serve now; in the future

☐ Competition for my service:

  - Other identical, similar, alternative services available
  - Number of competitors in my marketing area
  - Comparison of my service to services from others

☐ Marketing/promotion strategies for my service:

  - My target demographic, geographic, and business areas
  - My marketing/promotion methods to reach target areas
  - My "benefits" and pricing strategies
  - My position vis-à-vis my competition

☐ My planned selling activities:

  - How I will identify customer prospects
  - How I will identify decision-makers among prospects
  - How I will contact identified prospects
  - How I will negotiate contracts with identified prospects
  - Predicted number of sales now; in one, two, three years

Technological/procedural status. If your service is based on technology, is there a danger of early obsolescence? Or do you have security in the form of patent protection (your own or licensed), or a proprietary trade secret? Or do you rely specifically on skill, talent, and/or experience?

☐ Does my service rely on technology? On my skill? On my experience?

  - Describe my service.
  - Describe the degree to which the technology, service, or skill is exclusively mine.
  - Describe its strengths and weaknesses.
  - Describe its basic position relative to other services.

☐ What kind of protection do I have for my service?

  - Patent? Copyright? License? Other?

- Can others provide an identical service?
- Is there risk of obsolescence for my service method?

☐ Do I need regulatory or legal approval for my service?

Delivery of your service. How will you make your service available to your customers?

☐ Describe my physical facilities
☐ Describe where my work for the service will take place
☐ Name and describe my suppliers and how I will work with them
☐ Describe skills needed by those working with me
☐ Describe exactly how I will deliver the service

Your financial structure. Here is the opportunity to list those who will serve as your business advisors or consultants and to present your financial statistics—that is, your cost system, budgets and budget controls, cash requirements, key financial statements and projections, plus additional information that may be requested by lenders or potential investors (see Chapters 14 and 20).

☐ My auditor: name, address
☐ My lawyer: name, address
☐ My banker: name, address, contact officer
☐ Cost control and budget systems to be used
☐ My financing: personal, debt, equity
☐ My plans, if any, to "go public"
☐ My five-year financial statements and projections:

- Monthly profit-and-loss or income statements until breakeven, then by quarter
- Balance sheets as of the end of each year
- Cash budgets and cash-flow projections
- Capital budgets for facilities, equipment, other

☐ If I need financing:

- Funding request; desired financing, capitalization, use of funds, future financing
- Financial statements for past three years, or however long you have been in business (If you are just starting your business, your five-year statements and projections listed above can be used.)
- Monthly cash-flow financial projection, including the proposed financing, for two years
- Projected balance sheets, income statement, and statement of changes in financial position for two years, including the proposed financing

CHAPTER 9

Your Insurance Umbrella

Self-insurance, the willingness to pay for one's own losses, either personal or business, is for the rich and prosperous, not for an independent contractor just starting a service business. To ignore insurance, you must be able to pay for illnesses for yourself and your family, court judgments following lawsuits, losses by natural disaster, robberies, and more. Most businesses, even very large ones, cannot survive the financial impact of a major loss. They insure. So should you, not only at start-up time, but on a continuing basis.

There are two basic types of insurance, personal and casualty. Personal insurance deals with your life and your health; casualty insurance deals with your possessions and liabilities. A few of the larger insurance firms handle both types of insurance, while others will specialize in one or the other.

Your Insurance Advisor

Where should you start in developing your insurance program? Many people believe that you will be well advised to seek out an insurance broker, a person who represents more than one insurance carrier. In theory, the broker can pick and choose the combination of policies best suited to your specific needs and provide reasonable coverage at a price you can afford.

Look for an insurance consultant or broker in your town or city. Describe your activities, your present insurance program, and what you think you will be needing. Let this person advise you on the types of coverage you should have. But do not stop there. The right coverage can make the difference between business survival and insolvency. See a second broker. Get a second opinion. Compare suggested coverages and costs. If you still have questions, seek a third opinion.

Insurance for Your Business

Following is a handy checklist of things to consider as you plan your business insurance coverage program, based on a table in *Starting and Managing a Small Service Business* published by the SBA (see publication information in the Appendix).

1. Fire, smoke, and water damage insurance

   - Building(s)
   - Office furnishings and equipment
   - Display or show equipment
   - Files and records
   - Currency
   - Personal property
   - Employee property

2. Vehicle insurance

   - Damage (fire, collision, other)
   - Bodily injury (yourself, passengers, employees)
   - Towing
   - Theft (the car, its contents)
   - Property damage (caused by your car)
   - Liability protection

3. Life and health insurance

   - Worker's compensation
   - Disability
   - Key-person life (key-partner)
   - Hospitalization/medical care

4. Liability protection insurance (nonvehicular)

   - Service/product based damage, injuries
   - On/off premises injuries to employees
   - On/off premises injuries to non-employees

5. General-coverage floater insurance

- Theft/burglary
- Wind/hail/flood damage
- Riot/vandalism losses
- Explosion/lightning damage
- Plate glass damage
- Business interruption losses

Insurance for Yourself

Once you leave the security of regular employment, you also leave the company's medical and life insurance programs, as well as the pension program. You are on your own.

Health Insurance

Being a self-employed entrepreneur does not automatically mean that you cannot benefit from the economies of a group health insurance plan. There is more than one definition of what comprises a *group* for purposes of health insurance, as well as different requirements for the number of persons required to become a group.

If you cannot handle the costs of a regular medical insurance program at first, the most important single policy you can have is one that will cover major or catastrophic medical bills. One need spend only a few days in a hospital to be faced with a medical bill measuring in the multiple thousands of dollars. Major medical policies usually have $500 or $1,000 deductibles, with 80 percent payment or reimbursement of approved services exceeding the initial deductible amount.

The federal tax code allows those of us who are self-employed and carry our own insurance policies to deduct up to 25 percent of the policy cost in the adjustment section at the bottom of the front page of Form 1040. The remaining 75 percent, however, must be lumped with other medical deductions on Form 1040 Schedule A.

Retirement Plans

A retirement plan is a type of insurance to cover your living expenses after you are no longer professionally active. It is during your salad years, your peak earning years, that you will want to start a regular program of savings and investments for your senior years. There are a number of plans open to you.

Remember, if you have employees, the law may require that you provide pension plans for all of them if you are using your business to finance your own retirement plan. IRS Publication 560, *Self-Employed Retirement Plans*, listed in the Appendix, covers the subject in detail.

SEP-IRA Plans. One of the most satisfactory retirement plans for self-employed persons is the SEP-IRA (Simplified Employee Pension–IRA). Such plans require no initial or annual filing with the IRS or Department of Labor, as in the case of the well-known Keogh Plan. The SEP-IRA could well be your first retirement plan. It is inexpensive to establish and to maintain. Or it could serve as a second plan to allow you to make additional contributions.

With the SEP-IRA, you can vary the amounts of your contributions, according to your ability to pay. In lean years, you can skip making contributions, or you can make contributions for each tax year up to the date that tax payment is due, including extensions.

Annual contributions can be as great as 13.0435 percent of your Form 1040 net income, or a maximum of $30,000. This amount is deductible from your Form 1040 net income in the Adjustments section. You will, of course, pay taxes on what you have invested and what it has earned for you when withdrawal time arrives.

There are restrictions, however. You pay a 10 percent tax penalty if you make withdrawals before you reach age 59.5, except in cases of death or disability. Lump-sum distributions are usually taxed as ordinary income.

Keogh Plans. The other type of retirement plan that is popular with self-employed persons is the Keogh Plan. There are two types of Keogh Plans: defined contribution, and defined benefit. In the defined contribution version, your benefits are based on the amount that is contributed to the plan, adjusted for various gains and losses, income, expenses, and forfeitures. The other version, the defined benefit Keogh Plan, is any qualified plan (qualification through the IRS) not considered to be a defined contribution plan.

To establish a Keogh Plan, you must meet certain legal requirements and receive IRS approval of the plan and its provisions. Like IRA and SEP-IRA retirement plans, Keogh contributions are deductible (use the Form 1040 adjustments section). Maximum allowable annual contributions are 13.0435 percent of your Form 1040 net income, or a maximum of $30,000. Income taxes on the amount invested and what it has earned are not due until you withdraw them from the plan.

Hints for Insurance Shopping

Some states now have *plain English* legislation requiring that all consumer contracts (including insurance, leases, and purchase agreements) be written in plain and clearly understood English, rather than obfuscated in polysyllablic legalese. Even so, the meaning you attribute to a word in everyday conversation may not be its legal meaning in an insurance contract.

Marie V. made this sad discovery. She was driving her pickup truck, on the way to a customer, when she collided with a Volkswagen Rabbit at a four-way stop intersection. When the police arrived she admitted that she was at fault, having reached the intersection a second or so later than the other car. She was issued a summons and immediately went to the police station to pay the fine.

Ten months later she received notice that she was being sued for whiplash injuries to the other driver. She immediately called her insurance agent, expecting that the insurance company would provide legal assistance, and, if she should lose the suit, pay for the dollar-judgment against her, up to the amount of her insurance.

Not so. She made two mistakes. First, because the damage to both cars was very minor, she did not inform the insurance company at the time of the accident. Second, she admitted guilt for the accident by paying the fine without contesting the charges. The insurance company pointed to an obscure clause in the policy requiring *cooperation* by the insured party. She, they maintained, had failed to cooperate, by admitting guilt for the accident, which would place them in an unnecessarily difficult position if they tried to defend her.

There are several kinds of insurance to keep in mind as you discuss programs with insurers or insurance brokers.

Liability Insurance

If you can afford only one insurance policy, make it for liability coverage. Some companies will not deal with an independent contractor who does not have liability coverage for property damage or personal injuries caused by the contractor while on the company's premises. For your own sake, you will want protection from claims filed by business visitors, or by the casual passerby who stumbles on your sidewalk, slips on your icy steps, or falls into a hole or ditch located on your property.

Low-cost Insurance

Be careful. An attractive price does not guarantee an attractive deal. All insurance companies rely on the same actuarial statistics. If the premium is low, it probably means that coverage is limited or in some manner restricted. All too often an apparent price break is predicated on reduced payments. Such restrictions are not automatically bad. Examine the fine print carefully.

Does the policy cover those things of interest to you? These are your essentials. Does the policy cover things that are of little or no interest to you? These are your throwaways. You may need to shop around to find the policy that emphasizes what you want emphasized, but does not force you to pay for the nonessentials.

Stability of Insurers

If the insurance company goes out of business, your protection may evaporate. Do not let a famous name or gilded promises lure you into an unstable situation. Watch out for names that are *similar* to those of major insurance firms, but which may be fly-by-night rip-offs (not all states have strict rules governing insurance companies). Check with the office of your state insurance commissioner or state attorney general to learn if there have been complaints filed against the insurer. Or have your attorney check it for you.

Objective Advice

Who among us will not sell our own product or service as superior to those of our competitors. It is all too human, and insurance agents are human. Who can you trust? Most often it will be a person who has no personal axe to grind. An insurance broker representing a wide variety of insurers is most likely to offer objective advice to you. Or you might go to an insurance consultant who has no insurance-company affiliations.

Package Policies

Some insurers offer insurance packages that combine several types of coverage. Properly tailored to your needs as a small businessperson, such a package could be particularly attractive. Check carefully that it con-tains the protection you need and that you will not be paying for protec-tion you neither want nor need.

Blanket Policies

Blanket policies for commercial or industrial property can be written to provide all-risk protection for goods or supplies against a broad range of casualty hazards, such as freezing, flooding, earthquakes, seepage, landslide, war, radioactivity, dishonesty, theft, and more. Exclusions will be stated on the policy.

Difference of Conditions

Consider the so-called difference-of-conditions policy for insurance coverage of those situations not covered by your fire, boiler, crime, and other insurance policies.

Deductibles

The larger the deductible, the smaller the premium, which is a good way to save money. Be sure that you can handle self-insurance for the deductible amount. There is more than one kind of deductible, including stated-dollar amount, percentage of claim, or defined waiting period.

Rate Controls

You can reduce payments for casualty insurance by taking care to provide safe working conditions and by attending to such measures as timely hazard and trash removal. In your home, you will receive preferred rates if you have a kitchen fire extinguisher and a dead bolt on your doors. Ask your insurance agent or broker which measures will count in your favor, and which will not.

Hidden Coinsurance

You may be coinsuring and not realize it. Some fire and related casualty insurance policies require that the policyholder carry a specified amount of insurance based on the replacement value of the property. If you have such a policy and you cover a lower percentage of the replacement value than required in the policy, often set at 80 percent, you may find that you have less protection than you anticipated. Find out if the policy you are considering has an 80 percent clause. If it does, ask the agent or broker to explain to you in detail what it may mean to you.

Fire Insurance

Fire insurance policies should also provide protection against lightning, hail, wind, explosion, smoke damage, riot, vandalism, malicious mischief, sprinkler leakage, and damage from aircraft and vehicles.

Replacement Cost

Remember inflation. Consider that an ice cream cone that cost a dime in the 1930s costs well over a dollar today. Base your insurance coverage on today's actual replacement cost, not what you may have paid in some past time.

Business Interruption

Consider business interruption insurance to keep you solvent when calamity has shut down your service. The coverage should be ample to help you fight off insolvency until such time as you are once again in operation.

High-Crime Areas

Will you locate in a high-crime area as a way to lower your rental costs? If so, you may find that you cannot get regular commercial coverage. All is not lost. Look into federal assistance through the government's Fair Access to Insurance Requirements Plan.

Credit-Life Insurance

Will you be extending large amounts of credit to your customers? If so, you may wish to carry credit-life insurance to ensure that you will not go unpaid should a customer fail or die.

Key-Person Life Insurance

Are you essential to your business? Do you have an employee whose abilities and services are vital to your service? If so, you may wish to have key-person insurance coverage. If the key person dies, the proceeds of the policy provide a dollar-cushion until a replacement is trained or otherwise found.

Partnership Insurance

Partnership insurance is akin to key-person insurance. Its purpose is to cushion the financial blow if one of the partners dies, forcing liquidation of the partnership.

PART III

Finding Customers and Selling Your Services

CHAPTER 10

Prospecting for Customers

The first step in selling your service is to use your Marketing Plan strategies (see Chapter 7) to locate potential customers—that is, to build your prospect list. As you begin to identify who will receive your sales promotion messages and your in-person sales contacts, keep in mind the following questions:

- Does this person (firm) really care about my service?
- Why do they (or should they) care about my service?
- How can I reach this person (firm) with my message?

Building Your Prospect List

Your list of prospects most likely to need your service can be 10, 100, 1,000, or 10,000 names. For a very highly specialized service, the list might be closer to 10. A list of 100 to 1,000 is more likely. A list of 10,000 is a poorly qualified list, or it means that you are going into the commodity rather than the service business.

If the prospects you have listed are marginal, you may wish to have a large list. Through advertising, direct mail, and personal contacts, you will cull out the nonproductive names, leaving the top prospects for further follow-up. But this can be expensive and time-consuming.

Frank W. underwent this process when preparing a list of prospects for his direct-mail service. If you will recall, his first effort produced more than 3,000 names. By exercising greater care, he pruned the list to fewer than 100. Is he penalizing himself with the smaller list? Probably not. Not only has he greatly reduced the cost of contacting his prospect list, he has a better, more clearly focused universe upon which he can invest both time and money with maximum effectiveness.

Your prospect list can be designed to receive direct-mail promotional material and telephone calls, or for personal letter and in-person contacts. Either way, you need good names.

Where to Look for Prospect Names

Many of the same reference sources that you used when identifying categories for your marketing strategy (Chapter 7) will be helpful when you search for specific names with addresses. These were

- Telephone company yellow pages
- Local and regional newspapers and business magazines
- Local and regional business and industry directories
- Chamber of commerce directories

Look also at "A List for Direct-Mail Promotion," later in this chapter.

Names by Referrals

After you have been in business for a period of time, you will be able to discover new customers through referrals by present customers. When the time comes, do not be bashful; if you know you have a customer who is satisfied with the work you have done, say, "If you liked my work, I'd appreciate it if you'd let your friends and associates know about me and my service."

There are also noncustomer sources of referrals that can publicize you favorably. They will make your name known to those who would otherwise be strangers, so that you will not be a total unknown when you write or call. Among noncustomer referral sources are:

Family member referrals. Your spouse, your children, your parents, and other family members and relatives can comprise an important sales-promotion cadre for your business. Remind them to mention you and your service to their friends during social encounters. Remind them to mention you and your service during business or financial dealings.

Banker referrals. If you have done your homework conscientiously, and if your Business and Marketing Plans have impressed your banker, you may find your name being mentioned to your banker's associates, and, when the situation is appropriate, to others of the bank's clientele. Not only does this make your name known, but it gives you the valuable endorsement of a recommendation by a respected member of your local financial community.

Attorney referrals. If you have impressed your attorney with your business acumen and if you have spent advance time analyzing your legal needs, your attorney, like your banker, may mention you and your service to other clients, particularly to those who could benefit from the use of your service. Again, here is positive reinforcement for your image from a respected professional.

Investment advisor referrals. If you have investments through a local investment advisor, discuss your plans and objectives. Tell your investment advisor why you are going into business, how you hope for its growth and prosperity, and how, as the business and its profits grow, you will be seeking further financial advice. Your investment advisor will become another referral source.

News media mentions. This approach, sometimes called public relations, sometimes called press relations, will be discussed in detail in Chapter 11. The idea is to gain promotional mentions from local news media, such as newspapers, magazines, radio, and cable or regular television. It pays to establish a positive rapport with newspeople. Make appointments to visit them in their offices. Discuss the local business climate. Tell them about your plans. Get them to talk about their business relations to local commerce and industry. Ask how you can best cooperate with their organizations to develop news about your service that they will consider newsworthy.

Do not neglect those whom you contact socially or professionally. You do not have to be a bore to mention what business you are in. See that your message is broadcast to your accountant, your financial advisor, and noncompetitive businesses, even those that have no need for your services. Talk it up with past coworkers, your insurance broker, your suppliers. Make yourself and your business known to your bowling team, your golf foursome, your fishing and hunting companions, your exercise group or jogging mates, and your lodge or club members.

The more often people hear about your service, the more likely they are to suggest names to you, and to mention you to others who may be prospective customers.

A List for Direct-Mail Promotion

An effective way to promote a newly established business on a low start-up budget is with a direct-mail program, discussed in detail in Chapter 11. Naturally, the heart of a direct-mail promotion program is your mailing list—but not any old list. Mailings to those who are dead, retired, bankrupt, or otherwise uninterested in your service mean money down the drain. If your prospect universe is small and specialized, you can build your own list. If, however, you cannot find the names on your own, you may look for a list that has already been built.

Building Your Own Mailing List

List building, the accumulation of appropriate names and addresses, is at best tedious. Sometimes, however, it is the only way to produce a list that meets one's special business needs. At other times you will do it to save money. Following are suggestions for where you can look for names.

Local or regional publications. Look through past editions of local newspapers or past issues of area or regional magazines. Jot down the names and addresses of companies that appear to be prospects for your service; where names of people are given, include them. It is most effective to mail to a person. Look for business news of any kind, including promotions, transfers, lawsuits, public notices.

Local business/commerce directories. Many specialized publishers around the country gather information for publication in area or regional business directories. Many local libraries will have such directories on their shelves.

Advertise; offer a sample or a premium. You have seen them, those advertisements with a coupon inviting you to write in for a free sample or other premium. The purpose, of course, is to build a list of persons interested in whatever is being offered.

Your approach can be to offer helpful information tailored to be of interest mostly or only to those whom you wish to contact as prospective customers. Consider a brochure, a checklist, a report, results of a survey, or a newsletter.

Press release; offer a sample or a premium. This approach is similar to the advertising approach. Chapter 11 discusses the drafting and use of press releases.

Generate editorial publicity. Cooperate with your local media (newspapers, magazines, radio and television stations) to generate news items that in turn will generate queries. This approach is described in Chapter 11.

Study the yellow pages. You will find company-name prospects by category in the telephone company yellow pages. Unfortunately, many of these company names will not include the names of persons; and in most cases, zip codes are missing.

Local Hall of Records. Here is where you will look for names listed in the public record, such as business formations and bankruptcies, marriages and divorces, births and deaths, real estate transactions, and more.

Teach a class; run a seminar. Do you have special information or a skill that you can teach to others? If this information or skill is related to your business service, consider teaching a class or running a seminar. Those persons who attend will be either prospects for your service or associated with organizations that are prospects for your service.

Your sponsor can be your local chamber of commerce, a community-service organization, a local club or lodge, a senior citizens' group, a businesspersons' group, or some other organization that meets regularly and has at least some members who are interested in your message. Most program chairmen welcome volunteers. Insist on an attendance list. Failing this, offer attendees something related to your service, and give your mailing address.

Offer a prize; hold a drawing. You can promote this activity with a storefront display (assuming that you can find a cooperative local merchant with a storefront), and by advertising via newspaper, magazine, radio, or local cable time. You will have to be clever enough to limit interest in your prize or drawing to those persons most likely to be interested in your service. Obviously, each entrant must provide name and address.

Before you announce your contest, check with local authorities to be sure that you meet all legal requirements. Ask your attorney to determine if state laws on gambling and lotteries will affect you.

The Brokered Lists

There are mailing lists for rent that meet almost every conceivable objective. Your name is probably on several of these lists. Every time you purchase something by mail your name goes onto a list to receive future mail promotion materials, or to be sold to other mail-order firms.

Magazines rent their subscription lists. If you subscribe to a hunting-fishing magazine, your name will be on a list for sale to vendors of sporting goods. If you subscribe to computer or automotive or body-building magazines, your name will be on lists for sale to appropriate direct-mail advertisers. In theory, every purchase you make, every publication to which you subscribe, can put your name at the service of a dozen or a hundred direct-mail vendors.

Note the word *rent*. Most lists are not sold. The renter of the list prepares the material to be mailed and sends it to the owner of the list where mailing labels are attached. The only way the renter will know to whom the material was mailed is when someone responds to the material with an order or a query. For this reason, it is crucial that your direct-mail package include a response mechanism—that is, something that makes it both attractive and easy to respond. (See Chapter 11 for more on response mechanisms.)

More than 50,000 different mailing lists are indexed in the *Direct Mail Rates and Data Directory*, published by Standard Rates & Data Service. Many libraries have copies of this directory. Most direct-mail advertisers and virtually all direct-mail list brokers also have copies.

You will have numerous choices in how a specific list can be rented. Typical choices are categories or subcategories within the list, zip code selection, and every third or every tenth name (for test mailings).

Other List Sources

If you cannot find or afford the list you want, there are other sources. You can swap lists with related or similar but noncompetitive businesses or professionals. If you have no list to swap, you can try bartering your services in return for a list, or at least a one-time mailing from the list.

Some states rent their lists of automobile and drivers' license registrations to vendors with products or services of interest to automobile owners, or persons evidencing a certain degree of affluence because of the type of car they own. Other state-run licensing offices sometimes rent lists of professional license holders, such as dentists, lawyers, doctors, cosmetologists, architects, professional engineers, contractors, and others.

Another source of names is the membership lists of professional societies or trade associations. Be careful, however, about using such lists without permission. If the published list is copyrighted, you may be violating that copyright. Do not think you can fool the organization. Most lists are salted with dummy names. When your material reaches the mailbox for such a name, you are caught in the act.

CHAPTER 11

Promoting Your Services

Promotion is the heart of selling. It is what you use for visibility, to rise above the mass of competition. It is what distinguishes you from all others who purport to offer services like yours and benefits equal to or superior to yours.

In its broader sense, promotion is advertising, but it encompasses far more than paid announcements printed in magazines and newspapers, heard on radio, or seen on television. Promotion is anything and everything used to create a positive image for you and your service, and to make your universe of customer-prospects aware that you exist and are ready and willing to perform your service for their benefit. Promotion is what you use to bring new customers into the flock and keep current customers within the fold.

Chapter 7, "Your Marketing Strategy," and Chapter 8, "Mapping Your Business Plan," touched on image making, which will also be discussed in Chapter 12, "Selling with Proposals," and Chapter 13, "Selling Face to Face." This chapter will cover promotion through the use of:

- Résumés
- Testimonials
- Direct-mail campaigns
- Capabilities brochures
- Press releases
- Telephone contacts

- Space and time advertising
- Your own newsletter
- Writing for publication
- Meeting papers
- Technical reports
- Community involvement
- Proposals (see Chapter 12)
- Other exposures

Your Résumé for Business Promotion

When Roger S. left his job as a chemical engineer with a major chemical company to establish his own independent contracting business, his primary tool for attracting business clients was his résumé. His education and excellent academic record at a major university, his steady upward progression and frequent promotions within the hierarchy of his company, and his specific areas of experience and accomplishment gave his résumé an aura of authority and achievement.

Because he was concentrating his business development efforts on fewer than three dozen chemical manufacturing and petroleum refining installations in the Southwest, he felt that the personal touch, his résumé plus phone calls and personal visits, would be less costly and more effective than traditional space advertising or a direct-mail program. Roger had another advantage. He had participated aggressively in professional society and trade association meetings and was well known by chemical engineers and managers in virtually every company in the area.

The technique worked well for Roger. Within a month of the time he launched his service, he was in the black. His eventual failure as a businessperson (see Chapter 3) was unrelated to the way he made new-business contacts. His sense of self-promotion was excellent; his sense of business organization was dismal.

Building Your Résumé

Résumés are particularly suitable as primary business promotion tools for independent contractors who plan to concentrate on personal-service type contracts in which personal background, skills, and experience are at the heart of the service being offered. They are also effective when the service to be offered is complex or technologically sophisticated, and the universe of potential customers is concentrated geographically or limited in number. Resumés are also important secondary components used as "proof of capabilities" in broader scale promotional efforts emphasizing the service rather than the individual.

Contrary to popular opinion, the most successful résumés are "built"; they do not just happen. Your résumé is the result of your activities over a period of years, both planned and unplanned. If you are looking to the future and your own independent contractor business, consider what you wish to do, then determine what you will need in the way of document-able experience and provable capabilities. Seek out or accept those assignments that will provide the most desirable personal capability bona fides. Be active in both professional society and trade association activities. If possible, prepare articles for publication and papers for presentation at professional meetings.

The Content and Style of Your Résumé

The style, composition, contents, and appearance of your résumé will differ for different purposes and different audiences. If you were seeking industrial or commercial employment, you would probably focus on career objectives and what you have to offer toward those objectives. If you were seeking academic employment, you would probably focus on academic work, your areas of research interest, under whom you did your advanced degree work, your published papers, books, and reports, and seminar and conference participation.

Business services most likely to benefit from a well-designed and presented résumé are those that require special training and experience, such as engineering, architectural design, medical specialties, police procedures, legal specializations, accounting and auditing, advertising and public relations, and specific applications of psychology and psychiatry.

A business-development résumé for an independent contractor, however, has other objectives. Place yourself in the position of the person to whom you will send the résumé, the person who will make a serious business decision based on your résumé. Here is what the person will probably consider:

First-glance impression. First-glance impressions are lasting impressions. If your résumé fails to pass the first-glance test, it may never be read. Even if read, a poorly presented résumé will detract seriously from otherwise important content.

Is the résumé visually appealing? Is it neat? Is it literate? Do typos and obvious errors detract? Is it labeled and categorized to help guide the reader through its contents? Other detractions from the first-glance impression of a résumé are smudges and erasures, bad grammar, an overcrowded page with little margination, and faint photocopies.

Initial impact. Scores, even hundreds, of business-seeking letters, brochures, proposals, and résumés may come into your prospects' offices weekly. Which will be read in their entirety? Which are most likely to generate a favorable response? Which are most likely to result in a contract?

Impact is the secret. Not just impact, but clearly stated, briefly presented, quickly noted impact. What is impact for the purposes of business development? It is simply a statement or a promise that is of direct and immediate professional or commercial interest to the reader of the résumé.

Start your résumé with an impact statement, one that epitomizes the service that you are offering and the benefits that a user of your service can expect. But do not oversell, do not overpromise. Too much hype will detract from your credibility.

Capabilities statement. After the initial impact, keep the momentum going. Present your areas of capability in short, concise, but clear statements, either in a narrative paragraph or as a list of bulleted items. Do not worry about details, such as dates or places. These will come later.

Concentrate only on those items directly relevant to the service you are offering. You may be proud that you were the best soda jerk in town during the summer between your junior and senior years of high school, but if your service is computer programming, architectural design, or engineering maintenance, who, other than you and your mother and father, cares?

Back-up evidence. If the reader of your résumé was attracted by its appearance and if the initial impact statement carried him or her into and through your capabilities statement, the reader will now look for proof that you have the experience to back up your capabilities claim.

Here is where you present your educational training and employment history, complete with dates, places, company names, job titles, and, where appropriate, areas of responsibility, accomplishments, recognitions, and awards. As a part of the back-up evidence, you may include professional activities and memberships, with offices held, a statement of (but not a list of) patents held, articles or books published, meeting papers presented, and so forth.

Three suggestions:

1. Begin with those items most important to and most directly related to the service you are offering as an independent contractor. Do not

worry if the listing is not in chronological sequence. Start each entry of your listing with the most important concept—for example, the job title, the company worked for, or the job responsibility.

2. As mentioned earlier, concentrate on those items relevant to the service you are offering.
3. Keep the résumé brief—two pages at most. Most executive attention spans are limited, and a thick document is all too often laid aside for later (if ever) reading.

Printing your résumé. Yes, printing. Not typewriting. You may have a computer and laser printer you can use, or you may work with a commercial artist and/or commercial printer. This is no time to skimp.

Once the résumé is printed, examine it carefully. Ask friends, family, even strangers, to read it and comment on it. Watch for their reactions. Ask them what they think it says, to whom, for what purpose. If the message fails, or if there are errors, omissions, or other detractions, start over again. Again, this is not the time to skimp on effort.

Figures 11–1 and 11–2 show attractive, well-designed, one-page résumés. Note the effective use of side headings, and the no-nonsense listing of training, experience, and other qualifications.

Your Capabilities Brochure

A simple, low-cost capabilities brochure can be an effective supplement to or substitute for a personal résumé. The brochure is a promotion vehicle that carries your business message, describes the service you offer, tells of your experience or qualifications, and, most importantly, announces to the recipient what benefits can be expected by dealing with you.

Do not be frightened by the fancy, thick, four-color, catalog-sized capabilities brochures you have seen distributed by major corporations. Most of these are not business-development brochures. Rather, they are image makers designed to impress shareholders, stock-market arbitrageurs, and other corporations. What we are talking about here is a normal-sized sheet of good quality paper reduced to pocket, purse, or envelope size by folding into three sections, with appropriate printing on both sides.

Brochures of this nature are quite versatile. They can be included along with your personal correspondence, or sent along with your direct-mail program (described later in this chapter). You can use the brochure

HARRY S. DIXON, Ph.D.

ENGINEERS

950 CRESTON ROAD
BERKELEY, CALIFORNIA
94708-U.S.A.

528-8092
AREA CODE
415

SPECIALTIES
*
Investigations, Photography, Tests, Reconstructions, Reports

ELECTRICITY
Shock, Burns: How, Why, Code Violations. Lightning Damage: Or other cause?
Equipment Failures: Controls, Elevators, Hoists, Cranes, Heaters, Motors, Relays, Circuit
Breakers, Switches, Railroad and Security Warning Systems, Transformers, Wiring, Grounds,
Freezers, Refrigerators, Food Preparation Equipment, TVs.
Electrical Structure Failures: Poles, Radio Towers.

VISIBILITY
Evaluation of Seeing Tasks by Tests. Visibility of Objects, Adequacy of Warning Signs or Lights,
Effect of Glare.

FIRES AND EXPLOSIONS
Electrical or Other Cause. Code and Standards Violations.

AUTOMOBILE AND AIRCRAFT ACCIDENTS
Nightime Visibility Considerations, System Failures.

Bank References
Bank of America, University Branch.   Wells Fargo, University Office - Berkeley, Ca.

Education
B.A., Stanford University, 1931
Degree of Engineer, Stanford University, 1936
Ph.D., Purdue University, 1952

Engineering Registration
California, EE 2493
North Dakota, 246

Experience
Engineering Practice: International; 1931 to present:
To Insurance Industry and Legal Profession on Problems Involving Specialties;
To Engineers on Measurement of Underground Atomic Blasts, Specialized Analogue Computers,
Control Systems, Power Plants, Electrical Distribution and Transmission Systems;
Preparation and Evaluation of Electrical Engineer Professional Examination for California Board
of Registration, and New Jersey and North Dakota Boards.
Arbitrator; American Arbitration Association, 1967 to present.
UNESCO International Expert; University of Lagos, Lagos, Nigeria, 1964-65.
Professor and Chairman of Electrical Engineering Department: New Jersey Institute of Technology
Newark, New Jersey; 1952-56. North Dakota State University; Fargo, North Dakota; 1945-51.
Lecturer; University of California, Berkeley, California; 1951-52, 1956-57.
Aircraft Electrical Design Engineer; Douglas Aircraft Co., and North American Aviation, Inc., California;
1942-45
Instructor; Purdue University, West Lafeyette, Indiana; 1937-42.
Assistant Engineer; Northern California Irrigation and Reclamation Districts; 1934-37.

Publications
Properties of Materials, and Electrical Conductors Sections; McGraw-Hill Book Co. Engineering
Materials Handbook; 1958.
Papers on Corona; American Institute of Electrical Engineers Transactions; 1959.
Classified Reports in Aircraft Industry and on Legal and Insurance Matters.

Memberships
Fellow: American Association for the Advancement of Science.
Senior Member: Institute of Electrical and Electronic Engineers.
Member: Illuminating Engineering Society, National Society of Professional Engineers.
Associate: National Fire Protection Association. (Technical Committee Member)
Member: Aircraft Owners and Pilots Association, American Defense Preparedness Association.
Member: Tau Beta Pi, Sigma Xi, Eta Kappa Nu, Sigma Pi Sigma.
*Limited Physically

Figure 11-1. Accident-investigation engineer's one-page résumé

as a leave-behind reminder when you visit prospective customers. A copy
of the brochure can be included with each answer to a query from a
prospective customer. At meetings, conferences, and seminars, you can
leave a stack of your brochures on a nearby table or ledge, available for
attendees to see and take.

EQUIPMENT RESEARCH, INC.
ENGINEERING CONSULTING SERVICES

7217 Lindsey Road
Marine City, Michigan 48039
Phone: (313): 765-8778

GEORGE J. LEVOSINSKI   **REGISTERED PROFESSIONAL ENGINEER**

Education: Master of Science in Mechanical Engineering, Wayne State University, Detroit.

Bachelor and Master Degrees in Mechanical Technology, Warsaw Polytechnic, Warsaw, Poland.

MBA in Finance, Wayne State University, Detroit, Michigan.

Courses in Fatigue of Metals and Strain/Stress Analysis, and Human Factors in Engineering & Design, University of Michigan, Dearborn.

Seminars in Robotics. Courses in NC Programming. Courses in Finite Elements Analysis.

Various Seminars in Industrial Safety and Human Factors.

Certification in Safety from the Board of Certified Safety Professionals.

Courses in Fire Investigation at Madonna College, Livonia, Michigan.

Courses in Machinery and Equipment Appraising.

Experience: Finite element analysis of structures and components at Ford Motor Company, Tractor Division, using NISA and NASTRAN.

SUPERSAP at Equipment Research, Inc. presently.

Product safety reviews and analysis reports.

Accident reconstruction.

Varied experience in research and development of machine tools, construction and industrial equipment at EX-CELL-O, Babcock & Wilcox AMD Div., Ford Motor Company, Rockwell International and La Salle Machine Tools.

Testing of industrial and construction equipment at Ford Motor Company.

Testing of machine tools at Babcock & Wilcox — Automated Machine Div., and at La Salle Machine Tools.

Publications: • SME Technical Paper: Profit Maximization Through Optimal Facility Loading.

• Teach Control Pendant for Robots. This application paper on human factors in robotic controls was presented at the International Conference in Occupational Ergonomics, Toronto, 1984.

• Attorney's Guide to Engineering. Contributing author: Chapter 30, Machine Design. Matthew Bender, 1986.

• Listed in Who's Who in Technology 5th Edition in Mechanical Engineering & Materials Science, 1986.

Patents: U.S. #3, 744,924 on adjustable boring quill.

Affiliations: National Society of Professional Engineers
Society of Manufacturing Engineers
American Society of Safety Engineers
Society of Automotive Engineers
Human Factors Society
American Society of Appraisers

Figure 11-2. Equipment-research engineer's one-page résumé

In brief, your capabilities brochure will be your basic marketing tool, a promotion vehicle you should have even if you have no others. It creates and presents your business image. It explains what service you offer and the benefits you provide. It tells why you are qualified to offer this service.

Your Brochure and Your Image

The obvious objective of your capabilities brochure is to make prospective customers aware of the service you are offering. More specifically, its primary objective is to project a positive, attractive image to both current and prospective customers.

The image of service is always important, but not always easy to communicate accurately. In many minds, service is intangible, conceptually ambiguous, because one cannot touch, feel, smell, or taste service. Sometimes there is no true message of service, leading to fictional statements of benefits which, if promoted aggressively enough, are perceived as real benefits—for example, the use of sexual innuendo to sell male and female cosmetics, denim jeans, and even automobiles. Fortunately or unfortunately, according to your personal stance on such matters, fictional benefits are not effective for the promotion of the vast majority of independent contractor services.

Statement of image. Image projection and the earlier discussion of what business you are in (Chapters 7 and 8) are inexorably interwoven. Primary in creating a statement of image is a statement of benefits. After this statement is established, you can present how these benefits are derived and why you in particular are qualified to deliver them. Start by focusing on the following questions:

1. What are the *needs* or *wants* of prospective customers?
2. What *problems* do prospective customers face?
3. Which *needs* or *wants* or *problems* can you handle?
4. What is unique about the services you offer?

After specificying what your service is, consider the following image benefits messages:

- One-stop service for all needs
- Top quality at lowest cost
- Creative solutions for old problems
- No job too small, no challenge too great
- Fast turnaround for short-notice emergencies

Refer to these suggestions to help you define and present image impact messages with your brochure.

Help with Your Brochure

The basic elements required to create a brochure are writing, layout and typographic design, illustration, and printing. Each of these steps takes time, so get started as early as possible. You will want to have brochures on hand as you make your first solicitations for business.

You may opt for doing everything short of printing yourself. While you will save money this way, you are more likely to have an attractive, persuasive brochure if you have help. You may have a friend or associate who writes or designs sales copy.

If you decide to go first class and work with full-time professionals, get names from local business people who have effective brochures. Look at telephone yellow page listings under Advertising Agencies, Advertising Art, Artists—Commercial, or Writers—Business. Scan the local news-paper classified ad section where freelancers and moonlighters will be listed. Look at bulletin boards in local supermarkets or community gathering places. Talk to local printers; ask who they work with, who they recommend.

Discuss your service and business objectives in detail with the person or persons who might be working with you on the brochure. Look for those who appear to understand your needs and whose prices are reason-able. Suggest to them that while you are just starting in business with a simple project, as your service grows and prospers, there will be future needs for larger projects. Encourage them to work with you and grow with you.

What Goes into the Brochure

Do not expect copy writers or brochure designers or illustrators to be mind readers, do not expect them to understand the nuances of the service you will provide or of the needs and customs of the types of customers you are seeking. Invest time, first to be clear in your own mind, then to communicate ideas and concepts to those working with you on the brochure.

Coverlines. Coverlines make up the persuasive message that appears on the cover of your brochure. These are the first words seen by the reader of the brochure, and, if they are not convincing and relevant, they will be the last words read. Remember that your coverlines must tell what the reader wants to hear, not what you want to say. The latter is on the inside of the brochure, visible once it is opened. To test the effective-ness of your brochure coverlines, ask yourself:

1. Do they tell who will benefit from my service?
2. Do they specify the benefits clearly and quickly?

There may be no mention at all of specifically what your service is. Remember that you are selling the idea of specific benefits for a defined audience. How you accomplish those benefits will be presented on the inside of the brochure. Of course, your company name, address, and phone number can be in small print at the bottom of the cover.

The Rest of the Brochure

Assuming that your coverlines have snared the reader's attention and have generated enough interest to encourage the reader to open the brochure to view the inside message, you now have your opportunity to specify your service with particularity—how it works or what it can do— and evidences of your capability to provide the service. You also have a chance to elaborate or expand on the benefits to be derived from your service.

Here are questions you will want to consider as you and the copywriter prepare the inside copy:

- ☐ Does text relate to and expand on the coverlines?
- ☐ Is the writing clear, easy to understand?
- ☐ Is the style formal, or one-on-one personalized?
- ☐ Are the facts in your claims accurate?
- ☐ Are all important aspects of the service covered in the text?
- ☐ Can anything be misinterpreted?
- ☐ Will it generate further interest from the reader?
- ☐ Are specific benefits listed and explained?
- ☐ Does the text tell who and what your firm is?
- ☐ Does the text tell your (or your firm's) qualifications?
- ☐ Does it tell the reader how to contact you for details?
- ☐ Do you make a free premium offer to encourage response?

Evaluating the Brochure

Upon completion of the design, but prior to actual printing, you will want to inspect and analyze the brochure in view of your business methods and objectives, and the uses you have in mind for the brochure. Try the following questions:

- ☐ Does it have immediate visual impact?
- ☐ Will it stand out when next to others' brochures?
- ☐ Can the type be read at a distance of ten feet?
- ☐ Are type and illustrations clear and crisp?
- ☐ Am I trying to say too much on the cover?
- ☐ Can I use the brochure with a direct-mail program?
- ☐ Will it work as a reply to inquiries?
- ☐ Will it be a useful handout or leave-behind?
- ☐ Is its message both timely and timeless?

Considering the last item, *do not quote prices* in your brochure. Price listings will be meaningless for highly specialized services that must be tailored to specific situations. Also, as your fee structure changes with time, your brochure will become obsolete. You can, if you wish, end by saying something equivalent to: "Our fees are competitive. Let us give you an estimate for your next job." Or you can include an insert, which can be updated separately from the brochure itself, announcing your current fee structure.

Figure 11–3 is a four-panel brochure; Figures 11–4 through 11–6 are three-panel brochures; and Figures 11–7 and 11–8 are two-panel brochures.

In Figure 11–3, note the very simple front panel (far right at top). In this brochure, the *promise* is implicit in the word *Investigations*. The printing is in gold, and the background color is a deep blue. Inside the brochure is background about Acta Investigations, along with a discussion of applications of investigative services. In the center panels, the general scope of services is listed by clearly defined category. In the righthand panel, Acta lists additional services. Affiliations (memberships) are listed. Toward the bottom of this panel, space is left where a business card can be stapled, and at the very bottom, the address and phone number are listed.

The brochure in Figure 11–4 takes several different approaches. Its coverlines are given as questions, along with an atmosphere photograph to humanize the brochure. Name, address, and phone numbers appear at the bottom of the front panel. The center panel is used for a mailing label and postage stamp, allowing the brochure to be used as a mailing piece without need for an additional envelope. A *benefits* sales message is located on the lefthand panel. On the inside of the brochure there are two main messages: "Why Video?" to sell the service, and "Why Devine-Hall & Associates?" to sell Devine-Hall as the logical source of the video service. Again, an atmosphere photograph is used.

The Metallurgical Engineering Services brochure in Figure 11–5 has several attractive features. The company, its three main services, and its phone number appear on the front cover. The center panel is a helpful checklist, the type that could persuade the recipient of the brochure to keep it at hand for checking purposes. The lefthand panel gives a name to contact, the address and phone number, and a map to simplify locating the facility. Inside, the lefthand panel discusses the organization and its capabilities and lists the industries served. The center panel lists general categories of services provided and gives the address and phone number again. The righthand panel presents the specific laboratory tests available.

The brochure in Figure 11–6 uses a question on its front cover, phrased to state both the problem and its solution. The center panel could

SURVEILLANCE

Our highly skilled and experienced operatives have been trained to provide a discreet system for following the subject of an investigation. Generally, two operatives utilizing two radio-equipped vehicles, will be deployed in the following types of cases: matrimonial, corporate investigations, insurance, child-custody, and criminal matters. Unmarked vans equipped with night-vision devices, as well as video-taping equipment, are also available. We have the flexibility and resources to provide our clients with the services of a sole operative or those of a complete surveillance team.

Surveillance often times is the most revealing method of determining the truth in a given situation. For example, many long-term disability and compensation cases carry a tremendous amount of exposure. Surveillance of a claimant can save considerable sums of money by terminating undeserved benefits.

PHOTOGRAPHY AND VIDEOTAPING

We offer a full range of photographic services. Telephoto close-up photography, night photography, as well as other special needs, are expertly handled. The photographs are developed quickly, and the negatives are stored in our file so that the proper documentation of evidence is preserved regardless of the type of case.

Our agency offers a full compliment of video taping services for surveillance, personal injury cases, security and loss prevention, depositions, wills, and "Day In The Life" presentations. Monitoring and viewing equipment can be set up for office or courtroom presentations.

COUNTERMEASURE ELECTRONIC SURVEY

Our technicians utilize state-of-the-art electronic detection equipment for countermeasure sweeps to identify unauthorized listening and eavesdropping . . . over telephone lines, in offices, homes or vehicles. A thorough physical search is combined with technical electronic sweeps. Equipment such as spectrum analyzers, non-linear junction detectors, time domain reflectometers and radio frequency locators are deployed to assure your privacy. To locate wiretaps, all phone instruments and lines are checked to detect rewiring and tampering. Tests include triple-tone generator; on and off hook line tests and telephone analysis, identifies the location of the tap.

CORPORATE INTELLIGENCE & UNDERCOVER OPERATIONS

The competitive nature of business, as well as the constant change in the economy, has created a vital need for investigative assistance for businesses of all sizes. Our corporate investigations cover the areas of industrial espionage, theft, mismanagement, and patent/trademark infringement. We provide the following services to cut losses and to restore profitability to your company.

☐ Undercover operatives
☐ Employee interviews/interrogations
☐ Pre-employment background checks
☐ Security consulting
☐ Site investigations
☐ Asset investigations for mergers and acquisitions
☐ Theft deterrence
☐ Executive protection and emergency preparedness

Undercover Operations

Extensive information can be obtained on a long-term basis through the confidential placement of undercover operatives (working as regular employees) in your warehouse, store, or office. Our undercover program is tailored to your company's specific needs. Daily verbal, as well as weekly written reports, are compiled on subjects such as theft, morale problems, mismanagement, and drug abuse.

Acta Investigations offers its clients the following additional services:

☐ Celebrity protection and bodyguards
☐ Courier services for transportation of documents and valuables
☐ Use of our facilities to view videotapes, audiotapes, and confidential file material
☐ Attorney referral service
☐ Referrals to court qualified experts
☐ Notary Public

ACTA INVESTIGATIONS, INC.
CORPORATE OFFICE
1300 Post Oak Blvd.
Suite 1450
Houston, Texas 77056
(713) 680-8585
Fax (713) 961-4816

Figure 11-3. Four-fold brochure from a private investigator. When folded, the right panel is front, the next panel is rear, and the other two panels left fold to the inside.

Acta Investigations, Inc., is a full service investigative agency comprised of the finest, most innovative investigative talent in the private sector.

Our agents are former law enforcement, private loss prevention, and corporate security to assure you — the client — the most professional and experienced handling of even the most sensitive matters.

We provide our clients with:
☐ personal attention
☐ creative solutions to difficult problems
☐ prompt service
☐ confidential reporting
☐ comprehensive verbal and written reports
☐ concise accurate information

With these key elements, you can make decisions based on facts rather than speculation, and your job is made much easier. Our combination of experience, expertise, discretion and dedication assures you of the highest level of professionalism.

Acta Investigations, Inc., is licensed by the State of Texas as a private detective agency. All of its agents are fingerprinted and registered with the Texas Board. Acta is bonded as per state law. Additionally, our clients are protected by a full liability, errors and omissions, and malpractice policy up to $500,000.00

For your convenience we have categorized the primary areas of investigation separately, with brief explanations of each service throughout this brochure.

PRE-TRIAL AND LEGAL INVESTIGATIONS

We specialize in pre-trial investigation and case preparation for insurance companies, corporations, attorneys, and individuals. Investigations are handled expertly anywhere in the world.

Our services range from Criminal Investigations and Defense, Personal Injury Documentation (statements, photographs, diagrams, videotape), Environmental Law, Patent, and Trademark Infringement, Entertainment and Record Industry Matters, Matrimonial and Child Custody, as well as other types of legal investigation.

We can come to your assistance in last minute emergencies, travel worldwide on short notice, and provide you with a comprehensive report outlining our findings, complete with all documents, photographs and other evidence.

As always, results are what counts, not merely efforts, and we obtain results . . . fast.

INSURANCE INVESTIGATIONS AND DEFENSE OF FRAUDULENT CLAIMS

Acta Investigations, Inc. strives toward the reduction of insurance fraud. This fraud includes money taken from self-insured businesses, insurance carriers, and everyone that pays their insurance premiums, and represents an annual loss in the billions of dollars. Our surveillance and investigations will substantially mitigate an exaggerated claim, and will identify a fraudulent claim.

Through highly technical photographic and videotaped surveillances, unmarked surveillance vans, and pursuit vehicles, utilizing state-of-the-art equipment and experienced skilled investigators, we will obtain the necessary proof of an exaggerated or fraudulent claim.

A fully detailed report outlining our visual observations is provided with large color photographs for immediate review. Additionally, you will receive a separate videotape for each day of surveillance. We will gladly bring our monitoring equipment to you for your review, as well as supply you with your own copy of all tapes with our report. We preserve the original tape at our facility for future use in court or duplication.

Additionally, the following services can be utilized to thoroughly investigate a claim:
☐ Interview witnesses, claimants, and parties involved.
☐ Secure comprehensive signed statements
☐ Obtain autopsy and other official reports as needed
☐ Gather expert photographic and videotape evidence
☐ Accident reconstruction
☐ Legal photography

FINANCIAL AND ASSET INVESTIGATIONS

We have developed a high level of resources and information as well as many financial data bases that allows us to accurately and quickly locate assets for judgement cases, marital awards, and corporate "white collar" criminal cases.

Our investigators can locate virtually anyone, anywhere, for service of process, witness statements, and interviews. Our success rate for locating individuals is over eighty-five percent. . . . which is the best in the industry.

Whether you are attempting to satisfy an unpaid judgement, looking to increase or decrease alimony payments based on a changed circumstances, or checking backgrounds of individuals or corporations for a merger, acquisition, or other reason, we can provide you with answers to the questions.

The following information can be supplied as needed: • Judgement searches • Title & property searches • Drivers license checks • License plate lookups • Bank accounts • Brokerage accounts • Corporate searches • Income verification.

Background Investigations

We offer several levels of background investigations tailored to your specific needs, be it pre-employment screening, verification of investment, proposals, pre-marital checks or for any business or personal decision-making purpose. Information available includes civil and criminal history, financial history, driver's license records and employment verification.

Level One
Prior Work History Verification
Judgement Search
Driver's License Records

Level Two
Level one, plus:
References Interviews
Criminal Convictions

Level Three
Levels one and two, plus:
Financial Profile
Investigation/Verification of Assets

The above listed types of background investigations are fairly routine in scope. Considerably more involved and detailed background information can be developed depending on your individual requirements.

Figure 11-3 (continued). Back side of the Acta brochure. These four panels show when the brochure is unfolded.

Why Graphics?

- Professional Look
- Saves Time & Money
- Achieves an Organized Presentation
- The Cutting Edge

Have you ever seen or been in this situation before?

Graphic Arts is a form of visual communication. It is an effective way to simplify matters and captivate juries and judges. Graphics is also used for public relations, improving a lawyer's image in the profession. It can be used in giving information about a firm's qualifications in such areas as real estate, corporate, and tax law. The courts have said

"the public is entitled to know something about what lawyers are doing." Graphics can do this for you.

Devine-Hall & Associates
5450 Telegraph Rd., Ste 100
Ventura, CA 93003

Why Video?
Why Graphics?
Why Devine-Hall & Associates?

Devine-Hall & Associates
Law in Motion

5450 Telegraph Rd., Ste 100 • Ventura, CA 93003
(805) 658-2777 • (805) 682-6636
(805) 496-4044 • (800) 821-6457

Why Video?

- Saves Time, Money, and Strengthens Your case!
- Cost Effectiveness and Convenience with Expert Testimony.
- Visually effective demonstrative evidence applications.
- "Day in the Life": Subject, your client. The difficulties a paraplegic may encounter during his daily routine, or the recently injured whose suffering may not be as evident by the time your case goes to trial.
- Living wills may be videotaped for your clients who wish to insure their will will survive any possible challenges.
- Use in pretrial preparation. Two examples: Witness demeanor under cross-examination; associates playing "devil's advocate."
- More effective in presenting deposition testimony to the Court and jury than reading from the transcript.

Elizabeth Devine-Hall, trained in Video Depositions through the National Shorthand Reporters Association, National Judicial College, Reno, Nevada, 1980, presents Video in association with Barrie M. Schwortz of Educational Video, Santa Barbara, California, faculty member, Brooks Institute of Photography, and Documenting Photographer for the Shroud of Turin Research Project.

Why Devine-Hall & Associates?

- Full Service Reporting Company
- California Certificate Shorthand Reporters
- Key-Word and Key-Phrase Indexing
- Overnight Delivery
- Nine-Track Tape Conversion
- Interpreters / Translators
- Conference Suites
- Photocopying
- Transcription of Municipal Court Tapes
- Professional Service
- Overnight Exhibit Indexing & Reproduction

In this rapidly advancing computer age, litigation gets more complex and the law changes daily. It is imperative that counsel have someone he can trust to provide services, enabling him to focus on the success of his case without worry, in addition to the daily runnings of his office, graphics for trial, video...

David O'Grady
President
Central Coast Shorthand Reporters

Devine-Hall & Associates, a full service court reporting firm provides a professional team of reporters who prepare verbatim transcripts of matters heard in: depositions, court, hearings, arbitrations, statements and corporate meetings, thereafter producing accurate, timely and competitively-priced transcripts for its clientele.

Our firm emphasizes its responsibility and that of its associates to act ethically in all aspects of its activities, and seeks to expand in the legal community by promoting and augmenting its role.

In addition to our reporting services, our affiliation with Barrie M. Schwortz for Video and Dorothy Bacchilega for Graphic Arts is the answer to...
Why Devine-Hall & Associates?

Travel
We go where you go in global litigation.

Figure 11-4. A triple-fold brochure from a professional videographer. At top: right panel is front, center panel is for mailing, left panel folds inside. At bottom: the three panels open up at same time.

Top panel (front, right panel)

FOR MORE INFORMATION CONTACT:

DOUGLAS A. STOLK, P.E.
Metallurgical Consultant

903 N. Bowser Road, Suite 340
Richardson, Texas 75081

(214) 480-0033

OUR LOCATION:

TECH-CONCEPTS PARK

CHECKLIST FOR PRESERVATION OF
FAILURE EVIDENCE:

1. Keep fractured surfaces apart and untouched.
2. Avoid cleaning, brushing, sanding or chemically treating fractured parts.
3. Contact an experienced metallurgical consultant as soon as possible for instruction on proper protection, handling or shipping of the failed part(s).
4. Record a complete history of the circumstances surrounding the failure. Include drawings, sketches, names, dates and accounts of eyewitnesses.
5. Collect any documents of the parts, such as manufacturer's specifications, purchase orders, installation instructions, test results, service manuals, and maintenance records.
6. Call a trained failure specialist to the failure scene as soon as possible to photodocument the positions of the parts, fragments and the associated physical environment.
7. Store the parts indoors without exposure to moisture. If impossible to store inside, carefully cover fractured parts with plastic sheet to protect from the environment.
8. Cold section specimens at least (6) inches from any fracture surface. Use flame-cutting as a last resort--keeping the parts cool throughout sampling.

METALLURGICAL

ENGINEERING

SERVICES, INC.

Consulting

Failure Analysis

Laboratory Testing

(214) 480-0033

METALLURGICAL ENGINEERING SERVICES, INC.
Consulting • Failure Analysis • Laboratory Testing

Bottom panel (three panels open)

ORGANIZATION

Metallurgical Engineering Services, Inc. provides specialized engineering consultation and scientific analysis reinforced with complete laboratory test facilities for evaluation of metals, materials and processes. With 17 years of high-tech and heavy industrial experience, we are qualified to perform standard ASTM, MIL-Spec or customized tests for material certification.

Our staff stands ready to analyze your materials by use of metallurgy, electron microscopy, chemistry and engineering. We provide scientific analysis, test results and solid expert testimony for your legal requirements regarding physical materials, products and processes. Apply our teamwork to your most urgent or difficult challenges and enjoy the benefits of our specialized services. We invite you to meet our staff and tour our modern facilities.

INDUSTRIES SERVED

* Aerospace
* Attorneys
* Automobile/Aviation Accidents
* Communications
* Construction/Architecture
* Consumer Products
* Electronics Manufacturers
* Environmental Testing
* Forensic Investigators
* Gas, Oil and Coal Producers
* Metal Fabricators
* Mining and Exploration
* Municipalities
* Nuclear Power
* Petroleum Producers
* Refiners
* Semi-Conductor Fabricators
* Utility Companies

SERVICES

Consulting:

● Accident Investigation
● Certification (P.E.)
● Engineering Drawing
● Expert Testimony
● Facility Inspection
● Formal Presentations
● Literature Survey
● Litigation Support
● Product Evaluation
● Product/Process Research
● Professional Opinions
● Qualification of Tests
● Research and Development
● Site Evaluation
● Teaching Seminars
● Technical Writing

Failure Analysis:

● Accident Reconstruction
● Cause Determination
● Design Analysis
● Engineering Report
● Materials Feasibility
● Metallurgical Evaluation
● Microanalysis
● On-Site Investigation
● Photography
● Product Liability Analysis
● Safety Factor Calculation
● Sample Preservation/Storage
● Scanning Electron Microscopy
● Video-Taping

State of Texas Registered Professional Engineers
Member; American Society for Metals
American Society for Testing Materials

METALLURGICAL ENGINEERING SERVICES, INC.
903 North Bowser Road, Suite 340
Richardson, Texas 75081 (214) 480-0033

LABORATORY TESTING

Non-Destructive:

● Boroscope
● Compositional Analysis (EDX)
● Crack detection
● Density or Specific Gravity
● Dye Penetrant Inspection
● Electrical Properties
● Environmental Tests
● Flaw Detection
● Hardness Values
● Magnetic-Particle Inspection
● Metallurgical Analysis
● Mineral Inspection
● Particle Characterization
● Photodocumentation
● Proof Loading
● Scanning Electron Microscopy
● Surface Analysis
● Ultrasonic Inspection
● Visual Examinations
● X-Ray Inspection

Destructive:

● Abrasion
● Chemical Analysis
● Corrosion
● Emission Spectrometry
● Extractive Methods
● Fire Assays
● Geological Analysis
● Mechanical Properties
  * Bend   * Compression
  * Creep-Rupture * Drop Weight
  * Fatigue   * Impact   * Tensile
● Leaching
● Metallography
● Microhardness
● Mineral Identification
● Refining
● Sieve Analysis
● Thickness Measurement
● Weld Inspection

Figure 11-5. A triple-fold brochure from a laboratory testing service. At top: right panel is front, center panel is information, left panel folds inside with map. At bottom: the three panels open up at same time.

You be the judge.

Videotapes from actual cases, (made available through the courtesy of lawyers and clients with whom we have worked) are available for your viewing at La-Crosse Studios offices in Ann Arbor and Southfield. We invite you to meet our staff, see our work, and get answers to any questions you may have.

Please call for more information:
Southfield: 1-313-559-9140
Ann Arbor: 1-313-994-9292

Selected Clients

Collins & McCormick
Joselyn. Rowe. Jamieson. Grinnan.
Callahan & Hayes, P.C.
Frimet, Bellamy & Gilchrist, P.C.
Hughes & Trucks, P.C.
Jacobs & Miller
O'Brien, Moran & Stein
Terrence J. O'Hagan Law Offices
Robb, Lackey & Nusbaum
Trial Lawyers for Public Justice, P.C.
Sommers, Schwartz, Silver & Schwartz
Zett & Zett

Services available from LaCrosse Studios

Studio and location videotape production on 1/2", 3/4" or 1" format
16mm film production
Still photography
Videotape editing
Videotape transfers
Videotape duplication
Playback services, wide screen available

IACROSSE STUDIOS

Southfield, MI 48076
1-313-559-9140
3960 Jackson Road
Ann Arbor, MI 48103
1-313-994-9292

Will you lose
a case this year
because the jury
didn't see important
evidence on
videotape?

IACROSSE STUDIOS
media communications

How will you use video in your next case?

The uses of video production depend on the needs of the case you are working on.

- **Video Depositions**

  An excellent way to preserve testimony which might otherwise be lost because of the death or absence of a witness. The video tape allows the jury to see the expression and demeanor of witnesses while hearing the testimony, improving impact, credibility and retention. The existence of a video deposition as a potential impeachment weapon will deter unfriendly witnesses from changing or "forgetting" testimony. We have extensive experience in production and courtroom playbacks at trial.

- **"Day in the Life" Documentation**

  In personal injury cases, build the plaintiff's case with first-hand evidence of the effect that the injury has had on his or her daily existence. With minimum inconvenience to client and family, the LaCrosse production team will vividly illustrate how painful and disabling the injury is. These tapes can also be persuasive tools in negotiating a settlement and avoiding an unnecessary trial.

- **Location Re-enactments**

  Where evidence about the nature of an accident scene is crucial to your lawsuit, a videotape made on location can clear up possible misconceptions. Distances, relative locations, and shapes are all clearly demonstrated. Re-enactments can demonstrate the speed of vehicles, stopping distances, etc. Also adds the element of reality missing with maps, charts and photos.

Trial lawyers understand the problem.

If you do trial work you know how hard it is to get your whole case before the jury. Witnesses die, move away or just forget. Graphs, charts, and still photos often lack the immediacy to make much of an impression on jurors. Pain and suffering can be described but without the chance to really experience the plaintiff's plight, jurors are often unimpressed.

The impact of the "witness on the screen".

Television in the courtroom will help you put your case before the trier of fact more effectively. A video presentation commands the attention of everyone in the courtroom. Videotaped testimony of witnesses has more impact. Lawyers report that jurors seem to retain more of the testimony and remember more about how the witness looks and comports himself than with a live witness. Clearly, the use of video can strengthen almost any case.

Lawyers agree on LaCrosse for video.

Plaintiff and defense lawyers alike have been coming to LaCrosse Studios for over 20 years for high-quality videotape production services. Here are some examples of what they say:

"Our firm has used LaCrosse Studios for many years. They help us tremendously in settling cases successfully. We appreciate the extra time and effort LaCrosse takes to maintain a high standard of quality in video production. I rely on LaCrosse to fulfill our needs in this important area."

Stan Schwartz
Sommers Schwartz
Silver & Schwartz
Southfield, MI

"I also appreciate your time and effort in preparing the lawyer for his part in the video presentation. That awareness which you conveyed did a lot for my usually droll presentation."

Terrence J. O'Hagen
Attorney at Law
Ann Arbor, MI

"LaCrosse consistently offers the best service from the standpoint of professionalism, reliability, and ease of presentation."

Allen J. Philbrick
Conlin, Conlin, McKenney & Philbrick
Ann Arbor, MI

"The presentation of the Liuzzo case was dependent upon the excellent editing and technical skills of your studio and we are extremely grateful for the time you expended and for the superior quality of your work."

Anthony Z. Roisman
Director
Trial Lawyers for Public Justice P.C.
Washington, D.C.

"I have found (LaCrosse "Day in the Life" video presentations) to be of the highest technical quality and most effective in demonstrating the effects of injuries of our clients.... I would highly recommend (LaCrosse) to any professional who is seeking a high quality video presentation."

Richard F. Fox
Sommers Schwartz
Silver & Schwartz
Southfield, MI

Figure 11–6. A triple-fold brochure from a legal photographer. At top: right panel is front, center panel is for address, left panel with client listing folds inside. At bottom: the three panels open up at same time.

be used for postage and a mailing label. The lefthand panel offers sample videotapes for viewing, presents a *selected* list of clients as proof of qualifications, and lists the services available from LaCrosse Studios. The inside of the brochure is devoted exclusively to hard sell.

Figures 11–7 and 11–8 show how two-fold brochures can be quite effective, if one is careful and selective with the verbal message. Figure 11–7, from an accounting specialist, identifies the field served and the service offered on the front cover, along with address and phone number. On the inside, qualifications, experience, and areas of expertise are shown. Figure 11–8, from another firm, identifies the business and its services on the front cover and lists other services with the address and phone numbers on the back cover. On the inside, their primary service, corporate valuation, is described, along with Hempstead & Company's qualifications, a general statement of experience, problems that can be solved, and a description (not a listing) of clients.

Direct-Mail Campaigns

Direct-mail programs can benefit your business in at least two ways. You can create or purchase a mailing list (see Chapter 7), then mail new-business solicitation letters and brochures to the names on this list. Or you can use your customer list to mail reminders of your availability for future work.

Direct-mail professionals will tell you that there is an art in the design and presentation of a total direct-mail package, including a letter with an offer, an answer card or envelope (so-called response mechanism), plus some descriptive literature. Top people in the field can demand very large fees, far more than most start-up independent contractor services can afford. As an alternative, you can purchase any one of a number of books that purport to convert you into a direct-mail expert. In truth, you do not need to resort to either of these measures.

You can create your own effective direct-mail package by following a few simple rules.

The Direct-Mail Package

Direct-mail professionals will try to convince you that a long, rambling, and repetitive letter with a series of offers, each exceeding the previous one, complete and replete with a second color (often red), heavy indents, stars, and more are required for maximum response. Possibly true. Consider, however, that most direct-mail packages are sent to gigantic mailing lists, sometimes numbering in the millions. There is no way that such a letter can be specific for all recipients, so it will be designed to meet the varied needs represented on the list. If you build your own

Figure 11-7. A double-fold brochure from an accounting specialist. At top: right panel is front, left panel folds inside.

mailing list carefully and with a focus on those most likely to be interested in your specific offering, your problem is much simpler.

All you will need is a simple one-page cover letter, your brochure, and a return reply card. The only requirements are that your package attract favorable attention quickly, that it have a specific message, and that it exhort the recipient to respond, either with a specific offer, such as a one-time seasonal service or free inspection, or a promise to send something of interest, such as an information packet, a checklist, or the results of a survey.

Specialists in audit and tax matters for closely held businesses.

Kelleher & Company has been in business since 1972. The Firm specializes in the accounting and tax aspects of closely held businesses. The Firm feels that its major strengths are as follows:

- The credentials of its professional staff.
- The Firm has extensive experience in accounting and tax matters and dealing with and communicating with the Internal Revenue Service and state taxing authorities. The Firm's principal is an Attorney and CPA and the staff is experienced in data processing systems, tax matters, employee compensation, risk management/insurance and other matters common to closely held businesses. This expertise and ability to communicate reduces accounting fees and maximizes results.
- Convenient, down town location within walking distance of public transportation and parking.

Professional staff
John H. Kelleher, Attorney at Law, CPA
Thomas J. Marabella, CPA
William Ryan, Data processing specialist
Paul Mullin, Pensions and deferred compensation
Carl Huber, Risk management
Mark Wahlstrom, Insurance coverage reviews
Greg C. Takesian, Supervisor
Pat R. Ormond, Supervisor, insurance claim specialist

Yes, I am interested in discussing the following areas with you:

☐ S-Corporations - Advantages and Disadvantages
☐ Auditing and Financial Statement Analysis
☐ Benefit review and update
☐ Pension Plan Administration and Compliance
☐ Executive Tax Planning
☐ Evaluation of Property and Casualty Insurance Coverages

☐ Other Matters _____

Your Name _____ Firm Name _____
Address _____ City _____ State _____ Zip _____
Telephone _____

Figure 11-7 (continued). These two panels show when the brochure is opened.

Here are the minimum elements of a potentially productive direct-mail letter:

1. A letterhead to identify your business and to give your mailing address and telephone number
2. A salutation or short, to-the-point headline
3. Statement of problem to be solved by your service
4. Statement of special benefits from the service
5. Brief description of how the service works
6. Brief statement of your qualifications
7. Statement of offer; invitation to respond

Other Services

ESOPs

Employee Stock Ownership Plans serve as an attractive way to provide liquidity to shareholders of closely held companies, as a highly motivating employee benefit, as a financing source, and as a means of facilitating corporate buyouts.

Hempstead & Co. provides advice on the feasibility, design and implementation of ESOPs and ESOP transactions, as well as valuation services involving new and existing plans.

Mergers And Acquisitions

Hempstead & Co. serves owners and management considering the purchase or sale of a business. We provide advice on pricing and structuring the transaction as well as assistance in seeking and negotiating with qualified buyers or sellers.

Fees

Our fees are based on the complexity of the assignment and are established for client approval before work is begun.

More Information

Hempstead & Co. welcomes the opportunity to serve you. For references and additional information, please contact:

John E. Hempstead, ASA, CFA, President, or
Edward A. Wilusz, ASA, Vice President

HEMPSTEAD & CO. INCORPORATED
807 Haddon Avenue - Suite 23
Haddonfield, NJ 08033

Outside New Jersey: **800/541-3323**
In New Jersey: 609/795-6026
FAX: 609/795-4911

HEMPSTEAD & CO. *INCORPORATED*

Corporate Valuations You Can Rely On

HEMPSTEAD & CO. *INCORPORATED*

Figure 11–8. A double-fold brochure from a corporate valuation specialist. At top: right panel is front, left panel folds inside.

The response mechanism can be a simple mailing-permit postal card. You will pay postage only for those cards that are returned. Check with your post office to arrange and pay for a mailing permit.

Place your letter, a copy of your brochure, and your return card into an envelope (called *stuffing* or *stuffering*), address it, add postage (a stamp if the mailing is small or mailings are infrequent; a postal meter stamp or postal permit if your mailings are large or frequent), and your package is ready.

Your mailing will be more likely to avoid the circular file and reach its

Corporate Valuations

What Is A Valuation?
A valuation is an appraisal or determination of the value of a certain asset on a specific date. Hempstead & Co. performs valuations of business entities, securities of publicly or privately held corporations, partnership interests, professional practices and intangible business assets.

What To Look For In A Valuation
A competent valuation meets two tests. First, it reaches an accurate value conclusion. Second, it clearly and convincingly establishes how the conclusion was reached. A good valuation can be successfully defended and supported under critical scrutiny.

How To Get It
Quality valuations are accomplished by experienced, capable appraisers. Hempstead & Co. prides itself on its professional experience and expertise in the field of corporate valuations. As a financial consulting firm, our major specialty is valuing businesses and corporate securities.

Appraisals performed by Hempstead & Co. are frequently accepted as expert evidence in state and federal court proceedings. In accordance with the particular requirements of a client, we can present our valuation findings as written reports, fairness opinions, expert testimony, or as a combination of the three.

Professionals Who Are Qualified
The staff at Hempstead & Co. consists of a group of dedicated professionals with backgrounds in valuation, finance, accounting, economics, engineering and investment banking.

Professional designations held by Hempstead & Co. appraisers include Senior Member, American Society of Appraisers (ASA), and Chartered Financial Analyst (CFA).

When To Employ Them
Hempstead & Co. conducts valuations to satisfy requirements arising from a variety of situations, including the following:
- Allocation of Purchase Price
- Buyouts
- Charitable Contributions
- Dissenters' Rights
- Employee Stock Ownership Plans (ESOPs)
- ERISA Matters
- Equitable Distribution
- Estate and Gift Taxes
- Estate Freezes
- Fairness Opinions for Fiduciaries
- Going-Private Transactions
- Litigation
- Loss-of-Business Cases
- Mergers
- Public Offerings
- Recapitalizations
- Solvency Opinions
- Stock Option Plans
- Tender Offers

Clients Who Count On Us
Referrals from attorneys constitute the largest single source of clients for Hempstead & Co. Other valued reference sources for new assignments include previous clients, banks and trust companies, accounting firms and investment banking organizations.

Our clients range from professional practitioners and small businesses to large companies in many varied fields of endeavor. A sampling includes publishing, securities brokerage, insurance, leasing, banking, construction, real estate, consulting, wholesale distribution, retailing, mail order, and manufacturing. Our clients in government include the U.S. Department of Justice and the Internal Revenue Service.

Figure 11–8 (continued). These two panels show when the brochure is opened.

intended recipient if it looks personal. You can accomplish this by making sure that you have names of persons to accompany company addresses, use a postage stamp instead of a postal meter, type the name and address directly onto the envelope instead of with a paste-on label, and resist the temptation to decorate the outside of the envelope with a big red "FREE OFFER INSIDE." Your mailing will be most effective if you also have home addresses, thus avoiding efficient secretaries devoted to protecting their bosses from what they might think is junk mail.

If your list is targeted and up-to-date and your message is convincing, you should receive queries from at least 10 percent of those who receive the package. Another 10 percent may file the package for future reference. With perseverance, you have an excellent chance of converting one-quarter of the initial respondees into first-time customers. Then, if your service lives up to its billing, you should be able to convert half of your first-time customers into second-time customers.

Assume that you send out 2,000 direct-mail packages, and receive 200 responses. From the responses, you convert 50 into first-time customers and 25 into second-time customers. If your list held 10,000 good names, you would have the frustrating but happy dilemma of how to service 250 first-time customers. What does this suggest? If you have a large list, one likely to develop more business than your service can accommodate, make your mailing over a period of time in sections.

Selling by Telephone

Telephone selling, or *telemarketing* as it is often called, is an excellent way to introduce yourself to prospective customers. You can use the telephone for first contacts, or for follow-up contacts. You can use the telephone to solicit orders or to arrange on-site selling interviews. You will find the telephone to be particularly helpful as a way to prune a large list by identifying prospects worthy of further attention and by eliminating those with little or no potential. You will also find the telephone to be a helpful timesaver if your customers and prospects are spread over a large geographical area.

Properly handled, the telephone will enable you to create a personal rapport that does not exist with mute pieces of paper. When you are talking to someone by telephone, they almost always will respond to your questions or offers. Paper can be discarded or filed without a response.

While the telephone can be a friend, it also can be an enemy if not used properly. The rules for effective telephone marketing are simple, but seldom followed. You will waste your time, even create hard feelings, if you consistently interrupt key persons not concerned with the problems your service will solve, if you contact them at inconvenient times, or if you are aggressively insistent.

Here are a few suggestions for how to get maximum benefit from the telephone:

1. Try not to waste your time calling companies that have no current or conceivable future need for your service.
2. Seek out the identity of the person or persons most likely to be concerned with the problems your service can handle. Ask the company switchboard operator for the department and the person

within that department responsible for the activities of interest to your service.

3. Establish a time that is convenient for that person to talk to you. Early morning calls are best avoided. Try Friday afternoon calls, as the work week winds down. If the person you want does not answer, or does answer and is too busy to talk to you, ask for a good time for you to call back. *Never* leave a number and ask that person to call you.

4. When you do reach the desired person, introduce yourself and your business quickly and clearly. "I'm George Smith, President of Compressor Maintenance, Incorporated. Your office told me that you are the person I should talk to about compressor repairs and maintenance." The reference to "your office told me" lends legitimacy to your call. Even better would be "your secretary told me" or "your operations manager, James Brown, told me." The quick, clear introduction allows the other person to make a quick evaluation of interest, or to refer you to another person, if more appropriate.

5. When you know that you have the right person, and that person is willing to talk to you at that time, state the purpose of your call, getting to the point quickly. "Compressor Maintenance is offering a free get-acquainted inspection of your compressors."

6. Then the trial close: "When would it be most convenient for me to come to your plant? This coming Monday? Or would Friday suit you better?" Note the suggestion of alternative dates rather than a yes-no alternative.

7. Do not force the issue if the person is uninterested or sounds impatient. Sign off with courtesy: "Perhaps I caught you at a bad time. I will call again next week. Our offer is good for the remainder of the month."

As you talk, keep the following in mind:

1. Prepare your introductory script in advance and practice it so that you can sound natural as you introduce yourself and the reason for your call.

2. Do not start with that timeworn telemarketing cliché, "How are you today?"

3. Do not address the person by his or her first name.

4. Learn to listen (not just hear) as the other person speaks.

5. Keep your cool; do not be maneuvered into a verbal battle.

If the other person is receptive to further discussion or has asked questions about your service, do not hesitate to spell out your USPs (unique selling points). Remember, you are selling solutions, not techniques. This means learning the other person's problem and showing that you have a genuine interest. If your competition is mentioned, resist the urge to downgrade or otherwise poormouth them. It will hurt you more than it will hurt them. Above all, try for a commitment; ask for an appointment at the very least, but do not hesitate to ask for business.

Advertising Space and Time

Advertising placed in newspapers or magazines is called *space* advertising, and its cost is calculated by the space required for the advertisement. Advertising placed on radio or television is called *time* advertising, and its cost is calculated according to the time required to air the commercial.

Space and time advertising are most often used to reach very broad, nonspecialized audiences, such as the homeowners in an area, or automobile owners, or taxpayers. If the service you offer is specialized, but there are no specific lists you can use, you might want to try space or time advertising. Examples of such services are architects specializing in kitchen renovation and CPAs or attorneys specializing in estate planning. The applications are specific, but the potential customers cannot be identified with ease from among the general population.

Advertising Contents

The requirements for a good advertisement are much the same as those described earlier for the capabilities brochure. You must attract attention, and then offer some benefit or the solution to some problem. You must identify yourself and tell those who are interested how to contact you. Normally, however, the amount of text for a space or time advertisement will be less than for the brochure. Keep the following points in mind when placing such advertisements:

- Make a clear, specific offer.
- Cite the benefits you offer.
- Avoid hype; honesty is the best policy.
- Include a response mechanism (coupon for inquiries).
- Do not forget your company name, address, and phone number.

Figure 11–9 is an example of a simple yet attractive and effective space advertisement. As designed, it can be enlarged or reduced to fit various columnar widths, yet maintain its effectiveness. Note also that this layout can be used as a mailing piece, a leave-behind, a conference or seminar handout, or in conjunction with a direct-mail package.

Figure 11-9. Simple yet effective space advertisement that can be used in a number of publication formats, and also as a mailing piece or to accompany a direct-mail package.

Virtually every town and city in the United States has some person or firm offering expertise in the preparation and placement of advertising. They range from those willing to work with individuals and small companies to those who will breathe only the same air as is breathed by major corporations. Or, you can try your hand at preparing you own advertisement. If you choose the latter route, you can get typesetting at a local printer, sometimes even by the newspaper or magazine itself.

If your advertising is to go on the air, the radio announcer will read it for you. It is more complicated if your advertisement is to go on local or cable television. Here again, there will be local services. Your television station can make suggestions.

Responses and Inquiries

We have discussed the use of response mechanisms earlier. The same principles apply to both space and time advertising. If the readers or viewers of your message do not respond, you have wasted your money. The best way to generate responses is to offer something free, something of perceived value or usefulness. If the offer is related to your area of business activity, which it should be, then the persons who respond are said to be *qualified* responses. These responses are business leads to be followed up, and can be added to your mailing list.

A warning: If you do not act quickly on responses or inquiries generated by advertising, the responding person will either forget you or be irritated by your slowness to reply. If you cannot or will not take advantage of responses and inquiries, do not waste your time and money generating them.

Your reply can be as simple as a standard sales letter, a copy of your capabilities brochure, and the item you promised to send. Set up a tickler or reminder file to call them within two or three days of when they normally would receive your reply. Why so soon? Most of us, I am sure, have received something in the mail, and, two or three weeks later, a phone call asking if we received the item. Do we recall the item? Most often we do not. The sending of the item and the phone call are wasted.

Your Advertising Program

Not all advertising is aimed at generating responses. Other reasons include image building and building an aura of confidence, goodwill, and solid reputation. For those who sell consumer goods, the hope is that when you are faced with a wide variety of choices, as there are of coffee, toothpaste, or bathroom tissue, the latest name you heard and remembered will be the brand you will select. Most of these reasons will not apply to a newly formed or still small independent contractor service business.

What will apply, however, is the question of frequency. Most advertising experts will tell you that occasional and erratic advertising schedules are a waste of time and money. If you do decide to use space or time advertising, be sure that you have the funds for a continuity program featuring frequent exposures.

Local Press Publicity

Businesses that function primarily in a well-defined local area often can get their message across to potential customers through local news media—that is, the newspapers, magazines, radio, and television outlets that serve the area.

The techniques for obtaining favorable coverage by the news media are called press relations or public relations. This is where you create news announcements or articles tailored to influence public opinion favorably. Negative events, such as an accident, fire, burglary, bankruptcy, or lawsuit are not suitable for public relations announcements, even though such occurrences do become news items.

What Makes News?

There are event news, development news, informational news, and created news. Any or all of these can be used with various news media to publicize you and your service. Here are examples of *honest news* that most often is of interest to the local media:

- A new contract (be sure your customer does not object)
- A new service you are offering
- A new capability or facility for your service
- An unique accomplishment by your service
- Anniversaries for your service
- Association awards or elective offices
- Report of a talk or speech you made
- Your participation in a civic activity
- Change in your location
- Someone joining with you in your service

While the preceding are legitimate bases for news, what can you do that will entitle you to news coverage the remainder of the time? Simple. Invent news. Dishonest? Not at all, as long as your reporting of the invented news is accurate and true. For example:

- Develop a new special offer and announce it.
- Announce readiness to serve a new marketing area.
- Announce readiness to serve a new geographical area.
- Create a contest and offer a prize.
- Make a local business survey and announce the results.

The News Release

The most common way to see that publicity about yourself or your business is made known to the public in general is with a press release, an announcement that you send to the local media. If the news editors agree that what you have to say is of potential interest to a reasonable proportion of their audiences, they will print the information in your release, or at least an abbreviated version of it.

No great skill is needed to write a press release, but there are a few rules that will enhance its acceptability. Figure 11–10 is a hypothetical press release that would be likely to receive favorable attention from a newspaper or business magazine.

Referring to Figure 11–10 as a model, here are the basic elements of a press release:

1. Letterhead with address to identify source of release
2. Notice that the news is ready for distribution immediately
3. Name of person to contact
4. Phone number of person to contact
5. Dateline (city and date)
6. Simple, subject-identifying headline
7. Lead paragraph to tell who, what, where
8. Second paragraph for more detail: tells when and how; gives other credits when such are either due or important for an overall understanding of the item being reported
9. Final paragraph for a quick picture of company, company principal, and area of services
10. Signoff; can be –30– or ###

Here are some general guidelines for press releases:

• Type double-spaced, one side of paper only.
• Leave generous margins, a minimum of one inch at left, right, top, and bottom, to allow room for editing notes.
• Do not forget to include names, addresses, and phone numbers for follow-up contacts.
• Use a snappy, informative headline. Avoid cuteness.
• Write simple, straightforward prose.
• Be sure to tell who, what, where, when, why, and how.
• Signoff with ### or –30–.

Not all of your press releases will be used. Whatever you do, do not be a pest. If your news is published, fine. If not, take your lumps and try again in the future.

YOUR BUSINESS LETTERHEAD

Your Mailing Address

FOR IMMEDIATE RELEASE

Contact: James Brown

555-8888

LOCAL FIRM TO BUILD CITY CENTER KIOSK

Middletown, January 15, 19XX--James Brown Con-
structors (JBC) has been selected to build the Middletown Center Kiosk that was unanimously approved at the January 14
meeting of the Middletown Planning Board.

The new structure, which will house Middletown's newly
authorized Tourist Information Center, will be operated by the
Middletown Chamber of Commerce. Architect's drawings are
being prepared by XYZ Architects of Hightsburg. Construction is to begin in March, with completion scheduled for
early May.

JBC was founded April 19XX by James Brown, formerly
Construction Manager for ABC Corporation of Middletown.
JBC provides construction services locally for businesses and
residences.

###

Figure 11–10. Sample of a simple press release.

Photographs. If James Brown had an architect's rendering or sketch of the kiosk, he should have included it with the press release. If the press release had been personal information about Brown, such as an award, he should have included a picture of himself.

Do not waste your time with a Polaroid photograph. In most cases, it will not have sufficient contrast to be suitable for printing. If you want to send photographs with a press release and you are not yourself an experienced photographer, consider hiring a professional. Specify high-contrast, black-and-white (not color) glossy prints, preferably 4 × 6 or 8 × 10 inches.

Handle photographs carefully. All photographs should be labeled, as they will be processed separately from the press release. If you write on the backs of the photographs with a ballpoint pen, you may leave indentations that will show. Either use a felt-tipped pen, or, better yet, glue or tape a typed caption on the back of each photograph.

Before mailing, place photographs between two thin sheets of cardboard. It may sound obvious to say "do not fold," but as an editor I once received a photograph that had been folded so that it would fit into an undersized envelope.

Your Own Newsletter

The newsletter approach is an excellent way to remind people of your existence and continuing availability, and to do it in a pleasant, entertaining, and constructive, nonintrusive manner. A large number of businesses and professional people publish their own newsletters.

These are mailed regularly to past and present customers, as well as to prospective customers and others who might be influential in developing new business, such as through referrals (see Chapter 10) or testimonials (see later in this chapter).

The Newsletter's Appearance

The newsletter does not need to be gaudy with multicolor printing, photographs, and decorative typography. It does, however, need to be neat, grammatical, clearly written, well printed, informative, and on a good grade of paper. If you have a computer, you might want to produce your own newsletter using a desktop publishing program.

The Newsletter's Contents

In addition to careful writing and attractive appearance, there are two primary requirements for an effective customer-contract, business-development newsletter:

1. It should be aimed at a specific, identifiable, reachable universe of customers and prospects.
2. It should contain editorial content of interest to its intended recipients; it should tell of things that are aimed at customer needs and desires.

Here are some types of material that could go into a newsletter that will be read regularly by its recipients, helping them to remember you when it is time to parcel out contract work:

Public-service items. Report and discuss developments that will affect your customers and prospects. For example, industry developments, new federal or state laws or local regulations, new ways to accomplish things (particularly if you are ready to adapt these new ways to your own operations).

Current-problem items. Discuss some current problem that is affecting or will affect your customers and prospects, such as, weather conditions, taxes, labor, materials, supplies. You might consider a "guest columnist" for this feature.

Success-story items. Report a project completed or a problem successfully handled by you, along with careful statements about what was involved and anything unique about the way you handled the work. For example, you might mention new procedures, faster turnaround, lower costs, new materials. Be sure that the customer involved in the project gives you permission to write the item and has a chance to approve the final version—in writing—before it is published.

Profile items. Prepare a short profile on a person, company, industry, customer, or supplier. These can be items that have been suggested by others and submitted to you, or items you have prospected for. Again, get permission and final approval in writing before publishing a person's or company's name, or anything that might allude specifically to a person or company.

Short items. Use fillers for short open spaces and uneven columns. For example, a new service you are offering; someone who has joined your firm; new equipment, procedures, or facilities; recent contracts signed or completed; or an offer of something that is available to those who write in or call.

Figure 11–11 is an example of a newsletter prepared for distribution to customers and customer-prospects. The first three pages and half of

Current cases affecting estates, wills and trusts   *August, 1989*

Appropriate Interest Rate on Interest Free Demand Loans for Gift Tax Purposes Determined by Court

Donor established an irrevocable trust for the benefit of various family members and made non-interest bearing demand loans to each of the trusts. These loans were not reported by the donor as taxable gifts. Subsequently, the Supreme Court in *Dickman v. Commissioner,* 84-1 U.S.T.C. ¶13-560 (1984) held that an interest free loan did in fact give rise to a taxable gift and subsequently Congress embodied this result in §7178.

But for earlier years before this statute, the Service determined that the loans made by taxpayer were gifts, and concluded that the interest rate should be those set forth in Rev. Proc. 85-46, 1985-2 C.B. 507, as the higher of the (1) statutory interest rates for refunds and deficiencies under §6621 or (2) the annual average rate for Treasury bills. The taxpayer argued that the appropriate rate should be the lower rate of interest imposed on gift tax deficiencies.

The Tax Court held the Service was correct in using the interest rates set forth in the Revenue Procedure as a fair method of determining the reasonable value of the gifts resulting from the loans. The right to use money is a valuable right "readily measurable by reference to market interest rates" as the Supreme Court said in the *Dickman* case. The Service did not abuse its discretion in selecting this rate to measure the value of a gift through an interest free loan and was not required to use the lower interest rate under §483. *Eileen D. Cohen* 92 T.C. No. 65 (1989)

Trusts Established by Decedent Included In His Estate — No Evidence of Complete Bona Fide Transfer

Decedent was involved in a broad range of businesses during his life, and he controlled and kept records for each one. He maintained one main checking

account for all the businesses over which he had sole authority. He kept ledger sheets entitled "Trust" for his two children. From time to time he would credit amounts to this trust, including his promissory note. None of the trust's assets, however, were ever transferred to the son, and until he became the successor trustee did the son keep trust records or otherwise act as trustee.

Testator's attorney, the only co-trustee, died many years before decedent and although a bank was named as trustee, the bank was never notified of its appointment until decedent died. At the time of decedent's death, the balance of the son's trust amounted to approximately $388,000, while the daughter's trust was valued at approximately $104,000. The estate sought to exclude these trusts from the gross estate on the grounds that the gifts were bona fide and completed before death.

The Court ruled otherwise. The ledger sheets showing the trusts did not clearly prove the existence of a trust or that the beneficiaries of the trust owned that property. Rather, it appeared that the amounts created on the ledger sheets were at all times owned by decedent. At any rate, if he did not own title to the property, he certainly retained the income of the trust funds during his life under §2036 and this is enough to include the trust's value in his gross estate. *Estate of Maynard C. Wedum*. T.C. Memo 1989-148

Annuity Payable to Spouse Qualified for Marital Deduction

Decedent left her residuary estate primarily to a charity. But she established a trust for her husband to receive the income from the trust for his lifetime with the remainder to the charity. The trustee purchased an annuity for the husband paid from the corpus of the testamentary trust. Did this annuity qualify for the marital deduction?

Figure 11-11. Newsletter for professionals providing estate planning, wills, and trust services.

the fourth page of Figure 11–11 are devoted to helpful information of interest to anyone (for example, attorneys or bank officers).

Writing for Publication

Your byline on published journal and magazine articles can benefit you in at least three ways: (1) your name is widely seen; (2) the editor's accep-

§2056(b) provides that no marital deduction is allowed with respect to certain interests in property referred to generally as "terminable interests" passing from a decedent to a surviving spouse. The husband here had a right to an annuity of which he was the only beneficiary. No one else may receive annual payments from the annuity until the husband's death. The charity does not share any amount of the annuity as long as the husband is living. Thus, the annuity is not a non-deductible terminable interest. Reg. §20.2056(b)-1(c). Consequently, it qualifies for the marital deduction. *First Trust Company of Montana v. United States*, 89-1 U.S.T.C. ¶13,805 (D. Mont. 1989)

Testator's Belief That Daughter was Not His Biological Daughter Doesn't Invalidate Will Leaving Entire Estate to a Friend

Decedent died leaving his entire estate to his daughter A; but if she pre-deceased the testator, the estate was then to go to B, another daughter. Unfortunately, A was killed by a person or persons unknown. A week or so later the testator executed a codicil which left his entire estate to a male friend, cutting out his other daughter. When he subsequently died, the daughter challenged the probate of the will.

Ruled the court, the contestant must prove her case by clear and convincing evidence. There is a presumption of capacity, and the fact that the will left the estate to a friend and cut out his daughter is not by itself sufficient evidence showing that the beneficiary enjoyed the overmastering influence over a testator suffering from weakened intellect. The beneficiary under the will was not the testator's attorney, physician, pastor, or other person in a confidential relationship. And even if testator were mistaken in suspecting that his daughter was not his biological daughter, this is not the type of "mistake of fact" which would invalidate the will leaving the entire estate to a friend. Contestant has not carried her burden of proof and the will is admitted to probate. *In re Estate of Angier* 552. A.2d 1121 (Pa. Superior Ct. 1989)

Wife Not Entitled to Relief Under Equitable Distribution or Elective Share When Husband Died During Divorce, But She Could Raise Equitable Claim

In 1984, wife filed a complaint for divorce against husband on grounds of desertion. The complaint sought equitable distribution of property, alimony and counsel fees. But before trial, the husband died, leaving his entire estate to the children of his prior marriage. What is the wife's share of the estate?

Ruled the court, the wife has no right to take an elective share of the estate because husband and wife at the time of husband's death had been living separate and apart in different habitations. Similarly, the wife was not entitled to relief under the statute providing for equitable distribution of property on divorce because husband's death terminated the divorce proceedings.

However, the court noted, the wife still may obtain some relief. She was permitted to amend her pleadings to set forth any additional causes of action for an interest in the marital assets of the parties including claims that she is entitled to an equitable share of the marital assets on the grounds of quasi contract, quantum meruit, and other equitable theories including constructive trust, resulting trust, and unjust enrichment. The appellate court agreed. Let there be a trial on these issues of equitable entitlement as a way of reducing the harsh result from the statutes regarding equitable distribution and death while a divorce is pending. *Carr v. Carr,* 551 A. 2d 991 (N.J. App. Div. 1989)

Property Included in Decedent's Gross Estate as Property Subject to a General Power of Appointment

Decedent died after suffering from Alzheimer's disease for several years. He needed professional help to aid in daily functions. Under the spouse's will, decedent was given the right to use as much or all of the property as may be necessary for sickness, hospitalization, doctor's care, medication, and general comfort and welfare in keeping with the manner and mode of living to which decedent had been accustomed. He never exercised the withdrawal power given under the will. Did he have a general power of appointment requiring the property to be included in his estate at his death?

Ruled the Service, he did. A power to consume, invade or appropriate corpus which is limited by an ascertainable standard relating to health, education, support or maintenance is not a general power of appointment under Reg. §20.2041-1(c)(2). But a power measured by comfort, welfare or happiness is not limited by the requisite standard. "Support" or "support in reasonable comfort" are ascertainable standards, but not comfort and welfare. Consequently, decedent had a general power of appointment subject to tax at his death even though because of his disease he could not actually exercise this power. Under the applicable state law, there is not sufficient restriction and thus there is a general power of appointment taxable under §2041. Moreover, the legal or practical incapacity of the holder of power to exercise that power does not affect the existence of the power or prevent inclusion of property subject to the power under §2041, citing *Gilchrist v. Commissioner,* 630 F.2d 340, 344 (5th Cir. 1980). Consequently, the property subject to the power is includible in the decedent's gross estate. L.R. 8901006 (not a precedent).

Figure 11–11 (continued).

tance and publication of your article is an implied testimonial of quality; and (3) you can obtain reprints (copies) of your article to use in your direct-mail program, along with your sales letter and capabilities brochure.

Help for Your Writing

Even if you have never written for publication, there is no need to give up. There are people who will work with you to prepare finished articles.

The View From Washington

Debate Continues on Does a Capital Gains Tax Cut Raise Revenues?

The Administration's proposal to cut the capital gains tax rate on certain types of capital assets as a revenue raising measure still stirs doubt among many Democratic congressmen. The Administration, however, rules out linking an increase in the federal excise taxes on gasoline with the Administration's proposal to cut the tax rate on capital gains because the Administration maintains that a cut in capital gains will raise revenue and, therefore, does not need another revenue raiser as an offset.

Democratic experts in particular dispute whether a temporary cut in the capital gains tax will meet the goals of the Administration's proposal. Most of the testimony indicates that only about 25%, if that much, of a capital gains tax break would go to individuals with wage and salary income of less than $50,000. A temporary cut in capital gains tax rates is unacceptable to the Administration. The Administration, however, also does not want to make changes to expand the capital gains tax cut to include depreciable assets since this would be a revenue loser, they maintain.

Democrats Seek a Simple Tax Increase

Democratic legislators have proposed not trying to treat a capital gains tax cut as a revenue raiser — which they say is ridiculous. If there is a $5.3 billion shortfall in revenue, they say, let's simply increase tax rates on top bracket taxpayers, creating a 33% tax bracket that is not a transitional but a permanent bracket. The maximum capital gains tax would remain at 28%, a cut from the possible current maximum rate of 33%. As a matter of philosophy as well as the need to raise revenue, they favor a proposal to make the income tax more truly progressive.

Practitioners Disagree with IRS on Elimination of "Comfort Rulings"

A number of taxpayers and their counsel faced with large corporate transactions believe them to be covered by existing cases and rulings. Nevertheless, with so much money involved, they generally apply for and obtain a so-called comfort ruling. The IRS proposes eliminating comfort rulings, that is rulings that seem clearly to be covered by existing rulings or cases. The action is motivated by the IRS's current budget crunch and the fact that the IRS has limited resources to devote to taxpayer guidance and should not have to go over and over well settled ground. Practitioners, however, argue that there may be some slight differences that would cause their clients to face millions of dollars of liability at a later time. The whole point of the ruling system is to give assurances and not simply to provide a forum for the resolution of truly new and unanswered questions — because after 76 years of the personal income tax, there are not many of those left.

Proposed Repeal of ESOP Tax Break

A proposal has been made to repeal the 50% interest exclusion given to banks who lend money to employee stock ownership plans to finance the sale of stock to the plans, generally by wealthy stockholders. There has been, it is reported, considerable abuse of this section.

Tightening the Charitable Deduction May Be a Way of Raising Modest Revenue and Correcting Perceived Abuses

The Service, as part of its program to correct perceived abuses in charitable solicitations by tax exempt organizations is looking at a number of areas that present the potential for a donor to overstate charitable deductions. The Service will focus on payments to participate in celebrity golf tournaments (close to a personal expense with very little going to charity); purchases at church thrift shops and church art auctions (often abused by individuals claiming deductions where they are generally simply buying something); educational travel programs for professionals (high element of personal expense); inflated appraisals of donated property; sweepstakes solicitation by public television stations, and premiums offered in exchange for donations (deductible only to the extent the amount of the contribution exceeds the value of the property received).

Figure 11-11 (continued).

You provide the facts and the thoughts, the professional writer/editor presents your facts and thoughts in a form acceptable to the publication.

You can find writer/editors in the telephone company yellow pages. Or keep an eye on the classified advertising in your local newspaper, where freelancers (independent contractors) and moonlighters advertise their services. Another source of names is your local high school or college,

Estate Planning

Keeping Up With the Latest In Estate Planning Rules and Regulations Is Part of Our Job

Continuing professional education has become an established branch of legal and accounting practice as professionals strive to keep up with the enormous changes in the law. In the area of taxation alone, for example, practitioners must keep up not only with the radical statutory changes, both actual and proposed, but with some 6,000 pages of case material, about 2,000 pages of rulings and perhaps 500 pages of regulations, treasury decisions, committee reports and so forth, all of which are relevant in knowing what the tax laws alone are, and how they can most effectively be used to save taxes and avoid interest and penalties.

Of course, publishing this newsletter is one of the ways that we help keep estate planning professionals current with new developments in the law. We do the same with our own trust officers and employees. We encourage attendance and participation in lectures and seminars; we provide up-to-date material for continuing professional development; and, of course we require that our staff keep abreast of statutory and regulatory changes that affect their day-to-day work.

We believe that our principal competitors, generally members of your clients' families who might otherwise serve as executors and trustees, cannot really say the same. Also, we think that alertness to changes in the investment climate and economic opportunities is another important service that we can offer to your important clients. Again we very much doubt that our "competition" can make the same claim. In fact, we would venture to say that seizing one investment opportunity or avoiding just one important mistake would many times repay our tax deductible fees.

Won't you call one of our experienced trust officers for an appointment to see how we can most effectively fill the estate planning requirements of your important clients?

Figure 11–11 (continued).

whose teachers and professors can and will write with you in their spare time.

Opportunities to Publish

The practice of writing for publication is not limited to engineers, scientists, and business executives. Any type of service specialization will offer you ample opportunities to write articles. All that is needed is that you have something new and useful to say to the audience served by the journal or magazine, and that you can string sentences and paragraphs together in a logical and coherent manner according to the style of the publication.

The universe of subject areas covered by magazines and journals is virtually limitless. For almost any topic you can conceive, there are one or more publications serving those who have related professional, avocational, or intellectual interests. Topical areas range from religion to pornography and satanism, from nuclear science to garbage collection, from aircraft design and maintenance to janitorial services.

There are a number of directories that list magazines and journals, many of which will be in your local library. An hour or so with the directories will provide you with ample publication names toward which to direct your writing efforts.

How Articles Are Selected

Each magazine or journal has its own raison d'être, its own self-conceived mystique, its own sense of purpose and style. Each is directed toward a defined purpose for a definable audience of readers, and, if it is a trade publication, for the advertisers desirous of reaching that audience with their sales messages. The editors of these publications normally consider six basic requirements when accepting or rejecting finished articles or article proposals:

1. Is the author qualified to write on the subject?
2. Is the subject of the article useful or interesting for the readers of the publication?
3. Are the contents of the article timely and sufficiently detailed to serve the needs of the readers?
4. Has the publication already covered your area recently? Or, has it made a commitment to publish such an article?
5. Can the author write clearly and unambiguously?
6. Has the author followed the publication's style for organization, illustration, references, and so forth?

Doing Your Advance Homework

The first requirement for publication of an article is the proper selection of your target publication. What are you looking for? Readers interested in engineering? Medicine? Office maintenance? Municipal services? Undertaking? Within the category or categories you select (you may have messages to several discrete categories), which magazines publish the type of article you intend to write? Will your article deal with theory or practice; with how to do it or with how to design it; with physical installations or services? Examine the past six issues and analyze what it is the magazine wants in the way of articles and whether this *want* meshes with what you intend to offer.

Picture your target audience. Who is interested; who will care about what you have to say? Are these the persons who will read the publication you have chosen? Is this publication read by those persons for the purposes to be covered in your article? There is an illusion that because everyone is interested in health or automobiles or sports, every publication will be interested in health or automobiles or sports. Not necessarily true. If you are writing for a computer publication, forget about the common cold or construction-site accidents. However, you might have an article on computer-station furniture ergonomics, carpal tunnel syndrome for typists, or eye strain or radiation problems with monitors.

Know what you want to say; have a message. Mere knowledge of your subject area and your target audience is not enough. What is it you want to tell your audience? Why is it important to them? Why will they, or should they, care? Unless the editor is convinced that your article will enhance the value of the publication in the eyes of its readers, your chances of publication are slim indeed.

Know your subject. Know what you are talking about. Do not try to fake it. If you do not know some fact needed for the article, take time to find or learn it. If you do not know and cannot find or learn it, seek help from someone who does know it. If you still cannot find answers, either recast your article so that you do not need that fact, or look for another topic.

Planning Your Article

Say that you have selected the topic for your article. You have developed a clever bypass procedure for chemical plants and petroleum refineries to clean heat-exchanger bundles without shutting down operations. The topic is selected and you know how to explain the operation. Are you ready to write? No. You have more homework. Take the same six copies of the publication you studied while selecting which magazine would be your target. Analyze the style. You should look at five basic elements.

1. *Headline style*. Are the headlines mere labels? Do they contain action verbs? Do they emphasize the how-to aspects, or do they exhort the reader to do something?

2. *Deck material*. The deck comprises an expansion of the headline, a link between the headline and the article's introductory paragraph. In journals, the deck is frequently replaced by a paragraph summarizing the entire article.

3. *Article structure.* What is the sequence of elements that comprise the article? For example, many scientific journal articles have the following sequence: introduction with background material; statement of the work or experiment that was conducted; description of the equipment, materials, and instrumentation; experimental procedure; experimental results; discussion of results; summary; acknowledgments; list of references.

4. *Illustrations.* What kinds of illustrations are used? Line drawings? Photographs, or so-called halftones? Is there a fixed, or standard appearance to drawings and graphs, or does each article seem to follow its own style? Are the labels within the drawing typeset or lettered? You will learn more about such requirements when you receive the author's guide from the publication.

5. *References.* Do articles have no references, or a few or many references? The more scientific or academic the publication, the larger the number of references. Is there a standard style and sequence for how references are presented?

When you complete this analysis, you will be ready to outline your article and you will know what questions need to be answered before you begin the actual writing of the article.

Querying the Editor

Before you invest time and effort in an article that may not be publishable, write to one of the editors working with the magazine. Look on the magazine masthead (list of staff), usually located just after the table of contents, for someone with a *senior* or *associate* editor title. If the staff is very small, you might want to write to the *editor-in-chief.*

Introduce yourself: briefly identify who you are, what you do, and in what areas you are qualified. Then tell the editor that you are interested in writing an article for the magazine and specify the subject. Describe what the article will cover, to whom among their readers it will be directed, and what it will do for the benefit of their readers. Then ask if the editor is interested, and if so, ask for a copy of the magazine's author guide or article guide. Do this all on a single page. Yes; even editors have short attention spans.

If the editor is interested, you may be asked to supply more details, such as an outline of contents and a few sample pages for style. Or, the entire article may be requested.

Presenting Meeting Papers

It is hard to conceive of an established profession or major activities within major professions that are not served by one or more professional societies or trade associations. If you have not been a joiner in the past, now is the time. You may think you already know which organizations are of major interest to you. But you may be surprised if you study Gale's *Encyclopedia of Associations* with its thousands of listings. Say you are a mechanical engineer. Your society is the American Society of Mechanical Engineers, right? Well, partially. Here are a few trade associations related to mechanical engineering, any or all of which could have meeting and membership benefits of value to you as an independent contractor:

- Abrasives Engineering Society
- Acoustical Door Association
- Adhesives and Sealants Council
- Air Filter Institute
- Aluminum Siding Association
- American Boat Builders and Repairers Association
- American Institute of Maintenance
- American Pipe Fitting Association
- Association of Professional Draftsmen

And these are not even all of the *A* listings.

Writing Technical Reports

Small audiences involved in highly technical operations can be impressed with reports, white papers, and technical analyses, even those that are never published or presented at a conference. Each time you prepare a proposal (see Chapter 12), you are gathering background material and generating thoughts and information that could be expanded into a generalized report.

Watch out for ethical considerations, however. Be sure that your material does not violate a confidence. If there is a potential problem, either obtain permission (in writing, of course) from the person or firm involved or modify the facts to hide all specific identities. Or do not use the material at all.

Using Testimonials

The most credible source of recommendation concerning your abilities or the quality of your service is a positive testimonial from a satisfied customer, one who is pleased enough to be willing to tell others of your service.

You can wait for testimonials to come your way, which may be a long wait, or you can encourage testimonials. If you are confident that the customer was pleased with the outcome of your contract work, you can say, "I'd appreciate it if you'd let your associates know about me and my services." With luck, that person just may think to mention you at some opportune time, but do not count on it.

A better way is to ask, "May I use your name as a reference with my other customers?" or, "May I list your name on my brochure as someone I have performed contract work for?"

Parlaying Community Involvement

Community activities, particularly in towns and smaller cities, are important sources of positive-image visibility. Consider joining or otherwise becoming active in one or more of the following:

- Community-chest campaigns
- First-aid squad fund raising
- Volunteer fire department fund raising
- Fraternal organizations (Elks, Lions, and so forth)
- Church activities
- Senior citizen activities
- Hobby clubs
- Special interest groups
- Municipal government volunteer committees and boards

Look around. Ask questions. You may find other community activities that are even more suited to your time, interests, talents, and professional-business objectives. Volunteer to give lunchtime talks. Program chair-people will love you.

Other Professional Exposure

Everything you do that is seen and heard by others who know of you and what your service is becomes promotion, either positive or negative. Keep in mind that so-true cliché, "You never have a second chance to make a first impression." So whatever you do, do it right the first time.

In addition to all of the methods of promotion discussed in this chapter and elsewhere in this book, people will respond to your enthusiasm (or lack of it), to your attire (neatness, appropriateness), the appearance of your business forms (stationery, cards, invoices, purchase orders), and your telephone manner. A pleasant or constructive contact often encourages a second contact; unpleasantness or indifference seldom does.

CHAPTER 12

Selling with Proposals

It is content, not length, that creates a proposal. If you have been involved with major industrial or municipal proposals, very likely you picture a many-paged tome with numerous foldout diagrams or blueprints. A proposal is an offer to accomplish a specified task in a certain manner under specified conditions. The proposal may be a thick report, but it can also be a one-page letter with or without an attached sketch or a memo. A telephone call or an in-person chat can create a proposal.

Governmental bodies, both federal and local, and business firms frequently send out Requests for Proposals (RFPs) or Requests for Bids (RFBs) for work that will exceed a certain cost limit. But you need not wait patiently for an RFP or RFB before you submit a proposal.

When to Use a Proposal

A proposal is appropriate at any time or for any situation in which you see an opportunity to provide a service in return for payment. In fact, the proposal approach is merely another tool within your sales arsenal.

The proposal can be formal or informal. It can be long or short. It can be in response to a request, or it can be gratuitous. The kind of proposal primarily discussed in this chapter is relatively informal and for small- or medium-sized projects. Regardless of length and style, the proposal must:

- Create a positive image of you and your service.
- Provide all needed or requested information.
- Be clearly written and easily understood.
- Sell your service as the best one for the work to be done.

What Goes into a Proposal

The proposal should begin on your letterhead. Type the proposal double-spaced on one side of the paper only, with generous margins to allow the prospective customer room for notes and questions. Drawings, sketches, or photographs relevant to your proposal should be attached, along with a scheduling chart, such as PERT, as proof of your ability to plan. A complete proposal will contain statements about the following details:

☐ What is being proposed by whom to whom
☐ Problem or situation to be handled
☐ What efforts are needed to handle the problem
☐ Method proposed to accomplish the work
☐ Precise tasks involved in the work
☐ Anticipated end result and advantages to be gained
☐ Who is to do what (deliveries, orders, storage, and so forth)
☐ Your qualifications and facilities to accomplish the work
☐ Your plan for project management and control, with schedules
☐ Estimated charges (fees, supplies, and so forth) to do the work
☐ Request for a meeting to discuss and negotiate the proposal

The Proposal Introduction

The introduction is to introduce yourself and your qualifications, to offer a benefit, and to show that you understand the situation faced by the prospective customer. It should be brief, no more that two pages, if possible, with fill-in details to follow. The introduction should contain:

1. *Your name*, both for your business and yourself.

2. *Who and what you are*. Who are you? An independent contractor providing a specified type of service with specified benefits.

3. *Your credentials*. This will be a brief statement about yourself and the experience, training, or education that qualifies you to do the work. It can be as simple as "Five years experience in (whatever), with special training. Details to follow."

4. *What you have done before*. Mention a client or two, but only if you will not be betraying a confidence. Talk about the work you did when an

employee. Select an example that parallels or approximates the situation for which you are proposing your service. If you are programming computers, nobody cares that you were once an Eagle Scout or that you collect butterflies.

5. *What benefits you offer.* What is it your service can offer that is different from and better than services available from other independent contractors? What special offerings can you make to attract and excite the prospect? Speed? Economy? Guaranteed results? State-of-the-art technology?

6. *An understanding of the problem.* No one will sign an agreement with you if you cannot convince them that you understand both the broad picture and the details of the prospect's problem. Will you be working for the prospect's best interest? Of course; but show it by showing you understand and will satisfy the prospect's needs.

Your Approach and Methods

After the introduction, it is time for details. Here is where you will present your plans for accomplishing the work. Here is where you will set out the important aspects that need to be understood by the customer and then discussed as you negotiate the terms of your agreement. Points to be covered will vary, of course, with the type and complexity of work involved. In general, however, you should include sections that present:

- ☐ Project organization
- ☐ Project management
- ☐ Procedures to be used to accomplish the work
- ☐ Staff to be provided to accomplish the work
- ☐ Deliverable items included in the project
- ☐ Who is to be responsible for what
- ☐ Schedules to accomplish the work

Your Qualifications

Here is where you elaborate on the brief mentions made in your introduction. Here is where you win or lose the contract. Here is where you must convince the prospect that you are qualified for the work. Include:

- ☐ Resumé(s) of key participants from your service
- ☐ Current and recent projects of a similar nature
- ☐ Related projects that demonstrate quality and reliability
- ☐ Availability of necessary facilities and equipment
- ☐ Availability of needed resources and/or supplies

Your biggest hurdles will be the first few contracts, which you need to be able to demonstrate that your service can perform in a satisfactory manner. What many newly started independent contractor businesses either forget or ignore on purpose is the training and experience gained while employed by others. If you have left your former employer on good terms, you should not mind using your experience there as a credential.

The Wrap-up Request

Elizabeth A. had all the earmarks of a top-grade independent salesperson, or sales rep. She was attractive but did not flaunt her sex. She knew her product lines—industrial valves, fittings, and packing—better than the engineers who designed them. Her territory, the Los Angeles area, was both manageable geographically and filled with chemical plants and petroleum refineries, which were potential customers. She was energetic and enthusiastic. But she failed. Why?

Elizabeth was afraid of rejection. Her proposals were superb. Her presentations were models of effectiveness. But she could never bring herself to ask for an order. Rather, she hoped that one would be offered to her. To ask and to be refused would be the rejection she could not tolerate.

Every proposal, every presentation, every discussion, should be ended with a request. The request can be for an order, or it can be for another meeting for further discussion. This is called "closing" the sale. Without closing a sale, without making a request, you have little chance of success.

The Simple Proposal

Small projects call for small proposals. One would look the fool indeed if one presented a one-hundred-page proposal for a $100 project. Judgment is required. In many cases a one- or two-page letter or, as suggested earlier, even a memo or a phone call will suffice for a proposal.

Do not, however, be fooled into believing that all simple jobs can be handled casually. The project may be small, such as the installation of a small retaining wall, but who is liable for damages or death if the trench caves in? What if an innocent passerby trips and falls into the trench? What if you accidentally puncture a gas or water line, or strike an important telephone trunk line? Establish liability early. (See Chapter 22 for suggestions on contract negotiations and protection.)

The contents of a letter or memo proposal will be the same as that of any proposal, with an introduction, discussion of the project, and statement of qualifications. The style, however, will be more informal, and fewer details will be included.

A Few Helpful Suggestions

Fee Schedule

If you make no mention of costs, you may lose the customer. If you make too specific a mention of costs before you know all the details, you may run yourself into a loss position. Be careful of specificity at proposal or prenegotiation time. (See Chapter 22.)

Positive Approach

Present your case forcefully and positively, but never build yourself up by downgrading the competition, even if your prospect is doing so during your discussions. Never speak in unflattering terms about other customers, whether past, present, or future. Your prospect will wonder what you will say about him or her to your next prospect.

Honor Confidences

What some independent contractors fail to appreciate is that something may be told to you in confidence without anyone mentioning the word *confidential*. You may be within the letter of the law if you disclose such information to the customer's competitors, but you will be violating an important ethical rule of doing business as an independent contractor. Do not discuss one customer's business or methods with another customer, even one that does not appear to be competitive with that customer. A loose tongue can be bad for business.

Use Illustrations

Always consider the use of illustrative material with your proposals. The ancient Chinese knew: A picture is worth a thousand words. Perhaps more. Consider where you can use pictorials, flowcharts, graphs, cartoons, bar or pie charts, organization and scheduling charts.

Promise with Care

There is always the urge to present one's self in the best possible light. This urge can lead to exaggeration, and if the exaggeration is great enough it can be considered fraud, enough to void a contract and bring legal liability (see Chapter 16). Even if exaggeration does not create legal problems, consider the consequences if you use it to obtain a contract for a project that is beyond your *promise* of capabilities.

Use a Checklist

There is no shame in using a checklist to be sure that nothing is omitted from a proposal, or during an in-person follow-up to your proposal. Careful, meticulous professionals rely on checksheets or lists. Why should you be an exception? Design your checklist to:

- Help bring logical order to your efforts
- Help prevent rambling or misplaced thoughts
- Help expose sequential or factual inconsistencies
- Help create ordering and delivery schedules
- Help identify critical points in a project
- Help prevent expensive or embarrassing omissions
- Help speed the planning and writing process
- Help impress the prospect with your sense of system

In Summary

If you see an opportunity, do not wait to be asked for a proposal. Watch for prospects with problems who are looking for solutions, the type of solutions your service can provide. When you see such an opportunity, make your proposal. Start with a telephone call or letter, perhaps a brief in-person meeting. Follow up with a written proposal.

What makes a good written proposal? How will you know when a proposal is good or poor? Do you need to be another Henry David Thoreau or Ernest Hemingway? The answers are as simple as the questions. Keep the following in mind:

- Writing is bad only when it jars or fails to communicate.
- Proposals are bad only when they fail in their missions.
- Proposals are good when they are successful.
- If your style works consistently, then your style is good.

CHAPTER 13

Selling Face to Face

If you are already a super salesperson, you may wish to skip this chapter. But how many of us are super salespeople? How many of us are so good we need neither listen nor learn? Without selling, you will have no business. Regardless of how much advertising or promotion you do, most of your independent contracting agreements (sales, if you wish) will result from follow-up face-to-face selling and negotiation.

When it comes to selling one's services face to face, however, most professional people will demur, claiming that they have no selling experience. Not so. To many, *sell* is a dirty four-letter word. Not so.

Yet we all sell. Selling is essential to every aspect of our lives, personal and professional. Every day we sell ourselves as credible persons. We sell ourselves as caring friends, as loving family members. We sell ourselves as capable professionals to our clients or employers. Each time we deal with another person we are selling ourselves. If people cannot *buy* us as people, they are unlikely to *buy* our ideas, our performances, our friendships, or our love.

It is time to lay the "I don't sell" and the "I can't sell" fallacies to rest and to consider ways to enhance our innate selling abilities as independent contractors with services to offer.

Your Winning Image

You will note the frequent emphasis on *image*. As you have seen, image is involved in the marketing strategy and in developing promotional programs and materials. Image is important when we use proposals as sales tools. You will see that image is implicit during the negotiating process. Why so much emphasis on image?

To sell our services, we must first sell ourselves as persons capable of quality performance. We must project confidence in our abilities. We must project the image of a winner, as no one would trust dealing with a self-avowed loser.

What is image? It is the *you* that is sensed and seen by those with whom you talk and deal. Image is the persona you radiate, the aura that surrounds you. Image is the outer reflection of your inner self. Image is the summation of the perceptions of you by those around you. Image is the combination of appearance and verbal and body language.

What kind of people do you like to deal with? Stand back from yourself and take a good hard look. Are you the type of person you like to deal with? Do you inspire confidence and trust? If not, now is the time to start restructuring your image, both in your own eyes and in the eyes of others.

What Image Do You Want?

Should you be the thoughtful theoretician, or the brash derring-do performer? Do you need to be seen as a careful follower of directions, or as an innovator and solver of difficult problems?

You will find the answers in your own business. You will find the answers by identifying and analyzing those image attributes that are typical in those who are successful in the same or similar businesses.

What Makes Your Image?

"I am what I am, and there is no way I can be someone else," is the world's most common alibi for making no effort whatsoever. It is true that you may be born with certain genetic personality-trait proclivities, but you still have a great deal of leeway with how you enhance the positive possibilities and how you subordinate the negative possibilities.

Already, you have spent a lifetime developing the traits and mannerisms that characterize you today. Note the word *developing*. There is no barrier to redeveloping or modifying nonproductive traits and mannerisms. If you have a defeatist slouch, practice the erect stance of a winner. If your voice is soft and subservient, there are vocal exercises to add timber and resonance to your tones. If you tend to hem and haw as you speak, practice speaking without hems and haws. If you bury your points in endless preamble elaboration, practice starting with the point and then moving to the elaboration. Do not forget the value of a mirror as you engage in trait modification practice.

Signals of Positive Image

As a starting point, here are a few of the image signals seen in you by others. Think about which of these you lack or where improvement is possible. With careful soul searching and an application of determination and self-discipline, you may see significant enhancement of your image as a businessperson.

Believe in Yourself

Above all else, you must believe in yourself. If you do not, no one else will. Lack of faith in one's self or lack of self-confidence is one personality trait that is difficult to overcome when dealing with discerning service purchasers and negotiators. The shift of your eyes, the timber of your voice, the movement of your hands, the placement of your feet, the tension in your shoulders and jaw muscles are all giveaways.

Stop thinking and saying, "I don't think I can," or "I'm not sure if I can." Start with "I believe I can," and graduate to "I know I can." Limit yourself, of course, to the realm of the possible. This is no time to leap off the tallest building in town, flapping your arms, yelling out for the world to hear, "I can fly; I know I can."

Start with a personal audit of your professional strengths and weaknesses. Work on your weaknesses. Look for ways around those you cannot remedy. Look for alternatives or consider teaming with or hiring the services of someone who can plug the holes in your professional dike. At the very least, then you can be confident in the total effort behind your service.

Know Your Field

You would never deny that the launching time for your independent contractor business is no time to start learning how to perform the service you intend to offer. Yet you may find that the experience you had and the skills you developed as an employee are not completely adequate for a self-employed independent contractor.

The mere fact that you do not know 100 percent of everything that will or might be involved in providing your service is no reason, however, to give up your plans. It does mean that you need to create a total vision of the service you will provide, and under what conditions. Talk to others in the field. Try to prevent sudden, unpleasant surprises when you do become your own boss.

Look the Part

All of life is role playing, and the way we dress and the way we groom ourselves are essential to the role we intend to play. To some, role playing is synonymous with deceit. But wait. We all have many roles, different ones for different situations. Our manners in church are far different than at the corner bar. We have roles for employers, lovers, parents, and children—even for the beggar on the street and the snarling dog next door. Now you will have a role as a businessperson.

Looking the part is mostly dressing for the part. You would not show up for a ditch-digging job dressed in a tuxedo, nor would you show up for an executive meeting with dirty fingernails, wearing work shoes, coveralls, and a red bandanna. So dress for the part. Neat and clean? Yes, but also appropriately. For my first job as a shift engineer in a major chemical company, I reported to work wearing a tie and jacket. I was asked, "Do you have coveralls?" I replied, "Yes, I have my army fatigues." The response was, "Be sure to bring them when you report for work tomorrow."

Name Recognition

You may be able to provide the very best service in the entire world, but if prospective customers do not know your name or have never heard of you, business will lag. Remember that Chapter 11 contains a number of techniques you can use to promote name recognition for yourself and your service. You can also review the suggestions on the use of project proposals for image building in Chapter 12.

Many new-business founders are bashful, and they feel a moral revulsion toward self-promotion. They are crippled by the illusion that self-promotion is demeaning, that it is only for pushy, unpleasant people. Not so. One wins nothing by keeping one's image as a winner a secret. As the saying goes, "Don't hide your light under a bushel."

True, self-promotion can be obnoxious, but it need not be so. Honest statements of capability, skills, experience, or services offered can be welcome at the right time and in the right place, particularly if such statements are to the benefit of persons or businesses that can use your service.

Chapter 11 listed a number of effective and acceptable ways to make your name known, all of them forms of name imaging, both personal and business. Your first objective is to be known favorably; your second objective, failing the first one, is not to be seen as a stranger. Briefly, in review, name imaging can be accomplished by:

- Participating in industry and professional meetings
- Participating in industry and professional associations

- Participating in community activities
- Sending news releases to local media
- Giving meeting papers or publishing articles related to your service
- Creating advertising, newsletter, or direct-mail programs
- Using testimonials by past customers (To earn these, always meet your commitments and always deliver full value plus a little more.)
- Using references by persons of stature and influence

What Is the Problem?

It is the customer who defines *value received*, not the one who provides the service. It is the customer who must believe that a problem was solved or a need was filled. This means that your first challenge is to perceive the customer's need or problem, respond to the need or problem, then provide an acceptable solution. Herein lies a major hazard. Is the problem a technological reality, a personal perception, or a combination of the two?

Perception versus Reality

If you are truly technologically qualified to provide your service, you may find it difficult to accept a statement of a perceived problem that is based on personal or internal political realities rather than on what you would consider fact. Herein lies the difference between *needs* and *problems*.

The customer may say, "That unit must be ready to operate by the end of the month."

You know that to do so will require some overtime, even double time, from an expanded crew, and that short lead time will add to the cost of ordering supplies. You explain this to the customer.

"I'll accept that," is the reply. "I still want it to be ready to operate by the end of the month."

Halfway through the project, you learn that the unit meant to provide feedstock to your unit will not be online, nor will the unit your unit is to feed into. You rush to your customer with this information.

"I know that," is the reply. "Nothing has changed."

A few months later you understand. A company vice presidency had opened and it was your customer, the company supervisor whose unit was ready to operate first, who won the promotion. Was there a need? For the customer, yes.

Learn to Communicate

As professionals, we know how to speak and write. This, then, is communication. Or is it? Do we know how to listen? Even more important than mere hearing or listening, do we know how to encourage the other person to come forth with thoughts or statements relevant to our own interests? True communication works two ways: We transmit our thoughts; we hear, comprehend, and respond to the thoughts of others.

There are times when we all become so entranced with our own thoughts and our own visions that we impatiently wait for others to stop speaking so that we can continue with our own outpouring of words. Consider a compressor-maintenance service. Which of the two approaches is most likely to bring out the prospective customer's own thoughts, thoughts to which you can relate and respond:

"My service provides fast, reliable compressor maintenance."

"Do you have a problem keeping your compressors online?"

The first is a statement of the interests of the person providing the service. The second is an invitation for the listener to share thoughts with the questioner. Without the sharing of thoughts, how can one understand the prospect's problem? If one does not understand the problem, real or perceived or both, how can one offer an acceptable solution?

It should come as no surprise that the world's best conversationalists are those persons who have learned to listen 90 percent of the time, with the remaining 10 percent divided equally between expressing one's own thoughts and encouraging the other person to continue with his or her thoughts.

When the Customer Is Wrong

Your first responsibility to your customer is to provide an honest evaluation of what is needed to solve the customer's problem. What if the customer's understanding of the problem is inaccurate or incomplete? What if the customer is looking at symptoms, not causes; what if the customer's idea of a solution will work in the short term, but be unsatisfactory or more costly in the long run; what if what the customer has requested will not work at all, or will produce significantly inferior results?

What can you do to salvage the situation? Here are some ideas of how to meet and beat the problem as you try to guide the customer away from the fallacious perception:

1. Listen carefully to the statement of problems.
2. Respond sympathetically to perceived needs and solutions.
3. Ask questions to zero in on the cause of the problem.
4. Ask if the customer has considered other aspects or solutions.
5. Offer to make a confirming study of the situation.

6. Prepare calculations or an illustrative demonstration.
7. Express your own surprise as to what you have determined.

What if, despite all of your diplomacy and subtlety, the customer will not shift position? You can do the work the customer's way and walk away with your payment for services rendered. You can bluntly tell the customer of his or her error, and that your conscience will not allow you to take advantage of the customer. Or, you can find some excuse not to handle the work, such as overload, illness, lack of some specific item of equipment, and forget the contract.

Which is best? Who will be blamed? Whose reputation will suffer most if the work fails to answer the needs of the problem? The decision is yours.

Benefits to Offer

Before you receive a contract for a project, the customer will consider the benefits you can offer in comparison to those available from alternative suppliers of the service. Specific benefits to use for your marketing strategy were discussed in Chapter 7, while Chapter 11 discussed the use of benefits in your promotion program. The situation changes, however, when you are in a face-to-face negotiation with a prospect who is showing interest in what you have to offer.

Customers will respond to both positive and negative personal stimuli. Positive stimuli normally involve the desire for gain, such as profit, promotion, prestige; negative stimuli normally involve fear, such as monetary losses, demotion, loss of prestige. If such personal aspects are involved, try to learn about them, then determine if you can deal with them, short of kickbacks, bribery, or false promises.

Expected Benefits

What benefits, exactly, does the customer expect? Are these benefits really personal needs, as discussed above, or are they technologically real? Often it is a toss of the dice. If you guess right, you come up with a natural. If you guess wrong, it's snake eyes all the way.

Competitive Benefits

How will your benefits compare to those overtly and covertly offered by your competition? By now you should know what the competition openly claims, but what about closed-room negotiating claims?

Alternative Benefits

Is there a different or innovative way to provide the benefits requested by the customer? Does Mohammed come to the mountain, or does the mountain come to Mohammed? Do you enter the house of problems through the front door, the side door, or the back door?

Answers to these questions are sometimes difficult to discern. They may become apparent during negotiations, but not if you enter into the discussions with a rigid stance. Maintain your objectivity and flexibility. For example, consider the following exchange about what the competition is offering:

"I can finish the work in ten days. Nobody can do better than that."

"I wouldn't be so sure," is the reply. "I've been talking to other contractors, you know."

Is the customer telling you that your competition can do the work more quickly? Or, is the customer on a fishing trip for the best catch possible? Should you immediately change your offer to nine days or eight days? Maybe, but only if it is feasible, and not yet.

"I'd have to do some calculations to see if we can do it faster. Do you have a deadline you have to meet?"

"Yes, but I have some other things we need to discuss first."

Now you know that the time element is flexible. You also know that even if your competition has offered to do the work in less time, other factors remain important.

The other factors are discussed. At the conclusion, the customer says, "I like your approach and what you can do, but the time thing is still a problem."

Should you offer a time compromise now? Not unless forced into it by the customer. Giving in too quickly makes it seem that you were padding the time in the first place, which you may have been doing, but do not admit it. Try:

"Like I said, I'll have to make some calculations and check delivery times with my suppliers. I'll get back to you by Friday. Meanwhile, do you have an absolute completion deadline?"

You may get a date now, and it may be a date that the competition has promised, or it may mean that the competition was unable to meet an essential deadline. Go back to your office, make a few calculations and phone calls, if necessary, then shave a day or so off your time schedule.

Anticipate Needs

Your success rate for signed contracts will be greatly enhanced if you recognize the need to understand the specific needs of the business or industrial areas you intend to serve, as well as specific firms and individuals with whom you will be negotiating. This statement may appear obvious, but it is sad to realize how many start-up businesses have failed because the independent contractor thought that proficiency in his or her own area of activity was sufficient.

Look to business/industry needs. Consider the heat-exchanger cleaning service. What's to know, you wonder, other than how to clean an exchanger? Consider that some operations are batch (cyclic), others are continuous. Consider the different requirements of the chemical industry, the petroleum industry, and the utilities industry. Suppose that you are a computer programmer. You offer your programming services to any firm that can benefit from the special capabilities of a tailored program. Does a CPA have the same needs as a law office? As a grocery store? As a restaurant? As a wholesaler or distributor? As a chain of retail discount stores? As a dealer in automotive parts? Of course not.

Where do you find this information? Start with your local library. If your service is aimed at banks, start reading the banking magazines. If it is aimed at law firms, look through the legal publications. Talk to people who are in the business or industrial areas you wish to serve. Learn how they do things, ask about their problems. Attend meetings and conferences serving the business and industry areas of interest to you.

Look to prospective customer needs. Place yourself in your customer's position. Learn all you can about the customer and the customer's firm. Have they had recent problems, such as with pollution control, toxic substances, loss of business? What is the customer's competitive position? Has the company announced plans for expansion, construction, or consolidation?

How can your service relate to this knowledge about the company? Can you help them solve a problem? If so, tell them. Even if there is no apparent relationship between what you have learned and what you can provide with your service, your contact will be pleased and impressed that you took the time to learn about the company, and that you have an interest in its activities and welfare.

Moment of Truth: Face to Face

You have done your homework. Now comes the meeting with the prospective customer. What are the secrets of selling? One can fill a large-sized room with published books on how to sell. Here we will limit ourselves to a few key suggestions about the craft or art of selling.

Facing the Anonymity Curse

Being unknown is the most often met barrier facing someone who has only recently launched his or her business as an independent contractor. You may find the following responses:

- "I don't know you."
- "I've never heard of your company."
- "No one recommended you."
- "No one around here knows you."
- "I'd rather not take a chance on a new service."
- "We use ABC company, and we're quite satisfied."
- "You won't understand my problem."

Can you avoid the anonymity curse? Yes, but only with preparation. If you do not have an advertising or promotion program going, look for referrals or testimonials. Try to meet people at local business or professional functions. And get your promotion program in gear. Bootstrap yourself out of the nether-nether world of the unknown.

Facing the Smallness Curse

Are you worried that the smallness of your independent contractor service will hurt your chances? Do you think the sheer size of your competitors will bury you? If so, forget it. Get away from an "I'm too small" defensive posture. Sell the advantages of smallness; do not apologize for smallness:

- "To be small is to be flexible."
- "Small organizations make faster decisions."
- "Our overhead is lower."
- "We give big attention to small projects."
- "We aren't nine-to-five people."
- "We specialize."

Selling End Results

Do you have special benefits to offer? Compare the following. Which are subjective (what you want) and which are objective (what the customer will look for)?

- "I design interiors," or "I create interior visions."
- "I keep books," or "I make numbers talk."
- "I paint cars," or "I make old cars look new."

The customer is not as interested in what you do as in the results you can achieve. As noted throughout this book, the customer is not looking for a technician as much as for a provider of benefits, a solver of problems, a fulfiller of needs. Create an image that you are in business to help others.

Your Unique Selling Points

What special advantages can you offer? What are your unique selling points (USPs)? Consider:

- ☐ Superior quality
- ☐ Exceptional experience
- ☐ Quality/end-result guarantees
- ☐ Advantages of specialization
- ☐ Attractive prices or fees
- ☐ Fast turnaround
- ☐ High technology
- ☐ Convenient location
- ☐ Exclusive services

Selling Your Qualifications

There is an old joke about the job opportunity advertisement saying, "Wanted young man or woman with twenty years experience willing to start at the bottom and work cheap." This may very nearly describe your situation when you first start out in business. Your customers will want proof of performance in advance. They will look at your business experience and, seeing none or very little, will decide to wait until your business has a bit more seasoning, unless you find other ways to demonstrate your proficiency.

Here are some of the weapons available to you:

- ☐ Cite your past employment experience.
- ☐ Cite your relevant formal education.
- ☐ Cite special training courses you have taken.
- ☐ Show your understanding of the customer's situation.
- ☐ Provide a credible proposed solution.
- ☐ Provide referrals from past employers.
- ☐ Provide referrals from past work associates.
- ☐ Produce copies of published articles.

The Get-Acquainted Offer

"My business is new," you tell the prospect. "But I am not new to this kind of work. I had XX years experience at ABC Company doing the same kind of thing, but now I'm doing it on my own as an independent contractor."

"Do tell," the prospect answers, stifling a yawn.

"I'm making a special one-time, half-price, introductory get-acquainted offer to show you what I can do. If you don't like my work, you don't have to pay me."

"Hmmm," the prospect replies, now looking interested.

"But I'm not worried," you say. "I know my work. I'm confident you'll be satisfied."

How can the prospect refuse such an attractive offer? Will the prospect take advantage of your offer and not pay? Possibly, but most likely not. And if the offer does backfire, you do not need to repeat it to another prospect.

Sales Call Follow-up

Unless the service you offer is quite simple, chances are that several sessions will be involved before a decision is made, particularly if several possible contractors are being considered and interviewed. What is important is that you, as the newest of the contractors, are not overlooked or forgotten.

If negotiations are actively under way, you may wish to contact the prospect weekly or more often. However, what if the decision is being held until some as yet vague future date? How can you keep visible without becoming a pest? Here are some tried and proven methods:

- Send a follow-up letter after each meeting with the prospect.
- Write or call a congratulation for a promotion.
- Write or call regarding a new development in the field.
- Write or call as a reminder of an upcoming event of interest.
- Send a copy of your new or rewritten brochure.
- Put the prospect on your newsletter mailing list.
- Send a reprint of an article that you authored.
- Send a copy of a newspaper item about you or your service.
- Send anything else of interest, professional or personal.

Sales Call Checklist

You waste your time if you are not dealing with someone in authority within the prospective customer firm. Qualify your prospect ahead of time. Determine that the person with whom you will meet is the one specifically interested in your service, and that this person either has authority to make the purchasing decision or will make recommendations that are listened to by higher authorities within the organization.

Be sure that the prospect has the money for the job, and that the prospect has a sincere intention of doing business with someone. Once you have positive answers to these questions, it is time to schedule a meeting.

A sales meeting can be at the behest of the prospect as a response to your promotion program, or you may use a combination of mail and telephone to bring about the meeting. When you do meet face to face with the prospect, observe the following:

- [ ] Be prepared. Know in advance what you plan to offer.
- [ ] Organize your presentation. Avoid rambling.
- [ ] Listen carefully to perceived needs and problems.
- [ ] Be positive about yourself. Do not poormouth the competition.
- [ ] Speak out clearly. Do not mumble or hesitate.
- [ ] Maintain eye contact for credibility, but do not stare.
- [ ] Focus your presentation; avoid a shotgun presentation.
- [ ] Promise what you believe. Believe what you promise.
- [ ] Be scrupulous with the truth, the whole truth, nothing but . . .
- [ ] Use visuals, slides, graphs, photos, drawings, models.
- [ ] Mention similar jobs you handled successfully.
- [ ] Be specific, explicit. Avoid hype. Appeal to logic.
- [ ] Appeal to emotion: benefits gained, needs fulfilled.
- [ ] Avoid nonrelated personal feelings and convictions.
- [ ] Demonstrate the advantages of dealing with you.
- [ ] Show that you want to protect the prospect's money.
- [ ] Be flexible about meeting objections or unexpected requirements.
- [ ] Recognize when it is time to "close" the sale.
- [ ] Make a closing statement. Summarize the discussion.
- [ ] Ask for an order or a future discussion meeting.
- [ ] Leave something to remind the prospect of your visit, such as your brochure.

The use of visuals, mentioned in the checklist, is an effective way to enhance a sales presentation. A workable visual can be as simple as a handdrawn sketch, or as sophisticated as a working or scale model.

Close with a "heads I win, tails you lose" approach. Never offer the prospect the choice between *yes* and *no*. Present a no-lose alternative. There is a story about the Walgreen Drug store chain during the Great Depression. As the story goes, the countermen in the refreshments section were instructed that whenever a customer ordered a malt or milkshake they were to ask if the customer wanted an egg in their malt or milkshake for a nickel extra. Few customers were ready to pay the extra nickel, a coin that still had value in those days when a dime would buy a candy bar, a package of Wings cigarettes, or a triple-dip ice cream cone.

So the countermen were reprogrammed. They were told that whenever a customer ordered a malt or a milkshake, they were to hold up one egg in one hand and two eggs in the other hand, and say "One egg or two?" Most customers, overwhelmed at the idea of two eggs, settled for one egg and paid the extra nickel. This is similar to the "Shall I come over on Monday, or would Friday be better for you?" approach noted here earlier.

The leave-behind is particularly important. Always leave something to remind your prospect of your visit. It can be your brochure or other material you have prepared. Even your business card, which may end up in a telephone-number file, is better than nothing.

PART IV

What You Need to Know about Law and Contracts

CHAPTER 14

How to Find the Right Lawyer

Who needs a lawyer? You do, if you seriously intend to become a self-employed independent contractor in business offering a service in return for payment. You will face a dozen or more legal technicalities as you operate your business. Some you will recognize, others you will not. Some will involve complex legal concepts, others will be matters of simple common sense.

In short, at some time during your life as an independent contractor, you will need the advice and assistance of a lawyer. If you wait until some dramatic need suddenly arises before you select your lawyer, you will be forced into a panic decision, which is seldom a good decision. Even when you are faced with no legal problems, a lawyer can help you to plan for the future so that few if any legal problems need ever arise.

When You Will Need a Lawyer

An innocent failure to observe a simple *statute or regulation*, such as failure to procure a certificate of occupancy for the purposes of your business, could close down your business temporarily, and even permanently. Some legal omissions may simply evoke fines or penalties from local, county, state, or federal authorities.

You may face *civil legal actions*, actions by customers or others for breach of contract, or for personal injury or property damage. Some of

147

these can be avoided through using proper legal procedures. For others, you will need both pre-event and postevent legal protection.

Your lawyer can help you *form your business*, whether it be a sole proprietorship, a partnership, or one of the forms of incorporation. Your lawyer can help you select and record your *business name*, file for a Federal Identification Number, and related business requirements.

Your lawyer can help you to determine if you will need a *license* before you can offer your service as an independent contractor. Many professions require practicing licenses, including the law and various medical professions. Others that may not require a license when you are an employee will require that you obtain a license to practice your profession as an independent contractor. Depending upon the laws of your state, a license may be required for physical therapists, social workers, cosmetologists, architects, electricians, and more.

Will you need a local *permit* for your business? Permits vary widely, from certificates of occupancy to business permits. You can find out local permit requirements from your municipal clerk's office, or you can have your lawyer handle such matters.

How do you stand with local *zoning regulations*? Is the area you intend to work out of zoned to allow the type of operations required for your service? Your municipal clerk's office can show you the zoning map and regulations. What if you find that you are prohibited from practicing your service in your chosen area? Can you obtain a variance or exception to the zoning regulations? How would you petition for the variance? The services of a lawyer would be most helpful.

Is there a hidden "deed restriction" existing from some past owner of the property that prevents you from using the property for your service? Are there unexercised "easement" rights across the property that could become obstacles to the future use of your chosen location? Is there a *cloud on the title* held by the person leasing to you that could jeopardize that person's ownership and the rights leased to you? You will need the help of a lawyer to check out restrictions, easements, and clouds on titles.

What *federal and state regulations* have control over the way you provide your service? Consider personal safety (OSHA) and environmental safety (EPA). Are there others? Your lawyer can help you determine what will and what will not affect you as an independent contractor.

Will you *lease facilities*? Will your lease allow you to do what you intend to do? What are the relative rights and responsibilities between yourself and the lessor? Who is legally liable for maintaining the premises in safe condition? What are your continued lease obligations if the premises are partially destroyed by fire, storm, flood, or earthquake? Where will you stand if the lessor sells the property, or loses it through condemnation or eminent domain? You can sign a standard lease and wait for the hammer to fall, or you can let your lawyer help you protect yourself in advance.

As an independent contractor, you will provide your service under the authority of *contracts*, either oral, written, or implied. While most of the time there will be no trouble, a single major legal entanglement can destroy not only your business, but your professional and personal future. Do the contracts you sign provide basic protection? You will need the assistance of a lawyer to stay in safe operating territory. If you have doubts, be safe. Say, "I'll have my lawyer review it first."

How to Find Your Lawyer

Lawyers specialize, just as doctors, dentists, artists, or carpenters do. A law degree and a license to practice law do not ensure that a lawyer is an expert in contract law, nor do they mean that a lawyer knows or understands the problems of a small business. Even a lawyer who has had experience with the legal needs of a small business does not necessarily understand your particular type of business activity as an independent contractor.

How, then, do you find a lawyer who can serve your needs? Forget the telephone company yellow pages. Letting your "fingers do the walking" is little better than playing the slots at Atlantic City or Las Vegas. Most listings provide little if any help in finding the type of lawyer you need. Even if a few choice words appear along with the listing, these are the lawyer's claims, not testimonials to experience or capability.

Here are some suggestions for how to find the names of lawyers you can rely on to understand your needs:

Talk to Your Banker

Ask your banker for a list of three, four, or more lawyers or law firms known to the bank as able to handle the special legal needs of a small business. Even this may not be specialized enough. If you are providing architectural design or building construction, you will have particular legal advice needs. If you are a computer programmer, you will need a lawyer who understands copyright and patent law as applied to computer software.

Talk to Others

Talk to acquaintances who are in business. Introduce yourself to other small-business people in your area and nearby, particularly those who are not in direct competition with the service you intend to offer. Ask them about their lawyers, what they like about them, what they do not like about them, what their services cost. Discuss your needs with your accountant or financial advisor.

Look for Advice or Listings

In larger cities, there are organizations of retired businesspeople who offer their services free or at very reasonable cost to small businesses. Among them will be lawyers, as well as persons who can recommend lawyers. One such organization is SCORE (Service Corps of Retired Executives); also consider local offices of the SBA. Both of these are discussed in more detail in Chapter 24, "Secrets of Business Success." Look also for listings of lawyers by specialization from your local, county, or state bar associations.

Selecting the Right Lawyer

Once you have a name or names to contact, the next step is interviewing. Meet with one or more lawyers. Talk to them. Describe what you plan to do, and then query them to see how much they know about your intended line of business. See if you like them as people as well as respect them professionally. See if you can communicate with them, and vice versa. Never hesitate to ask specific and searching questions. Pussyfooting not only will derive very little specific information, it may even produce misleading impressions.

There are several areas in which you will need answers:

Fees and Expenses

What is the lawyer's hourly fee? Is there a charge for the get-acquainted interview? If so, how much for how long? What is the fee schedule for future consultation? For trial preparation and court appearances? For contract drafting and review? For incorporation? Is a retainer fee involved? If so, how much is it and what can you expect in return? Will the lawyer expect you to sign a contract for a guarantee of personalized legal service? How are expenses over and above basic fees charged, and for what types of services?

Compatibility

Do you like the lawyer as a person? Regardless of the lawyer's skill and experience, if you do not like him or her as a person, if you are uncomfortable with that person, if you cannot communicate with that person, it will not be a good business relationship.

Understanding

Small businesses have special problems, needs, and opportunities that differ from those faced by large corporations. Does the lawyer understand the special needs of small business, or your type of small business? Deal in specifics; do not settle for generalizations. If the lawyer refuses to discuss those topics of particular interest to you, it could mean that he or she is not truly interested in your business, or that he or she does not know enough about the specialized law of small businesses.

Experience

What specific small business experience does the lawyer have? What kinds of businesses? What kinds of situations within these businesses? While client confidentiality may prevent the use of client names, it should not prevent a general discussion of those experiences that bear most directly on your intended operation.

References

Will the lawyer give reference names for you to contact? How do these referenced persons feel about the lawyer? Are the legal services satisfactory? Is the lawyer available when needed? Does the lawyer listen well and communicate well in return? Under what circumstances did the referenced persons utilize the lawyer's services? What difficult situations did the lawyer help to resolve? How reasonable are the lawyer's fees and other charges?

CHAPTER 15

The IRS versus Independent Contractors

The Internal Revenue Service has developed an obstacle course designed to frustrate you in your efforts to conduct business as an independent contractor. If you cannot meet their tests to differentiate yourself from an employee, you will lose your status and benefits as an independent contractor. Your client may well be described as your employer, confounding your desire for independence and saddling the client with the very paperwork, personnel chores, and payments of tax and benefits expenses it thought were being avoided by dealing with an independent contractor.

The Sad Saga of Stuart A.

Consider the potential situation of Stuart A., an independent contractor dealing under the name Fairway Airways, which provided consultation, planning, design, installation, and maintenance services for heating, ventilating, air-conditioning, and refrigeration systems used in office buildings, factories, and public facilities. In March he negotiated a lucrative contract to provide building-wide air conditioning for the offices of Save-a-Dollar Supermarkets, a medium-sized grocery chain with retail outlets in five states. It was to be Stuart's biggest job to date.

The contract took into consideration the size of the job to be done, the staff and facilities available from Fairway Airways, and the support available from Save-a-Dollar. Other than the usual clauses defining the scope of the project, design, scheduling, and payment arrangements, there were to be several special contract clauses.

1. The size and scheduling of the project would require more people than the 12 employees available from Fairway Airways. As Save-a-Dollar's maintenance department was temporarily overmanned, Save-a-Dollar would assign a crew of eight plus two shift foremen to work with Fairway Airways. The only restriction was that both the Fairway Airways staff and those assigned from Save-a-Dollar would be required to work according to Save-a-Dollar schedules and regulations, and all had to honor provisions of the labor contract currently in effect at Save-a-Dollar.

2. The Save-a-Dollar crew assigned to the project would be provided with tools and equipment from the Save-a-Dollar supply room. Both Save-a-Dollar and Fairway Airways workers would have full use of the locker room, showers, cafeteria, and medical facilities operated by Save-a-Dollar for its employees.

3. In order to reduce expenses and to expedite completion of the project, Save-a-Dollar would order the materials and supplies required, benefiting by its larger buying image and the deliveries and discounts it could demand.

4. Because of a tight schedule, Fairway Airways would agree to devote its full staff and facilities to the work at Save-a-Dollar.

5. Payment to Fairway Airways at the completion of the job would be guaranteed to be no less than cost plus 15 percent. To keep the costs at a reasonable level, Save-a-Dollar would keep complete time and materials records, with Fairway Airways reporting daily on standard Save-a-Dollar accounting forms.

Enter the IRS

How would the IRS react to this contract at tax time? In all probability, the IRS would cite Save-a-Dollar for multiple delinquencies in withholding and FICA taxes, and the state would come after Save-a-Dollar for delinquencies in worker's compensation and unemployment insurance payments. Upon closer examination, it would be discovered that the IRS was including Fairway Airways personnel among employees of Save-a-Dollar. The result would be that Save-a-Dollar would have to pay an additional $3,800 in taxes, insurance, and benefits for each of the twelve Fairway Airways employees.

"But Fairway Airways is an independent contractor," both firms would argue. However, the IRS would be adamant. Save-a-Dollar had exercised controls over the methods and conduct of Fairway Airways to an extent that made the contractor's employees *de facto* employees of Save-a-Dollar, regardless of what either or both firms called Fairway Airways.

How the IRS Judges Employees versus Independent Contractors

The IRS test to determine whether or not a person is an employee or an independent contractor focuses on a single point: Who has control? Even more important, who has the right to exercise control, even if this right is not exploited. IRS agents are expected to consider twenty common-law factors listed in the IRS training manual. As related to the Save-a-Dollar/ Fairway Airways contract, these are:

1. Who tells how to do the work? To the IRS, an independent contractor is hired for his or her ability to perform specified work meeting specified standards without the need for detailed supervision by the hiring party. The IRS can claim that Save-a-Dollar exercised excessive control over the direction of the work.

2. Who trains the worker(s)? Do the independent contractor's workers know how to perform their work, or must the contracting party train them? The Save-a-Dollar workers provided for the project were trained by Save-a-Dollar.

3. Is the work a part of regular business? Simply stated, does the work provided by the independent contractor substitute for work reasonably conducted by company-paid employees? The fact that Save-a-Dollar did provide part of the work staff leaves this question open to debate.

4. Who must do the work? Is this a personal-service contract that must be performed by a particular person, such as, for example, the painting of a portrait? Save-a-Dollar and Fairway Airways have no problem here.

5. Does the customer provide assistants to work with the independent contractor? If the customer hires, supervises, or pays persons to work with the independent contractor, independent operation is questionable. Save-a-Dollar's contract is quite vulnerable on this point.

6. Is the relationship continuous? Save-a-Dollar faces no problem here—not yet.

7. Who controls the hours of work? Save-a-Dollar, obviously. This test is debatable, as it would be difficult to work on company premises when the company facility is closed.

8. Is it a full-time arrangement? No. This test is closely related to number 6 above. No problem here.

9. Where is the work done? This is a pointless question, particularly when contract work must be performed on a client's premises.

10. Who schedules the work? Who directs the sequence in which work is done? Overall scheduling is by the request of the client; day-to-day scheduling should be by the contractor. The contract is probably safe on this point.

11. Does the independent contractor have to make reports? Of course; progress reports are standard and satisfy reasonable needs for information. Just be sure that they are done your way, not the client's way. Fairway Airways may be vulnerable here.

12. How is the independent contractor paid? Is payment hourly, weekly, by commission, by the job with benchmarks for progress payments? If one is paid like one of the client's own employees, one may well be considered an employee of the client.

13. Who pays for travel? This is not relevant to the Save-a-Dollar/Fairway Airways agreement, but might be an issue for independent manufacturers' or sales representatives.

14. Who provides tools and materials for the work? The Save-a-Dollar contract is vulnerable on this point.

15. Whose facilities are used to perform the work? Who provides the special machinery or equipment needed? Fairway Airways made provisions for its staff, Save-a-Dollar for its staff. There is possible vulnerability here.

16. Can the independent contractor lose money? One of the important signposts of an independent business is the chance of losing money on a job, as well as of making money. A cost-plus contract must be very carefully drafted to avoid this IRS trap.

17. Can the independent contractor work for more than one customer at a time? Here is true independence, the freedom to work for anyone and everyone. Was this violated by the terms of the contract? Perhaps—then again, perhaps not, since the prohibition was for the duration of a single job only.

18. Can the independent contractor work for anybody and everybody? This is a virtual duplication of number 17 above.

19. Can the customer fire the independent contractor? One can fire employees only. One must find a way to cancel or breach a contract to get rid of an independent contractor.

20. Can the independent contractor walk off the job at will? This is the flip side of number 19 above. An employee can quit at any time. A contractor is in breach of contract if work is not performed according to the contract.

Does the Save-a-Dollar/Fairway Airways agreement jeopardize the independent contractor status of Fairway Airways? Yes, it has a number of unwise provisions. Would the IRS prevail? Perhaps, but there is some hope of relief under Section 530(a) of the Revenue Act of 1978 as amended.

Section 530(a) says that a person can be considered an independent contractor if there is a reasonable basis not to treat the person as an employee, and if the hiring party has not treated the person or other persons performing substantially similar work as employees before, and if the hiring party has reported amounts paid to the person on a timely filed Form 1099.

Play It Safe

You may or may not be protected under Section 530(a). Rather than be sorry, keep in mind this checklist of important do's and don't's when you are negotiating a contract:

- ☐ Do seek payment by the job, not open-ended and by the hour.
- ☐ Do set your own working hours, where possible.
- ☐ Do have your own company headquarters.
- ☐ Do insist on written contracts for each job.
- ☐ Do make public solicitations for other customers.
- ☐ Do keep your own accurate financial and business records.
- ☐ Do hire your own staff to work on projects.
- ☐ Do avoid responding to "help wanted ads."
- ☐ Do have your own business cards, stationery, invoice forms.
- ☐ Do arrange for your own liability insurance.
- ☐ Do have your own professional licenses and business permits.
- ☐ Do work separately from client employees, where practical.
- ☐ Do define the scope of work to be done clearly in writing.
- ☐ Don't become an extension of your client's business.
- ☐ Don't become a full-time pseudo company employee.
- ☐ Don't be prevented from contracting with others.
- ☐ Don't use a client's tools, where practical.
- ☐ Don't accept fringe benefits from clients.
- ☐ Don't accept employee-like favors from clients.
- ☐ Don't let clients hire your assistants for you.
- ☐ Don't set up a regular work-hour pattern with clients.
- ☐ Don't use clients' identification symbols or logos.
- ☐ Don't accept out-of-contract expense reimbursements.
- ☐ Don't make regular use of clients' office space.
- ☐ Don't participate in client staff meetings.
- ☐ Don't accept detailed employee-like work instructions.

CHAPTER 16

The Anatomy of a Contract

A contract may be formal or informal, written or oral, explicit or implicit, simple or complex. However, if you want to protect yourself from the major consequences of even minor misunderstandings arising during even simple work projects, you will insist on a formal written contract in which the scope of work, terms of party responsibility, and provisions for expenses and for payment are clearly and explicitly stated.

If your services as an independent contractor are relatively standard and easily described, you may wish to have an attorney draft a standard contract for you, much as for real estate brokers and landlords. Differences are handled by filling in the blanks. If your services are complex, incorporating numerous aspects, schedules, payments, and such, you will be wise to have your contracts reviewed by your attorney before you commit yourself to them. There are a number of legal hazards that you may face if your contract is vague, inaccurate, incomplete, or otherwise in error or lacking in foresight. These are described in detail in Chapter 17.

Contracts come in many forms. One must consider what kind of a contract is involved. For instance, was it a unilateral (one-sided) contract or a bilateral (two-sided) contract? Was it an express contract, an implied contract, or a quasi contract? Was it a prime contract, or was it a subcontract to a prime contractor? Was it a general contract or a personal services contract? These aspects are discussed in detail later in this chapter.

While no single article, book chapter, or even book can make you into an expert on contracts, it will help you greatly, both while negotiating a contract and while working with your attorney, if you understand the basics of what you are doing when you sign a contract.

What Makes a Contract?

Not every agreement is a legally enforceable contract. Among the points of law a court will consider when a contract is contested or there is a claim of breach are the following elements:

- ☐ Were the parties clearly identified?
- ☐ Did one party make a bona fide offer?
- ☐ Was there acceptance and/or ratification of the offer?
- ☐ Was a counteroffer and acceptance involved?
- ☐ Was there mutuality of understanding and intent?
- ☐ Was there coercion or undue influence involved?
- ☐ Was there a "consideration" in return for the contract?
- ☐ Did the contract fully define the agreement?
- ☐ Were the parties' duties clearly specified?
- ☐ Was the agreement firm, or was it an agreement to agree?
- ☐ Was there an illegality involved in the contract?

The Parties to a Contract

The persons or organizations involved in the negotiation and signing of a contract are known as the parties. If the terms of a contract are to be legally supportable, it is essential that the parties are carefully and properly identified in such a manner that there can be no doubt as to who is meant.

Two persons can shake hands and produce a legally binding contract. Or, there can be scores of parties, as for a complex development project, such as a large office building or a shopping mall where a number of specialized prime contractors and their respective subcontractors are involved.

Several firms or persons may back the project, either under contract between themselves, or as a joint-venture corporation. There could be an architectural prime contractor, as well as prime contractors for the foundations, excavations and grading, roads, buildings, sidewalks, sewer and water lines, and so on. Prime contractors will in turn hire subcontractors for detailed specialties, such as hauling, storage, electrical and plumbing work, roofing, flooring, tile work, glazing, heating and air conditioning, and more. You, as an independent contractor, could be a prime contractor or a subcontractor.

What Makes an Offer

There is no legal mystery about offers. An explicit statement of willingness and readiness to perform an act in return for a consideration (another act or payment) is most likely an offer. But it must be specific and definite.

"I will program your computer for $1,000," is an offer.

"Will you pay me $1,000 if I program your computer," is a question, not an offer. It is an invitation for the other person or party to make an offer to you, or to open negotiations.

"I program computers for $1,000," is not an offer. It is an advertisement.

"Give me $1,000 and I will program your computer," is specific and definite; hence it is an offer waiting for an acceptance.

The Acceptance versus a Counteroffer

Neither is there a legal mystery about what makes an acceptance to an offer. An acceptance is a specific and explicit agreement to act in the manner that was proposed by the offering party.

If the response to your offer to program a computer for $1,000 is, "Yes, I will pay you $1,000 to program my computer," it is an acceptance of your offer.

"I might consider having you program my computer for $1,000," is not an acceptance. It is an invitation to negotiate.

"I'll give you $900 to program my computer," is not an acceptance. The offeror's terms have been rejected, and the response cancels the offer and itself becomes an offer, known as a counteroffer. The original offeror is now in the position of becoming the acceptor, or negotiator, or counterofferor.

"I might consider having you program my computer for $900," is not a counteroffer, as it is not a definite statement of position. Rather, it is a request to negotiate.

The Role of Ratification

Ratification of a contract is acceptance and approval of the terms of the contract. One can ratify a written contract by signing it, or ratify an oral contract by saying "Yes" or by shaking hands. But there are more subtle ways to ratify a contract, some of which may come as unpleasant surprises to the legally ratifying party.

You can ratify a change in a contract by waiver. That is, you can allow the change to occur and continue by failing to insist immediately on the original terms of the contract. If the other party is violating contract terms, do not be bashful. Do not rely solely on contract terms that say your failure to act is not a permanent waiver. Speak out, write a letter, have your attorney lodge a formal protest. Protect yourself. Silence or other inaction leads to the implication that you accept the violations as legitimate contract changes.

An action involving you without your consent can be ratified and converted into a legal agreement if you accept it. Acceptance can be, as in the paragraph above, through implied consent by inaction. Or, it can become a legally binding contract by your oral or written statement saying that you now agree to the uninvited action, and authorize it to continue.

There are other actions that may ratify an action to convert it into a legally binding contract. Past practice between you and another party on a continuing basis, or accepted practices in the trade or business within which you operate, can be accepted as ratification of an ongoing series of actions, even though no offer was formally made and no acceptance was ever communicated by the other party. If you have such an ongoing arrangement and you want to end it or modify it legally, do so with a written notice to the other party.

Were the Terms Mutual?

Agreement, understanding, and mutuality of intent are essential elements of an enforceable contract. If there was no agreement, there is no contract. If there was a major misunderstanding that destroys the mutuality of intent, there is no contract. Contract terms forced upon one party by the other party may make the agreement void. Coercion of any form destroys mutuality, as does the exploitation of undue influence, the hiding of important facts, or misrepresentation of facts that go to the heart of the contract.

One of the first things a court of law will consider during contract litigation is the intent and mutuality of the agreement. If the intent is clearly stated and defined within the "four corners" of the contract, the court is most likely to support the contract, barring other defects. If the intent is vague or ambiguous, corroborating evidence will be sought to determine the intent. If even submittal of evidence does not clarify the intent or indicate the existence or absence of intent, the court may find that it has no basis upon which to base a judgment.

What Makes Consideration

Consideration in contract law language is something of value given by one party in return for something of value from the other party. There is a chance that a contract will be declared invalid if consideration is missing. If you, as an independent contractor, offer to provide a service, the service itself is your consideration. When the customer agrees to pay for that service, the payment is the customer's consideration.

While payment for services constitutes the mutual consideration in most business agreements, there are other forms of consideration recognized by law. For example:

An act in return for a promise. You promise to provide a service in return for some action by the other party. The act can be prepayment of money, but also can be transfer of some other object or action of acceptable value to you.

A promise in return for a promise. You promise to provide a service in return for a promise from the other party; for example, "I'll program your computer if you will pave my driveway."

A forbearance in return for a promise. You promise to withhold an action that is within your legal rights in return for a promise by the other party. "I'll program your computer for no charge (the forbearance) if you will give $1,000 to the Community Chest (the return promise)."

A modification of a past promise in return for a new promise. This involves a change in position by both parties, with added consideration by both parties. "I'll program two of your computers for an additional $500."

A new agreement to replace a former agreement. This involves the total abolishment of the previous agreement in favor of an entirely new (not merely modified) agreement.

Different courts in different states at different times have different definitions of what constitutes consideration. It is best to check with your attorney if you have any doubts as to the legal validity of the consideration involved in an agreement. In almost every situation, however, there must be some trade in obligations, such as providing a service, paying for a service or product, a change in position by either or both parties, or some combination of such actions. Some courts require only token consideration, such as one dollar, while others will consider the adequacy of consideration relative to the value of what is received.

Is the Agreement Complete?

Before a contract can be defended in court, it must be shown to contain the specific details with which the court can determine performance and liability. Normally, the most you can expect from a court judgment is an interpretation of what is contained explicitly and specifically within the contract. If no completion date is specified in the contract, the court will not arbitrarily create a completion date, although one could be inferred, as in the completion of a structure in time for a specified event. Here are some of the potential hazards you may face when drafting a contract:

- Failure to describe work involved with clarity and in detail
- Failure to specify completion schedules with specificity
- Failure to specify payment terms and times with specificity
- Failure to provide for unexpected obstacles or emergencies
- Failure to specify which party holds liability and for what
- Failure, as subcontractor, to avoid prime contractor problems

What Kind of Contract?

Contracts, like people, cars, dogs, and cats, come in many sizes and shapes. Some are oral, some are written. Some are express, some are implied. Some are by agreement, some are by court order. And more. You can commit yourself to a contract or a change in an existing contract with a memo, a letter, a handshake, the nod of your head, or by your actions or inactions.

The Unilateral Contract

Avoid creating a unilateral contract, as it is hardly a contract at all. Rather, it is you promising to provide a service, or actually providing that service, without a promise in return. The recipient of your largess is under no obligation to you. A good example most of us have experienced at one time or another is the receipt of a book or object in the mail, with the request for a contribution or payment. If you did not request or otherwise solicit that book or object, you are under neither an obligation to pay for it nor to return it.

"I'll program your computer for $1,000. Okay?"

If there is no reply, no action to imply acceptance of your offer, but you program the computer anyway, does the owner of the computer owe you $1,000? No. When you made your promise to program the computer, were you obligated to do so? No, not without an acceptance. There was no meeting of the minds; no mutuality of intent.

You go ahead and program the computer. The owner tries out the program, and says, "Nice work." Does he now owe you $1,000? No. Still no commitment. "Sure," he then says, "it's worth $1,000." Does he now owe you $1,000? No. Not yet. "I'll pay you $900 for your work." Does he now owe you $1,000? No, but he has now committed himself to pay you

$900. What began as a unilateral contract with no mutual obligation has now been converted into a bilateral contract with a commitment.

There may be times when it seems that it would be good business to provide a free service as a form of advertising or business development. Be careful. Not only do you stand a very good chance of not being paid, you may be sued for illegal entry or trespassing. You may do it for free, but be sure that you have authorization from the recipient of the service.

The Bilateral Contract

Bilateral, as you may guess, means two-sided. When the word *contract* is mentioned, what most of us are thinking of is the bilateral contract whereby there is an offeror (one or more) and an acceptor (one or more) in return for consideration (token or more) for a mutually understood and agreed upon objective that is to be accomplished by mutually agreed upon methods with mutually agreed upon schedule, performance, and payment.

At least two parties must be involved. Each must make a commitment to the other. Each must provide something for the other. The result is a promise for a promise, such as a service in return for a payment. Both parties are obligated to perform.

The Express Contract

Most of us think of the bilateral contract as an *express* contract. If both parties express their intentions, either orally or in writing, to enter into the contract, there is an express contract. This expression of intent must be communicated between the parties in complete form.

For your business as an independent contractor, the express contract should be the only form you use. And it should be in writing. When the terms and expectations of the two parties are memorialized in writing, the chances of error, confusion, omissions, misunderstanding, or forget-fulness are minimized. Each party knows what to expect from the other party.

The Implied Contract

As mentioned earlier, you can have a contract without ever saying or writing a word. It will be your actions and responding actions by the other party, or it will be past trading practice or accepted practices of your profession or type of business that will create a legally enforceable mutual obligation. This obligation will be called an implied contract.

If, during the course of doing continuing business with a person or company, an ongoing pattern is established, this pattern can be implied to be a contract for continuance or repetition of the actions that created the pattern. For example, you have received eleven consecutive monthly requests to monitor and adjust the air circulation system for a major downtown office building. While the twelfth notice does not arrive when you expect it, you provide your service the twelfth time. The building manager refuses to pay for month twelve.

"We didn't ask you to come in," he argues.

"But I've been doing the same thing for eleven months," you reply. "I assumed that your letter was late."

"We don't want you anymore. If we had wanted you, we would have told you."

Do you have a contract for month twelve? Very likely you do have an implied contract based on the course of trading. Should you be paid for your services? Again, very likely. Would you win a judgment for payment in a court of law? No careful lawyer will promise that you absolutely will win. You do, however, have an excellent case on the basis of the continuing course of business.

Where, then, should you stand on implied contracts? As an independent contractor, avoid the implied contract wherever possible. Express contracts are much safer. In the case above, the careful businessperson would have made a phone call or a visit before plunging in to provide the service.

Court-made Contracts

Courts do not generally make contracts. However, there are exceptions to this rule, such as the implied contract. In most cases, the implied contract is an interpretation of some present or past agreement. There is another form of court-made contract, however, that is even more tenuous.

Consider the so-called quasi contract. This form is in truth not a contract at all by any of the definitions associated with contracts, yet it is as legally binding as any in-writing express, mutually accepted contract.

The quasi contract is a court-ordained obligation forced onto one party for the benefit of a second party in the interests of fairness and equity. The quasi contract is rare, and usually comes about when some person or organization is taking unfair advantage of a second party. You are unlikely to become involved in such a contract unless you are extremely naive (and taken advantage of) or extremely aggressive (and taking advantage of others).

The Subcontract

If you work under contract to someone who in turn has a major (prime) contract with the intended recipient of the benefits of your service, you become a subcontractor. Or, if you have negotiated a contract that requires services that you cannot provide, you may contract with specialists to provide the needed extra services. They will be subcontractors to you; you, in turn, will be the prime contractor.

An example of subcontracting would be when a major computer hardware manufacturer has a contract to provide a computer network, plus special-application software, training, and maintenance. The hardware firm, the prime contractor, may contract with an independent contractor for the programming, with another independent contractor for the training, and with a third independent contractor for the maintenance services.

Before you sign on as a subcontractor, insist on seeing the prime contractor's contract. There may be provisions in the master contract that would be unattractive to you as a subcontractor, such as payment for your completed services when the prime contractor has breached or in some other manner defaulted on the prime contract. The problems faced by the subcontractor occur most often in construction projects (see Chapter 19 for a discussion).

Before you, as a prime contractor, sign with subcontractors, be sure that there are no intervening obstacles within your own contract. For example, in a personal services contract, discussed next, you may be prohibited from assigning the work to another person or firm. In such cases, you either forget about subcontracting, or obtain written permission from the party for which you are providing the service.

The Personal Service Contract

Suppose that you have received a contract to create a computer program that is specific to the needs of your customer. You have been selected because of your reputation and on the strength of the work you have done for other customers. You find that you are overextended, so you contract out the programming work to another independent contractor. Okay? Probably not.

A contract with you to provide a service based on your known personal and unique capabilities is most likely a personal services contract. To subcontract your duties would be similar to Michelangelo's subcontracting the painting of the Sistine Chapel ceiling to Joe Green (Giuseppe Verdi), a fine musician and composer, but a horrible painter.

If you do subcontract the work, you will be in breach of contract. The customer can terminate the agreement immediately. If you subcontract the work *sub rosa* and the results are either poor or merely so-so, and the customer learns of your action, you can be sued for breach of contract and damages. The damages could be compensatory, such as hiring another programmer to do the work you failed to do, and perhaps even punitive (or exemplary), as civil-court punishment for your flagrant disregard of the terms of the contract.

Is there a remedy for your situation? Yes, there are two remedies, in fact. You can either obtain written permission for a substitute to do the contract work, or you can have your attorney try to relieve you of your contract obligations with as little pain as possible.

The Purchase-Order Contract

One type of contract that comes as a surprise to many businesspersons is created by the specifications that appear on the rear of many purchase orders. Usually these specifications are in fine print and are ignored by the recipient of the order. Beware. Never ignore such writing. If you find the terms repugnant, you have several basic alternatives.

You can mark out the fine print and sign your name with "deleted" or "terms not accepted." Some firms will cancel the purchase order if you do this. You can try to mark out or revise only the ones that bother you most. This also may be rejected by the one who issues the purchase order. Or you can try to negotiate the changes most important to you. Experience has shown that one never knows what revisions to standard contract forms (so-called boilerplate) will be accepted until one asks.

Related to purchase-order contracts is the fine print you will find on parking-lot stubs or sporting-event tickets, whereby the ticket-holder waives all rights to sue for injury or loss.

Trust Me, but Put It in Writing

An oral contract is just as valid legally as is a written contract. However, the exact terms and understandings of the oral contract may be difficult to prove without witnesses. Even if there are witnesses, no two people will remember an event in exactly the same way. Also, with an oral contract, there is no touchstone to which one can refer to refresh one's memory of details. There is good reason for the well-known legal oxymoron: An oral contract is not worth the paper it is written on.

Except for the most simple of contracts, nothing much more complicated than "I'll cut your grass for $20," try to avoid the oral contract. If you have no choice, immediately write a letter to the other party outlining the agreement as you understand it. Ask that party to either agree or modify your understanding in writing. A simple expedient is to send two copies of your letter and to ask the other party to sign and return one of them to you.

Killing Prior Agreements

When you sign a contract, the law assumes that all prior related agreements are merged into the latest contract. It further assumes that any verbal agreement made just before or contemporaneous with the signing of the contract is incorporated into the latest contract. If prior written agreements or prior or contemporaneous oral agreements do not appear in the signed written version, the court assumes that they were not meant to survive the signing.

This is the Parol Evidence Rule. *Black's Law Dictionary* defines the Parol Evidence Rule as follows: " . . . when parties put their agreement into writing, all previous oral agreements merge into the writing and a contract as written cannot be modified or changed by parol (oral) evidence, in the absence of a plea of mistake or fraud in the preparation of the writing."

Simply stated, what you see is what you get. If you wanted it to be part of the contract, you would either put it into the writing of the contract, or you would refer to the prior document within the contract.

Never sign a contract until you are sure that it is the *complete* agreement. Any words, explanations, or promises by you or the other party are erased upon your signing the contract. If something was left out or there is no written reference to it in the contract, you must prove it was omitted either because of fraud or by mistake. Sorry, but ignorance, stupidity, or failure to consult with and tell the full story to your attorney are not acceptable excuses.

Here is a very personal example of how the Parol Evidence Rule can work against one party and for the other. Say you have located a building you wish to lease to house your business. It is perfect for your purposes and available at a price you can afford. The location is good, all utilities are available, and it is within reasonable distance of your home. One problem remains. An old barn stands at the rear of the property. Not only is it an eyesore, bad for your business image, but it is in obvious danger of collapse. As such it is a safety hazard.

"I'll lease it," you say, "if you'll get rid of that old barn."

"No problem," the owner replies. "It'll be down in a week."

Then you sign a lease contract. The barn remains standing.

A month passes. "That damned barn is still there," you complain.

"What barn?" is the reply.

"Hold on a minute," you yell. "You promised to take down that old barn on the rear of the property."

"I did? Well, sorry, but it's not in the contract."

Angry and frustrated, you go to your attorney. You tell your story. "Make him take it down," you demand.

Your attorney looks at your lease. "I don't see anything about taking a barn down," he says.

"He promised."

"When?"

"Just before I signed the lease."

"Not after you signed?"

"No, just before."

"Not after he signed the lease?"

"No, just before."

Your attorney sighs. "Sorry, friend. Looks like you are out of luck. The Parol Evidence Rule. The court will assume that if it was important to you to have that barn down, it would be in the contract you signed. You'll have to prove fraud or mistake."

"It was fraud when he promised and didn't intend to do it," you reply.

"Can you prove it? Were there any witnesses to your conversation and mention of the barn?"

"No. But it was an obvious mistake."

"Does it prevent you from using the building and the land? Does it prevent you from doing business?"

"No," you admit.

"Then the only mistake was yours, and it's not the basis for legal action."

There are exceptions. Fraud and mistake have already been mentioned. If the wording of the contract is ambiguous, the court may allow presentation of extra evidence to prove your point. If you can prove that the other party used illegal means to induce you to sign the contract, you have a chance. Or, if there are glaring omissions from the contract, omissions that basically void the other benefits of the contract and are of a nature that no reasonable person would have allowed, the court may allow oral testimony to fill the contract's *four corners*.

The Importance of a Written Contract

Your written contract plays roles even more important than to shield you legally. If the truth be told, in most cases a contract is not much better than the continuing goodwill of the parties to the contract as a tool to enforce compliance by your customer. Remember, it also enforces compliance by you. Where the contract is of greatest value is to protect you from unexpected liabilities in the event of accidents or unpredictable obstacles that prevent proper completion of the work.

You do not need a complex document to provide a legally enforceable written contract. There are situations where you can hold the other party legally liable by use of a letter or written memo, even the minutes of a meeting. So if you cannot persuade the other party to sign a contract that is couched in legal terminology, discuss alternatives with your attorney. Ask what is needed to give legal authority to informal writings.

There are situations, however, where your contract must be in writing. The Statute of Frauds requires a written contract for the sale of land or the sale of an interest in land. The Statute also requires a written contract for any agreement that will require in excess of one year for completion, or where there is a promise to pay the debts of another person.

CHAPTER 17

When Contracts Are Sick

Even the most carefully drafted contract can fail. Some contracts are born crippled, some start out healthy, but become sick along the way. A contract can be or can become illegal. A contract can be based on misunderstandings or mistakes. A contract can be the result of coercion or unfair advantage.

Never forget your silent partner, Murphy the navigator. Things will go wrong at the most inopportune times. Blame Murphy. Equipment will break down in the middle of a job. Blame Murphy. Supplies will arrive late or will not meet specifications. Blame Murphy.

You can head Murphy off at the pass if you pay meticulous attention to details during the contract negotiating and document-drafting steps, as outlined in Chapter 22. Even then, a contract can fail, the victim of unforeseen events or intervening impossibility.

The Need for Specificity

There are three basic reasons why specificity of terms is important when drafting a contract.

To calculate damages resulting from breach of contract the court must be able to determine the essential facts of the contract. If the completion date is omitted, there is no way to calculate damages incurred because of completion delays. If materials or supplies are not carefully specified, there is no way to calculate damages resulting from the use of substitute materials or supplies.

Wording so vague as to obfuscate the basic intentions of the contracting parties can destroy an agreement as *void for vagueness*. If the writing does not clearly present the terms and expectations of the parties, the contract cannot bind the parties.

Equally ineffective is "an agreement to agree." It is not binding, for example, to say, "The parties to this agreement will at the appropriate time establish a schedule of completion." This statement is an agreement to seek a future agreement. It is neither definable nor supportable and provides no basis for the calculation of damages.

Examples of Specificity

Chapter 22 lists a number of contract terms that must be presented in detail in the final document. Here are a few examples of when specificity is important, and why.

Anticipate and allow for delays. Your contract should make specific provisions for stoppages or slowdowns beyond your control because of illness or accident, review delays by the customer, labor stoppages or slowdowns, and more. Each type of service will have its own potential delay hazards. It is up to you to learn what these are and keep a checklist in mind while negotiating. If you have a specific completion schedule, which will be true for most contracts, you must have specific provisions to excuse you for failure to adhere to that completion schedule because of events that are not of your doing.

Anticipate and allow for obstructions. Obstructions of many kinds can also prevent you from maintaining the agreed-to work schedule. These can include labor trouble, equipment breakdown, public disturbances, material or supply shortages, blockage or failure of transportation and deliveries, or acts of nature or government. What if you are faced with impossibility or impracticality of completion? Anticipate and allow for both foreseeable and nonforeseeable obstructions.

Anticipate the effects of changes. What if the customer company's objectives change? How will that affect you? What if the person you have dealt with leaves, the department is terminated, or the firm goes bankrupt, becomes insolvent, or is sold? Where will you stand? Anticipate changes and protect yourself with specific clauses in your contract.

Anticipate confusion in responsibilities. Recognize the probability of confusion and disagreement if your contract is not specific about who is to do what, how, and when. Who is to rent equipment, you or the customer? Who is to order supplies? Who will hire additional personnel needed? Who will obtain work permits? Be specific. Leave no doubt.

Anticipate how you are to be paid and reimbursed. Be sure of specific language about payments, both amounts and timing. Be specific about the conditions and timing of customer reimbursements for materials and supplies you order for the work. Will payment or reimbursements be related to steps toward completion of the work? If so, be sure that they are designated specifically and clearly.

Contracts Sick at Birth

There is an untold multitude of reefs and shoals to navigate around and avoid in the contract-law ocean. Following are a few of the more commonly met hazards, and how you can avoid them.

Lack of Mutuality

Be sure that you and your customer are in mutual agreement as to the objectives of the contract and the terms you have negotiated for the accomplishment of these objectives. Mutuality means much more than mere understanding. Mutuality means agreement free from coercion, duress, trickery, or unfair advantage.

Misrepresentation/Fraud

If one party lies, and the lie becomes a basic reason for the other party to agree to the contract, there is no meeting of the minds, hence no mutuality. Misrepresentation or fraud can arise in several ways.

1. A fact material to the contract is knowingly misrepresented.
2. A fact material to the contract is omitted or hidden.
3. A material change in facts is withheld from the other party.
4. A fact is stated with reckless disregard for truth or falsity.

To be actionable in a court of law, the misrepresentation must be made with the intent to cause the other party to enter into the contract, the misrepresentation must directly or indirectly be to the detriment of the other party, and the injured party must have relied on the supposed truth of the misrepresentation as a basis for signing the contract.

It is quite tempting to deal in hyperbole when bidding for a contract, particularly when one is new to the field. Carried to an extreme in excess of commercial "puffery" (for example, "I am pretty good at what I do"), such as misrepresentation of one's experience, ability, facilities, or other capabilities required to perform the terms of the contract, it can become fraud. As noted earlier, misrepresentation need not be an outright lie. It can be a half-truth or failure to disclose facts significant to the contract. A contract based on fraud is automatically void.

Unintended Misinformation

What if one or both parties unintentionally provide misinformation during contract negotiations? There is no fraud. If the misinformation is not materially important to the completion of the contract, the agreement will most likely continue as written.

However, what if the misinformation goes to the heart of the contract? What if it makes it unreasonable or impossible to complete the contract? While the contract is not fraudulent or illegal, it has the elements of impossibility, or, at the very least, impracticality. Such a contract is not automatically void, as for misrepresentation, but it is voidable. The parties can continue the contract agreement, or either party can request that it be made void.

A voidable contract can be replaced by a new and accurate agreement by the mutual consent of both parties. The old contract can be rescinded, either by mutual consent, court action, or binding arbitration. Or it can be corrected (reformed), also by mutual consent, court action, or binding arbitration. If the parties enter into a new contract, there is recision of and satisfaction of the prior contract, an action called *accord and satisfaction*.

Clerical/Arithmetic Errors

Clerical errors, typing errors, and such are not uncommon in contracts. Normally there is no material effect on the agreement, but there are exceptions, as when a key date, value, payment, or responsibility is incorrectly noted. Arithmetic calculation errors on a construction contract bid can be financially devastating.

Are you stuck with such an error, even though it would mean a major financial loss for you? Not necessarily. There is legal precedence for construction bids where courts have allowed reasonable correction of the figures. But don't rely on it. Check and double-check your figures. Read and reread the contract several times before signing. Have it read also by a contemporary, an employee, your attorney, your accountant, or a knowledgeable family member.

Misunderstanding/Misinterpretation

What if your customer refers to something you think you understood at the time, but later you learn that you grossly misunderstood the meaning or implication of that reference? And what if this misunderstanding will have a major impact on the completion of the contract?

Such an occurrence means that there was no true meeting of the minds, no mutuality of understanding and intent. Whatever you do, do not sacrifice yourself or your business without first making an attempt to resolve the problem. If you can prove your misunderstanding, and if it truly does go to the heart of the contract, the court may allow the contract to be rescinded or reformed.

Illegalities

There are contracts prohibited by law, or under the somewhat vague mantle of *public policy*. These contracts are void at birth, and will not be enforced by the courts. Included are:

Restraint of trade. Included are agreements that lessen the opportunity for free competition, such as collusion for price fixing, geographic allocations of service areas, and excessively harsh non-compete agreements.

Harmful to the public. Included are agreements that work against the public well-being, such as red-lining, racial unfairness, pollution, and illegal dumping.

Commit a tort, cause an injury. Courts will not uphold any contract with the objective of injuring another person either physically or economically, or to produce any other type of legal or civil wrong against a third party.

Obstruction of justice. A contract is illegal if its objective is to impede police action or the fair and free operation of our judicial system.

Usurious bargaining. One cannot have a contract that involves the encouragement or practice of lending money at rates defined by the state as excessive and usurious.

Inducement of official misdeeds. An agreement to induce misdeeds by public officials, either through bribery, force, or other forms of force or coercion, is illegal. Lobbying, whose purpose is to influence legislation or other legal matters, is not prohibited if it does not attempt to induce illegalities.

Exemption from misconduct. A contract that purports to relieve a wrongdoer from responsibility for willful misconduct or injuries caused by negligent misconduct is against public policy.

Unfair Practices

There are contract practices that are not illegal according to statutory (legislative) law, but which are prohibited by common (court-made) law. These include unfair practices such as forcing a person to agree to and sign a contract using duress, fraud, or unconscionability. Duress encompasses force, fear, threats, or economic pressure; fraud was discussed earlier; unconscionability is the use of unfair advantage or position of power to force a contract.

Party Incompetency

If you sign a contract with a person who is incompetent at the time of signing, the contract is usually considered to be voidable; that is, at the petition of the incompetent signer or his or her representative, the contract can be voided.

While mental disease, senility, idiocy, or other mental failings can be the basis of incompetency, there are other bases for such a claim. What if you sign a contract after the seventh martini? What if you sign immediately after taking a drug (either prescription or so-called "leisure-time") that leaves you only partially aware of what you are doing? Were you incompetent? Most likely, but it will be up to you to persuade the court.

What if you sign a contract with a child who is thirteen years old. Consider that this is a very bright, precocious child with a full grasp of the facts and implications of the contract. Any contract with an infant, a person not yet legally an adult, is automatically suspect. Not only is there a better than even chance that the contract will not bind the infant, it most likely will be voidable at the behest of the infant or the infant's legal guardian or custodian.

Statute of Frauds

The Statute of Frauds became law in England in 1677 and has been adopted in more or less modified form in nearly all of the United States. Its provisions of greatest direct interest to you as an independent contractor are that a written contract is required (1) for the sale of land or sale of an interest in land, and (2) for a contract that cannot under any circumstance be completed in less than a year.

When Contracts Are Breached

Did you do what the agreement specified? Is your customer satisfied with your work? Or does the customer feel that you failed to live up to your agreement—that is, are you accused of breach of contract?

Breach of contract means failure, without legal excuse, to perform any promise that forms the whole or a part of a contract. Contract breaches come in several forms:

1. Material (major, fatal to objectives)
2. Partial (minor, not fatal to objectives)
3. Continuing (ongoing)
4. Constructive (implied)
5. Anticipatory (obviously coming)

Material Breach

A material breach is the most serious of all breaches. Performance is so lacking that the objectives of the contract are not being met, and may never be met. The injured party has the legal right to sue for total breach and termination of the contract, with a judgment for appropriate damages to be paid by the offending party.

Partial Breach

If you have delivered substantially the heart or essence of the contract, but have failed to conform to certain lesser aspects of the contract, then the breach is partial. You may be penalized for your omissions, or you may receive an order for specific performance, but you are still entitled to a major portion of your remuneration since your efforts have substantially benefited your customer.

From this concept comes the term *substantial performance*. For substantial performance, the court will protect your rights, but also the rights of the customer.

If, on the other hand, your customer has breached the contract, the same legal consequences exist, but in reverse. It is possible, however, for both parties to breach a contract, each in a different way.

In contrast to material breach, a partial breach does not automatically bring with it a termination of the contract. Examples of partial breach are failure to paint a structure or the use of the wrong color of paint, the leaving of trash around the construction site, or some other failure or lack that does not cause the end product of the contract to fail.

Continuing Breach

A breach that is repeated at short intervals or endures for a considerable length of time is called a continuing breach. Such a breach is most likely to occur when a contract is for a series of repetitive services, such as the weekly maintenance of a central air-conditioning system.

Possible court remedies include money awards to the injured party, orders for specific performance, or injunctions.

Constructive Breach

The word *constructive* is a legal fiction used where the law infers something that in reality does not exist. For example, at one time possession required the physical holding of an object. You could own something, but unless you were present, you did not possess it. Now the concepts of ownership and possession have been merged so that you can be at a distance from the thing you own, yet still possess it. This is called *constructive possession*.

Constructive breach takes place when one party is disabled from performing the contract through some act or statement, even though the action or lack of action to cause the breach has yet to take place. It is closely related to anticipatory breach, discussed next.

Anticipatory Breach

This type of breach takes place when something happens that in some way assures that one party will not fulfill contractual obligations. Bankruptcy or insolvency can be the basis for anticipatory breach, as can an open and clear renunciation of the duty as stated in the contract.

The legal recourses for anticipatory breach are similar to those for constructive breach.

Determining Breach of Contract

If your work falls short of the terms of the contract, your customer is not obligated to pay you for these shortcomings until you have corrected them, or until you and the customer come to some other settlement. If, however, you cannot come to an agreement and the shortcomings still exist, you may find yourself involved in either a lawsuit, mediation, or binding arbitration.

On the other hand, if your customer can find no fault with your work, you should be paid. Failure to make payment is a breach of contract on the part of the customer. What if some latent or hidden flaw or deficiency in your work becomes evident at a later date? Do not be surprised if there is a future demand for satisfaction.

Satisfactory to Whom?

As related to a contract, the word *satisfy* has both a legal and an emotional meaning. Legally, you have satisfied a contract when you have completed the work in accordance with the terms of the contract. Emotionally, you have satisfied a contract when the customer is pleased with the results. If you satisfy a contract legally but not emotionally, you are safe, but the result is bad for business.

If you want to provide both satisfactions to be safe to practice good business, be as thorough and careful as possible during negotiation of contract terms. Be sure that there are no uncomfortable surprises, either for you or for your customer.

Completion Date Breaches

The most simple provision is for the work to be completed by a specified date, with allowances, of course, for delays (see discussion in Chapter 22). What is less simple is where completion is scheduled according to some other event, with this latter date unknown at the time of contract signing, such as the next time the Dodgers beat the Cardinals.

Whatever the completion date, protect yourself from breach of contract by allowing sufficient time, then add time for the unexpecteds. Beware of *time is of the essence* statements in the contract. This means that all work must be completed by a specified date, no matter what delays or obstacles are met along the way. Even a minute late, in theory, means a breach of contract.

Consider all possible delays that are beyond your control (again, see Chapter 22). Provide time to allow for such delays. Insist that the contract contain provisions that will forgive you for delays caused by unexpected events or conditions.

Customer Interference Breaches

Your customer, even without malice or intent, can interfere with your work so that you are prevented from meeting the terms of your contract. The interference can be as simple as delays in examining and approving blueprints, or as complicated as failure to order supplies or materials in time.

Under such conditions, there is a fair chance that the court will discharge you from your obligations under the contract. Note, however, that the interference must create more than mere frustration or irritation. The interference must be legally actionable. It must create a situation of partial or total breach.

Impossibility Breaches

There are times when events or conditions make it impossible to complete the terms of a contract. What is impossibility? One person's impossibility may be another person's inconvenience. What caused the impossibility? Was it the result of control or lack of control by one party, or of the inadequacy or inability of one party? Was it a physical impossibility, or a commercial burden?

Shortages of material or labor, or delivery problems, usually are not construed to be the causes of impossibility. When the laws of nature intervene, however, one has good basis to establish impossibility and claim relief from the duty of performance. You will not escape if the impossibility is because you have committed yourself to a project for which you are unsuited.

Unfortunately, courts are not always consistent in their rulings. Where one court would find a situation to be one of impossibility, another court might hold you to the terms of the contract. The safest answer is to protect yourself at contract negotiation time.

Acceptance of Breaches

If you are not alert, your customer's breach of your contract might become accepted and enforceable. If your customer is a week late in making a payment and you do not complain, you may have ratified a change in the contract allowing week-late payment henceforward. If you have a right to make a claim based on a term in your contract, but fail to insist on your right to that claim, you may have waived your right to that claim.

Do not lose your rights by failing to call attention to the other party's breach of the contract. By allowing the breach to continue through your failure to act, you may have ratified a different way of performing the work or of being paid.

Breach of Contract Remedies

A contract breach can be remedied by judicial, mediation, or binding arbitration action. Such actions are quite different from criminal prosecutions for crimes against the state.

Taking Your Claim to Court

The object of a civil proceeding is to make the injured party whole again, at least as whole as is possible with a money judgment, or to obtain a court order to prohibit or to command an action.

The award of a money judgment can be *nominal*, such as one dollar to say that the court recognizes a breach, but that you suffered no significant loss. The award can be *compensatory* to cover your costs or to place you monetarily in a position equivalent to that which would have existed if the contract had been honored. Or the award can be *punitive* as punishment for grossly unacceptable behavior. The biggest problem with a money award is that it is up to you to collect the money.

Another form of court action is an order for *specific performance*. Such an action legally compels the breaching party to continue with and adhere to the terms of the contract. This type of award is rare, as it places the court in the uncomfortable and often untenable position of supervising the remainder of the project.

When deciding for or against a lawsuit for failure to pay, or to force action, one must consider both the positive and the negative aspects. On the positive side, you win either money or action. On the negative side, your legal fees may be large, especially if the other party chooses strenuous resistance in court, and these fees will come out of what the court awards you. The publicity for your business can damage your image with prospective customers. Your attention will be distracted from business. A great deal of time, much of it cooling your heels in courtrooms, will be subtracted from your working time. And you might not win.

Filing a Mechanic's Lien

The law creates a security interest for you, the independent contractor, in property you have installed. If your customer does not pay you, you can exercise this right with a mechanic's lien. This can give you the right to foreclose on the property, an entire house or building, if necessary, and sell it to retrieve the value due to you.

The balance, if any, goes to the recalcitrant customer. This process is not as simple as it sounds. You will need the help of an attorney. The same positive and negative arguments noted for a court action apply to a mechanic's lien. In fact, if the other party resists your claim, there will be a court confrontation.

Mediation/Arbitration

Contracts frequently have clauses calling for either mediation or arbitration in the event of a disagreement between parties. Arbitration is formal and can be binding on the parties involved, whereas mediation is informal and is not binding.

Arbitration is most often arranged through the American Arbitration Association (AAA), and it is binding. That is, both parties agree in advance to abide by the decision of the arbitration panel, and both agree that the decision is binding so that it cannot be appealed in a court of law. Arbitration as a way to settle disputes can be made mandatory by including an arbitration clause in your contract. Here is the wording suggested by the AAA:

> Any controversy or claim arising out of or relating to this contract, or the breach thereof, shall be settled by arbitration in accordance with the _____ [see following Note] _____ of the American Arbitration Association, and judgment upon the award rendered by the arbitrator(s) may be entered in any court having jurisdiction thereof.

Note: For a construction contract, fill in the blank with "Construction Industry Arbitration Rules." For a commercial contract, insert "Commercial Arbitration Rules." For other types of contracts, contact the AAA at 140 West 51st Street, New York, NY 10020–1203; phone 212–484–4000; FAX 212–765–4874. The AAA also has 32 branch offices in major metropolitan areas across the United States, from Arizona to Washington.

The arbitrator is selected by the two disputing parties from names on a list provided by the AAA. Depending on the size and complexity of the dispute, there may be a single arbitrator or a panel of arbitrators. Arbitration proceedings emulate many of the forms used in trial courts, but with less formality. Statements of claim and counterclaim are presented, along with evidence, witnesses, and testimony.

Arbitration is not free, although it most likely will be faster and less expensive than a court trial. There is a fee to the AAA, a fee for the arbitrator, and payment of expenses for each party's attorney and witnesses.

Mediation does not produce a binding result. Rather, it is a process in which the disputing parties submit their differences to a neutral third-party (the mediator) who works with the parties to help them reach a settlement of their dispute. If an accord is not reached as a result of the mediation, either or both parties are then free to take their cases to arbitration or a court of law.

Mediators are selected from among attorneys, retired judges, and experts in various professional and business fields. Each of them is trained and evaluated by the AAA. For use in the mediation procedure, the AAA has established a number of guidelines which are available at no charge. Guidelines include those for commercial, construction industry, family, and insurance dispute resolution. There are more, all available to you if you contact the AAA.

The AAA-recommended mediation clause that you can incorporate into your contracts is:

> If a dispute arises out of or is related to this contract, or the breach thereof, and if said dispute cannot be settled through direct discussions, the parties agree to first endeavor to settle the dispute in an amicable manner under the _____ [see same Note as for the arbitration clause, but substitute the word "mediation" for "arbitration"] _____ of the American Arbitration Association, before having recourse to arbitration or a judicial forum.

What Is Your Best Choice?

Your best choice is to avoid contract disagreements entirely. At least you should avoid serious disputes that cannot be settled amicably by calm discussion between reasonable people. You can accomplish this by (1) careful and detailed negotiation of the agreement, (2) careful drafting of the contract, and (3) careful performance of the work.

If you cannot avoid a dispute, mediation is the quickest and least costly way to settle, but it is not binding. Arbitration is faster and less costly than most court trials, but the finding of the arbitrator cannot be appealed. The judgment of a court trial can be appealed to a higher court, but the time lag may be very long because of overloaded court calendars, and attorney's fees can become very large.

CHAPTER 18

The Sales Rep Contract

A popular service favored by many independent contractors with mechanical or engineering backgrounds is to sell equipment, materials, and supplies to industrial factories and plants. Such a person is usually called a "sales rep" or a "manufacturers' rep." The sales rep normally represents the makers of a number of parallel but noncompeting product lines. For example, a sales rep selling to the chemical process industries might handle pumps from one manufacturer, valves and fittings from a second manufacturer, and gaskets and packing from a third manufacturer.

In the business, the sales rep is usually called a *rep*. The manufacturer represented by the rep is usually called the *Principal*. The rep's revenue is derived from sales commissions paid by the Principal, not from the purchasers of the products. The rep is responsible for all business expenses associated with sales calls, travel and entertainment, office facilities and services.

The manufacturers using sales reps have the advantage of not bearing the office, salary, benefits, and travel expenses of having their own sales staff. This is particularly advantageous for a manufacturer who seeks sales in an industry or a geographic area where there is not enough potential business to justify a full-time field salesperson, or where a new product is to be test marketed before committing to the expense of a company sales representative.

Is There a Contract?

Too often, the rep fails to insist on a written contract to solidify his or her business relationship with the Principal. Often there is no more than a hurried discussion, an oral agreement, and a handshake. Other reps will sign a canned contract thrust upon them by the Principal. It is easy to guess who is favored by such a contract.

A number of sales rep organizations have created standard contracts, and they urge their members to take the lead in presenting such contracts to the Principal they plan to represent. One such organization is MANA (Manufacturers Agents National Association, 2021 Business Center Drive, PO Box 16878, Irvine, CA 92713).

Even with a good contract in hand, one designed to protect your legitimate interests, it is important that you know and understand the significances of the various clauses in the contract so that during negotiations you can use good judgment regarding those clauses you should insist on, and those which you are safe compromising.

The Question of Commissions

As mentioned earlier, sales rep compensation traditionally is in the form of commissions based on the dollar-value of the sale. Say that you persuade ABC Chemical Company to purchase a $100,000 compressor made by XYZ Compressor Company, your Principal. XYZ then delivers the compressor, ABC pays XYZ the $100,000, and you, the sales rep receive your $10,000 as a 10 percent commission. It's all quite simple. Or is it?

When Is a Commission Earned?

You send the ABC order to XYZ headquarters and request payment of your commission. The sales manager at XYZ objects.

"It's just an order," he explains. "We haven't delivered, and ABC hasn't paid."

You wait, as you know delivery on such a major item as a $100,000 compressor will be slow. At the end of two months, you again call the XYZ sales manager.

"How about my commission for the ABC sale?" you ask.

"Oh, that," the sales manager replies. "We turned down that order. No sale, no commission."

Have you earned the commission? Or is the sales manager within his rights in denying you the commission? If you have a written contract, you can find out in a few minutes. If there is no written contract, then the relationship between you and your Principal will be defined according to industry practice.

No question, an order is not a sale until there is a delivery and a payment. But once you have received the order and transmitted it to your Principal, can the Principal reject the order? Most Principals insist that acceptance or rejection of an order is at their discretion. Is this reasonable? Consider:

- ABC might have a bad credit record.
- XYZ might not be able to meet the delivery schedule.
- XYZ might not be able to meet the materials specifications.
- XYZ might have other priority customers to serve.
- XYZ might be planning to phase out the compressor business.

Can you protect yourself from denial of orders by your Principal? Yes, to some extent, but not completely. Be sure that your contract contains a statement such as "Approval of orders developed by [your name] will not be unreasonably withheld," or "Orders developed by [your name] can be rejected by Principal only for valid business reasons."

Will these contract clauses prevent rejection of orders? They might help you in a court of law if you are about to lose a very substantial commission and you are reasonably sure that there is no legitimate reason for rejecting the order. If you do this, however, you will have destroyed your future working relationship with the Principal.

The most likely benefit to you will be indirect in that such a clause could make the Principal more cautious. Even more important, you will realize that Principals frequently have legitimate reasons for rejecting an order, and you will learn the truth of that old adage, "Don't count your chickens until the eggs are hatched."

Should you sign a contract that says your commissions are not earned until the product is shipped? Practically speaking, yes. You have little choice. Should you sign a contract that says your commissions are not earned until the Principal has been paid for the shipped product? Again, the practicalities say yes. If you are paid following delivery, but the customer never pays, then you will owe your commission back to the Principal. By then you may already have spent it.

Are you seriously at risk with such an arrangement? Not with a reputable Principal. Check around before you commit yourself to a Principal. Talk to other reps. Talk to potential buyers of the Principal's products.

When Prices Are Discounted

Should you receive full commission on discounted products? Be sure that this subject is covered in your contract. You may be asked to accept a lower commission rate for discounted sales. Is this fair? That is for you to decide. Discounted items will be easier to sell, but your profit will be smaller.

When You End the Relationship

Back to the ABC-XYZ scenario: You obtain four excellent orders for XYZ equipment, totaling $500,000. Your commission, if everything goes according to plan, will be $50,000. But there are delays. The usual two-month delivery time is past, and the signs are that there will be another three-month delay. You are caught in the middle. You have already given a 30-day notice to XYZ that you will no longer represent them. This means that delivery will not take place until well after your arrangement with XYZ is terminated.

Does this mean that you have lost your $50,000? Perhaps. Perhaps not. What does your contract say? Is there any provision for payment of commissions based on orders taken before termination that are delivered after termination? If not, you can kiss your commission goodbye.

But wait! Is it possible that XYZ got wind of your intention to leave them to handle rep sales for QRS Intermetallics? Is it possible that the delay in delivery was planned to prevent you from collecting your commission? "Of course not," you say. "They'd lose their sale." Would they? What if the customer was assured that they would receive a $25,000 discount if they accepted late delivery? Collusion?

When You Breach the Contract

Again the ABC-XYZ scenario and the $500,000 order: Without telling XYZ, you have been selling a competitive product line made by QRS Intermetallics. XYZ learns of your perfidy and immediately terminates your contract with them.

You can forget your commission from the ABC sale, regardless of what your contract says. You have violated and voided your contract. It no longer exists.

When XYZ Merges with QRS

QRS Intermetallic persuades XYZ management to merge. The surviving firm is now QRS-XYZ Intercompressor. The compressor model produced by XYZ is being dropped for the more advanced model designed by QRS. Your contract was with XYZ? Is it still valid with QRS-XYZ? What happens to the $500,000 order you earned for XYZ from ABC?

If ABC will accept substitution of the new QRS-XYZ model in place of the XYZ model, you may still have a shot at your commission. But only if the new firm will honor your contract. After all, XYZ no longer exists. Where will you stand? It depends on your XYZ contract. Did it have a provision specifying that if the company was sold or otherwise acquired, it carried with it the obligation to continue your contract? It should have. Then you would have the legal basis to claim the commission and, if your claim is denied, take your claim into a court of law.

Protective Sales-Rep Contract Checklist

You have seen just a few of the potential hazards of sales repping with inadequate contract protection. Entire books have been written on the subject (see reference in the Appendix to *The Salesman's Legal Guide* by Sack and Seinberg, or contact MANA, mentioned earlier in this chapter).

Your best protection is to have contract assistance from an attorney who is familiar with sales rep contracts. Lacking this, your next best protection is to consult with an experienced sales rep, one who has lived through more than one unpleasant experience with a Principal. Lacking either of these, take the following checklist with you during contract negotiations:

- ☐ What is the commission rate?
- ☐ When is the commission earned? When is it paid?
- ☐ What credit do you get for customer-returned goods?
- ☐ When is an order considered accepted for commission purposes?
- ☐ How are commissions for discount-priced orders handled?
- ☐ Can the Principal change commissions unilaterally?
- ☐ Does the Principal make advance payments against commissions?
- ☐ What is your specific territory?
- ☐ Are you limited geographically? By type of industry? To specific prospective customers?
- ☐ Is your territory exclusive to you?
- ☐ What if other reps for the Principal sell in your territory?
- ☐ Will you get commissions for orders obtained within your territory but delivered in the territory of another rep?
- ☐ If so, will you get full or shared commissions?
- ☐ What if another rep's order is delivered in your territory?
- ☐ If so, will you get a shared commission?
- ☐ Can you take orders outside your territory? Where?
- ☐ Does a Principal prevent you from also representing a noncompetitive Principal? Watch out for your "independence."

☐ How can you terminate the contract (escape clause)?
☐ How can the Principal terminate the contract?
☐ How long in advance is notice given for no-fault termination?
☐ Will you receive commissions on orders delivered after termination of the contract? Under what conditions?
☐ Will you be provided with suitable samples and literature?

In Summary

No two situations will be identical. Some of the preceding will not apply to a specific contract, and other items that are important may not be listed. But if you and your attorney cover all of the bases in the checklist, you will have a far better contract than most sales reps have.

CHAPTER 19

The Construction Subcontract

For very large projects, the number of subcontractors will greatly out-number prime contractors, the hirers of subcontractors. As a newly established business offering a specialized niche service, you are much more likely to be a subcontractor than a prime contractor for large jobs. While subcontracting is usually thought of in relation to construction, in fact it can apply to any project involving a complex interrelation of a number of skills and specialties.

Dangers of Subcontracting

The subcontract can be either a blessing or a curse. It can be the means of generating revenue through work on large projects for which you cannot bid. Or it can create legal hassles, liabilities, or loss of income.

The goal of a well-constructed subcontract, according to *Contract Documents* (see description in the Appendix), published by the Associated Specialties Contractors, Inc. (the ASC)* is as follows:

*Located at 7315 Wisconsin Ave., Bethesda, MD 20814–3299, phone 301–657–3110. A member organization comprising the Mason Contractors Association of America; Mechanical Contractors Association of America; National Association of Plumbing, Heating, and Cooling Contractors; National Electrical Contractors Association; National Insulation Contractors Association; National Roofing Contractors Association; Painting and Decorating Contractors of America; and Sheet Metal and Air Conditioning Contractors National Association.

Contract documents should promote harmonious and efficient cooperation to accomplish the objectives of both parties rather than entrap the unwary. In practice, however, carelessly worded language and ambiguities entrap one party or the other because the parties were unknowingly far apart in their comprehension of what the words meant when the job was bid and the contract signed.

In most cases, subcontract agreements bind the subcontractor to the terms of the general contractor's agreement with the owner.

What does this mean? First, lack of communication between parties can "entrap the unwary." Second, if the general (prime) contractor has a bad contract with the owner, or agrees to provisions deleterious to the subcontractor, the subcontractor may be left without protection.

Are there defenses for the subcontractor? Yes. First, never sign on as a subcontractor under a prime contractor's basic contract until you and your attorney have had the opportunity to see and study the prime contractor's contract with the owner-customer. Second, be sure that the prime contract covers all contingencies. Third, be sure that you understand fully the meanings and consequences of the clauses within the prime contract. What if the prime contractor refuses? It is your decision. Play ball blindfolded, or leave the game.

Elements of a Prime Contract

Again quoting from the ASC's *Contract Documents*:

Owners need a completed facility for a predictable cost. Contractors and subcontractors can best deliver the facility on time and within budget when their risks are limited by equitable clauses which they clearly understand at the time of estimating.

What are these all-so-important clauses? They include:

- Payments
- Retainage
- Performance time
- Scheduling
- Avoidance of (or compensation for) interference
- Efficient (timely) contract administration
- Submittals
- Changes
- Design change responsibility
- Site inspections
- Notices

- Claims
- Disputes
- Damages incurred by either party
- Waivers
- Suspension of work
- Termination of contract by either party
- Indemnity
- Insurance
- Warranties
- Inspections and tests

Fortunately, much of this work has already been done for you in either of two nationally recognized standard subcontract agreements. They are:

- *AIA Document A401–1987* (Standard Form of Agreement Between Contractor and Subcontractor) designed by the American Institute of Architects (AIA)
- *1966 AGC-ASC Standard Subcontract Agreement* developed by the Associated General Contractors of America and the ASC

According to the ASC, the AIA Document A401–1987 is regarded as the most equitable and workable of all *standard* subcontracts by its owner, the AIA, and by subcontractors and their associations. It contains many provisions to protect the mutual interests of owners, contractors, subcontractors, and lower-tier subcontractors.

As for the 1966 AGC-ASC Standard Subcontract Agreement, the payment language is not as effective from a subcontractor's point of view as is the AIA subcontract agreement. But language similar to that in the AGC-ASC subcontract agreement has been tested in courts in several states and, in general, has been interpreted favorably for subcontractors.

Getting Paid for Your Work

One of the greatest obstacles that the subcontractor must overcome is getting paid on time, or even getting paid at all. The ASC has suggested four good criteria for payment clauses between the prime contractor and subcontractor that will protect your rights as a subcontractor:

1. A clear statement of your entitlement to be paid in full upon satisfactory completion of your work.
2. The percentage the prime contractor retains of your earned progress payments should be no greater than the owner's retainage of earned progress payments to the prime contractor. Retainage is

the right to withhold a specified percentage of progress payments as a way to assure that the work will be completed.

3. Prompt pass-through to you of your share of payments to the prime contractor by the owner, including payments for stored materials.

4. Statement that you are to receive payments to which you are entitled within a specified or reasonable period of time, even if the prime contractor has not been paid for any reason that is not your fault. Avoid a *conditions precedent* clause that says the prime contractor must be paid before you are paid.

Basic Contract Clauses

While the problem of payment is foremost in the minds of most subcontractors, there are other contract danger spots in the controlling contract between owner and prime contractor.

No-Damage-for-Delay Clause

Example: Subcontractor signs contract, agreeing to complete work within 30 days, with a penalty provision for late completion. Owner's drawings are in error. Subcontractor is 15 days late completing the work, held up while owner's engineering department produced corrected drawings. Is Subcontractor subject to the penalty for late completion?

The no-damage-for-delay clause is popular with owners. It is a way for them to avoid liability for their own delays caused by design errors or omissions, excessive change orders, administrative delays, or other interferences by the owner, the architect, or other prime contractors associated with the project.

Is the subcontractor liable? Yes, if the contract contained such a clause without forgiveness of delay caused by the owner. If you decide to accept a no-damage-for-delay clause in the contract, first try to determine the history of promptness and/or delay or interference by the owner in past projects.

Open-ended-Scope Clause

A subcontractor signed a contract to design a new integrated, multi-user computer system for ABC Company. Halfway through the job, ABC established a new department, incorporating 13 more work stations. The basic system, file-server, and printer auxiliaries had to be redesigned. When work was 90 percent complete, ABC again changed the specifications. What would have been a 60-day job became a 150-day job. The subcontractor submitted a request for modified payment to match the extended time needed.

An open-ended-scope clause normally states that the contract documents do not necessarily indicate or describe all of the work required for full performance or completion of the work. This kind of clause is dangerous because of its vagueness, an open invitation for trouble.

Is the subcontractor entitled to the additional payment? Probably not, if the contract contained an open-ended-scope clause. Definitely avoid such a clause. The owner is allowed to make all kinds of changes, additions, or modifications for which you may or may not be paid.

Indemnification Clause

It is virtually impossible to avoid indemnification clauses in contracts. Protect yourself, however, by a statement in the clause that your indemnification responsibilities will apply only for those actions or inactions that are directly your fault.

Design-Verification Clause

Another danger point. Such a clause will state that the contractor(s), including, of course, the subcontractor(s) examined the drawings and specifications carefully, and verified their accuracy. If you agree to such a clause, you become responsible for any design deficiencies.

Site-Investigation Clause

Yet another danger point. When you sign a contract with a site-investigation clause, you are saying that you have investigated the site prior to bidding and are aware of problems and risks not clearly indicated in the drawings and specifications.

Without question, this can be a legitimate sharing of risks, but only if it does not imply responsibility for latent or other physically unobservable problems, or risks not identified in the contract documents.

Lien-Rights Clause

The lien-rights clause is the most direct and possibly the most effective tool available to a subcontractor to insure payment for work done. It gives you a legal lien (claim) on what you have contributed to the overall work, and, with court authority, the theoretical right to sell the project, even the entire project, to obtain fair payment.

You want this one. To help you, it must reach back to the owner through the owner-prime contractor contract.

Waiver-of-Claim Clause

This type of clause can be a troublemaker. Such a claim states that when you accept final payment for your work, you release all claims against the customer—that is, the owner.

Such a claim can become coercive. The customer can withhold payment until you agree to a waiver of all claims that may have developed out of changes, delays, or other items within the contract that normally entitle you to relief. Avoid it if you can.

Termination Clause

While the right of an owner or prime contractor to terminate an incompetent or defaulting contractor is reasonable, in practice the terms of termination can be quite harsh. If you are terminated as a subcontractor by any clause in the contract or for a breach of any kind, you may then be made to bear the cost of hiring a substitute to complete the work, a substitute who may not work as economically as you would.

Watch out for a termination clause that allows the terminating party to seize tools, materials, and equipment you have on the job site. The right to terminate a subcontractor should not contain abusive and unreasonable terms.

Strike Clause

Some contracts require that in the event of a strike, the contractor must provide other manpower, either union or nonunion, to facilitate completion of the work.

If you rely on union help, try to delete such a clause. If this is not possible, insist on language that will not require you to take actions that would conflict with your own labor agreements.

Consequential-Damages Clause

A danger point. While it is reasonable for you to be financially responsible for your own failings or shortcomings in performing the work called for in the contract, experience shows that costs incurred through consequential-damage clauses can snowball to reach phenomenal sums.

Either delete such a term or rephrase so as to negate the financial consequences to you of losses or damages to the owner due to partial or complete loss of use of the project, loss of interest, loss of revenue or anticipated profits, financial damage to the owner for failing to meet customer requirements, or other near- or long-term consequences of your failure to perform.

Flow-Down Clause

This is a clause to bind the subcontractor to the prime contractor, and vice versa, in the same manner that the prime contract binds the prime contractor and the owner.

Such clauses can be harmful, but in most cases they are helpful to the subcontractor.

Force-Majeure Clause

A force-majeure clause enumerates excusable causes for delay and allows specified time extensions.

Properly written, such a clause will protect you from the responsibility for delays or costs that result from change orders, actions or inactions of others that are not your fault, the so-called acts of God, floods, fires, explosions, strikes, boycotts or other labor disputes, lockouts, and acts of local, state, or federal governments.

Differing-Site-Condition Clause

You want this clause. It can protect you from liability or breach when site conditions are materially different from those shown in the contract drawings or specifications, or differ in any other manner that neither party could reasonably expect.

This clause is important to you. It could save you from a great deal of pain.

Claims Clause

Another clause you want. A claims clause clearly establishes your right to collect for any damages you may incur as a result of acts or failures to act by the prime contractor, owner, architect/engineer, or other contractors or subcontractors on the same project.

Dispute Clause

You want this clause, too. It assures that you have the same rights regarding disputes with the prime contractor that the prime contractor has with the owner. Arbitration or mediation may or may not be included.

Other Contract Elements

As well as the legal party-interrelation clauses already noted, there are factual elements that should be included in all contracts. Without them, there is confusion of rights, responsibilities, and liabilities. These include:

☐ *Ability to pay.* Be sure that the owner has the ability to pay the prime contractor, and that the prime contractor has the ability to pay you. Do not hesitate to investigate and to ask for documentation.

☐ *Drawings.* If drawings are needed for the work you will do, be sure that the contract contains specific mention of what drawings are needed, when they are to be submitted, and the required form of the drawings.

☐ *Insurance.* The contract should be specific about the type and amount of insurance you will need, and those items of potential or shared liability for which you should seek insurance protection.

☐ *Site facilities and utilities.* Will water, electricity, temporary power, lighting, heat, and sanitation facilities be provided for you at no charge? If not, you need to know in advance so that you can allow for these costs in your bid.

☐ *Job cleanup.* Of course, you are responsible for the after-job cleanup of your own identifiable scrap. But be sure that the contract clearly states that you will not be held responsible for a prorated portion of the general cleanup of the premises, or for the disposal of central scrap piles.

☐ *Storage and work areas.* Will the contract provide you with adequate space in which to work and to store your equipment and materials? If not, you need to know in advance and allow for the additional expense in your bid.

☐ *Legal compliance.* Who is responsible? You are for your own work. Before you bid, you should be familiar with and ready to comply with all relevant local, state, and federal laws, regulations, and installation codes. Do not, however, let the contract make you responsible for the failure of plans provided by the owner or prime contractor to meet local, state, and federal laws, regulations, and codes.

☐ *Hazardous substances.* If your work requires the use of hazardous materials, such as toxic chemicals, explosives, asbestos, and PCBs, on the work site, it is your legal obligation to prevent the exposure to these materials by your workers or others in the vicinity.

☐ *Warranties.* You will have little if any control over the warranty language of your contract. What you can do is make sure that your warranties to the prime contractor are no more onerous than the prime contractor's warranties to the owner.

The Big Picture

These few pages hardly cover every aspect of subcontractor contracts of importance to you. There are other aspects to consider, such as:

- Direct payment by owners
- Title company funds disbursement
- Change order procedures
- Preconstruction conferences
- Punch lists
- Temporary job utilities and services
- Hold harmless clauses
- Scope bidding
- Concealed shipping damages
- Construction progress delays

Of course, not all subcontractor jobs are so complex as to require attention to every one of the items discussed in this chapter. There is a great deal of difference between laying a new front sidewalk and participating in the construction of a 1,000-car municipal parking garage. For the sidewalk, a handshake might suffice. For the municipal garage, you could be looking at a 100-page legal document.

When should you seek out legal advice? You will have to be the judge. If your maximum loss is a few hundred dollars and there is no additional potential of liability or consequential damages, take a chance. If you lose out, grit your teeth, smile, and try to be smarter next time. If your potential loss can be measured in the thousands of dollars, let your lawyer help you protect yourself.

PART V

Putting It Together and Making It Work

CHAPTER 20

Budgeting for Survival and Growth

Accurate records of expenses and income are essential for the long-term success of any business enterprise, even if you are the sole person involved in the delivery of your independent contractor service. Records not only serve to tell you how your financial situation is today, but also can be used to guide and predict your business and personal financial situations next week, next month, next year, and so on.

A large proportion of the new business efforts that do not succeed fail because the owners were unaware of their income problems up to the moment of insolvency. The biggest single reason for failure is lack of income caused by faulty bidding, which in turn is caused by failure to consider and keep track of all business expenses (both direct and indirect) and to add a fair margin of profit to generate income to cover personal living costs.

This chapter covers accounting for your business and personal expense records for the purpose of business control, although specific expense items will also be discussed in relation to taxation in Chapter 21. This chapter concerns:

- Recognizing business and personal expenses
- Creating and using budgets
- Other financial reports and their uses

Your Expenses: Business and Personal

Most of your business expenses will be tax deductible (see Chapter 21), while most of your personal expenses will not be tax deductible. For both, however, you will need to keep careful records, not only to defend your tax returns should you be challenged by the Internal Revenue Service, but for the simple purpose of knowing where you are financially today, and where you are headed financially in the days, weeks, months, and years to come.

If you do not have a full understanding of the total cost of doing business, as well as of your personal income needs, you will not know how to negotiate profitable contracts. You will not know if your bid will make a profit, or be a loser.

Elements of Business Cost

The two major elements of business expenses are direct costs and indirect costs. *Direct costs* comprise labor costs, materials costs, and miscellaneous expenses, such as fees, rentals, and permits. *Indirect costs* comprise such expenses as wages and salaries (including your own), benefits, taxes, facilities repair and maintenance, and general supplies and equipment.

Some direct costs are fixed, such as monthly rental or insurance payments. Others are variable and may change with your seasonal business cycles.

Direct business costs. A direct cost is any expense that you incur specifically and exclusively for a given project. Included are items such as:

- ☐ Materials used specifically for the project
- ☐ Supplies used specifically for the project
- ☐ Equipment rentals or leases, prorated to the project
- ☐ Labor costs (including your own) prorated to the project
- ☐ Costs of deliveries and pickups for the project
- ☐ Special fees or permits required for the project
- ☐ Travel and per diem for food and lodging for the project
- ☐ Performance bonds required for the project
- ☐ Special liability riders to your insurance for the project
- ☐ Any other expense directly attributable to the project

Indirect business costs. Indirect costs, sometimes called general costs, are those that are related to the cost of being in business and that cannot be exclusively identified with a specific project. You will have these expenses as long as you maintain a business, even if you have no projects and no income. Indirect costs normally are divided into *personnel* and overhead (nonpersonnel) categories.

Personnel business costs. These are the expenses you incur if you employ others to assist you in the conduct of your business. If you do not require employees, or if your assistance is under contract with other independent contractor services, you can ignore many of the following expenses.

- ☐ Salaries and wages
- ☐ Employer's contribution to Social Security taxes (FICA)
- ☐ Insurance, including:
  Worker's compensation (state requirement)
  Unemployment (state required)
  Group medical program
- ☐ Fringe benefits, including:
  Pension plan participation
  Paid time off (vacations, holidays, illness, other)
  Performance bonuses
- ☐ Independent contractor fees, including:
  Legal consultation fees
  Part-time bookkeeper fees
  Accountant/financial consultation fees

Business overhead costs. Those nonpersonnel expenses that you incur regardless of projects underway, just to stay open for business, are the overhead component of your indirect costs. They include:

- ☐ Rentals (facilities, parking, furnishings, equipment)
- ☐ Utilities (heat, electricity, water, telephone)
- ☐ Insurance (casualty, liability, business interruption)
- ☐ Licenses and permits
- ☐ Depreciation of capital assets
- ☐ Property taxes, local assessments
- ☐ Regular office supplies (stationery, forms, etc.)
- ☐ Postage and delivery
- ☐ Advertising, promotion, marketing
- ☐ Business development (lunches, entertainment, gifts)
- ☐ Repair, maintenance, cleaning services
- ☐ Business-related travel in general
- ☐ Printing, copying, etc.

☐ Subscriptions and reference materials
☐ Membership dues and fees

Personal Overhead Costs

Few of us bother with detailed personal living budgets while on salary. Somehow we seem to make everything work out by instinctual spending controls. This should change, however, as you plan to enter into your own independent contractor business. As you calculate your salary (or "draw") from your business, you need to keep in mind your fixed and variable personal living expenses, some of which are quite obvious, such as food and shelter. Others, however, you might overlook.

Fixed personal expenses. Your fixed personal expenses are those over which you have very little immediate control. At best you could move to less-costly lodging, keep a low thermostat setting, turn off lights not in use, or take showers instead of baths. Major savings in fixed personal expenses would require major adjustments in life-style.

☐ Rental or mortgage payments
☐ Utilities (heat, electricity, water, telephone)
☐ Insurance (homeowner's, automobile, medical, life)
☐ Taxes (income, real estate, personal property)
☐ Loan interest (credit card, bank, automobile, other)

Variable personal expenses. If you must cut personal expenses during the developmental days of your business, your greatest opportunities for savings will be found in your variable personal expenses, such as:

☐ Food, beverages
☐ Clothing, accessories
☐ Laundry, cleaning
☐ Magazines, newspapers
☐ Pets and their care
☐ Personal care (cosmetics, toiletries, sundries)
☐ Recreation, entertainment, travel, vacations
☐ House repairs and maintenance; lawn care
☐ Garbage and trash removal
☐ Home furnishings, appliances
☐ Car expenses (fuel, oil, repair, registration, licenses)
☐ Child-care expenses (allowances, lessons, camp, school)
☐ Medical expenses (doctors, dentists, medications, hospitals)
☐ Contributions (church, charity, PBS)

Budgets: Essential Business Tools

We all know about budgets. A few of us even have personal expense budgets to guide us in our month-to-month expenditures. Few of us, however, use our budgets to forecast our medium- and long-range financial futures. In business, however, the situation is different. Your budget forecast, even before you actually launch your business, has several essential functions. Your budget forecast is a planning and guidance tool.

Your budget forecast forces you to recognize the expenses you will have. It forces you to analyze your market potential so that you can forecast sales and income. Without a budget that incorporates both direct and indirect costs, your project-cost estimates will be a little more reliable than Russian roulette or a roll of the dice. When you are in operation and actually delivering your service, a budget forecast will show you where you are spending too much and where you are bringing in too little. It will help you to coordinate the total activities of your business.

There is more. Your operating budget when compared to your budget forecast will show you how religiously you have adhered to your growth plan, perhaps even where you should revise your growth plan or modify the way you are doing business. Your operating budget will let you know when you have reached break-even operation, and then when you have graduated into that glorious realm of profitability. And it will let you know when you have reached the point of total payback of initial investment and are operating in the clear.

Your operating and forecast budgets will alert you to an impending need for outside financing early enough to avoid financial gridlock. They will help you to anticipate cyclic or impending cash-flow problems, and to make plans for cash survival by establishing and using a bank credit line or some other infusion of operating capital. Potential lenders or investors will need to see and respect your budgets before they will invest their money in your operation.

Creating Your Budget

Unless you have experience in business accounting, you should work out your budget procedures and forms with your financial advisor, preferably a CPA familiar with the recordkeeping needs of small businesses and individual independent contractor entrepreneurs. If, however, you want to tackle budgeting by yourself, or you plan to use an accountant but want a better understanding of what will be involved, the United States Small Business Administration (SBA) has published two very helpful booklets, both of which are listed in the Appendix: *Financial Management: How to Make a Go of Your Business,* and *A Handbook of Small Business Finance.*

Remember, a budget is a guide to what should be; a budget forecast is your prediction of what the future holds for you financially. Elements of a budget are revenues and expenses, direct and indirect, as discussed at the beginning of this chapter.

Financial Reporting Forms

Figures 20–1 through 20–4 are simplified examples of various financial reporting forms that can be prepared using a combination of investment and debt figures with operating and forecast budget figures.

The Balance Sheet (Figure 20–1). This form provides a picture of the financial health of a business at a given moment, usually at the close of the basic accounting period (calendar or fiscal year). It lists all known assets and liabilities.

ABC Company
December 31, 19_ _

BALANCE SHEET

ASSETS		LIABILITIES	
Cash	$ 1,896	Notes payable, bank	$ 2,000
Accounts receivable	1,456	Accounts payable	2,240
		Accruals	940
Inventory	6,822		
Total current assets	$10,174	Total current liabilities	$ 5,180
		Total liabilities	5,180
Equipment and fixtures	1,168	Net worth*	7,440
Prepaid expenses	1,278		
		Total liabilities and net worth	$12,620
Total assets	$12,620		

Figure 20–1. Simple balance sheet. Based on Fig. 2–1, *Financial Management: How to Make a Go of Your Business,* SBA Small Business Management Series No. 44. (*Assets – Liabilities = Net Worth)

ABC Company
December 31, 19_ _
STATEMENT OF INCOME

Net sales		$68,116
Cost of services sold (direct costs)		47,696
Gross profit on sales		$20,420
Expenses (indirect costs):		
Wages	$6,948	
Delivery expenses	954	
Bad debt allowance	409	
Communications	204	
Depreciation allowance	409	
Insurance	613	
Taxes	1,021	
Advertising	1,566	
Interest	409	
Other charges	749	
Total expenses		$13,282
Net profit (gross profit less expenses)		7,138
Other income (e.g., interest)		886
Total Net Income		$8,024

Figure 20-2. Simple statement of income. Based on Fig. 2-2, *Financial Management: How to Make a Go of Your Business*, SBA Small Business Management Series No. 44.

Balance sheet *assets* include cash, merchandise, inventory, land, buildings, equipment and machinery, furniture, patents or trademarks or copyrights, and the like, plus money owed to the business—that is, accounts receivable. They are usually arranged in decreasing order, according to how quickly they can be converted into cash. Assets can be broken down into

- *Current assets*: Cash, securities, accounts receivable, inventories, prepaid expenses, and other items that can be converted into cash within one year in the normal course of business.
- *Fixed assets*: Land, plant, equipment, machinery, leasehold improvements, furniture, fixtures, and other items with life expectancies measured in years.

ABC Company
December 31, 19_ _

PROFIT-AND-LOSS STATEMENT

Sales	$120,000
Cost of goods sold	70,000
Gross margin	$ 50,000
Selling expenses:	
Salaries	$ 15,000
Commission	5,000
Advertising	5,000
Total selling expenses	$ 25,000
Selling margin*	$ 25,000
Administrative Expenses	10,000
Net Profit	$ 15,000

Figure 20-3. Simple Profit-and-Loss Statement. Based on Exhibit 4, *A Handbook of Small Business Finance*, SBA Small Business Management Series No. 15. (*Selling Margin = Gross Margin – Total Selling Expenses)

- *Other assets*: Intangibles, such as patents, royalty arrangements, copyrights, exclusive-use contracts, and notes receivable from officers and employees.

Balance sheet *liabilities* are those amounts owed by the business—that is, funds acquired through loans or purchases on credit which are yet to be paid out by the business. Liabilities are usually listed in order according to how soon they must be repaid. They can be broken down into

- *Current liabilities*: Accounts and notes payable, accrued expenses (for example, wages and salaries), taxes payable, portions of long-term debt due within a year, other obligations to creditors due within a year.
- *Long-term liabilities*: Mortgages, intermediate and long-term bank loans, equipment loans, and other money obligations due to creditors in longer than a year.

Net worth on the balance sheet is the difference between assets and liabilities. Net worth is the owner's equity, namely the owner's personal

ABC Company
For Three Months Ending March 31, 19_ _
CASH BUDGET (Forecast–Actual)

	JANUARY		FEBRUARY		MARCH	
	Budget	Actual	Budget	Actual	Budget	Actual
Expected cash receipts:						
1. Cash sales						
2. Accounts receivable						
3. Other income						
4. Total cash receipts						
Expected cash payments:						
5. Raw materials						
6. Payroll						
7. Other direct expenses						
8. Advertising						
9. Selling expense						
10. Administrative expense						
11. Plant and equipment						
12. Other payments						
13. Total cash payments						
Summaries:						
14. Expected cash balance at beginning of month						
15. Cash change (4 – 13)						
16. Expected cash balance at end of month (14 + 15)						
17. Desired cash balance						
18. Short-term loans needed (17 – 16)						
19. Cash available for short-term investment (16 – 17)						

Figure 20–4. Simple three-month Cash Budget (also called Cash-Flow Sheet) spreadsheet for actual versus forecast cash expenditure comparisons. Based on Exhibit 12, *A Handbook of Small Business Finance*, SBA Small Business Management Series No. 15.

investment plus any profits and minus any losses accumulated by the business.

Statement of Income (Figure 20–2). This form is a measure of a business's sales and expenses over a given period of time. It is normally prepared at the end of each month and the end of the business year (calendar or fiscal). Its purpose is to show operating results for the reporting period.

Net sales are gross sales less returns and allowances. *Gross margin* is net sales from which *cost of goods sold* (cost of inventories) is subtracted. *Operating profit*, not shown in Figure 20–2, is calculated by subtracting selling and administrative expenses from gross margin. To obtain *net profit* (the figure from which your business income tax is computed), *other income* is added and *other expenses* are subtracted. The *net profit after tax* is *net profit* less the income tax due and paid to federal, state, and local authorities.

Profit-and-Loss Statement (Figure 20–3). Also known as P/L statement, this form is a variation on the statement of income shown in Figure 20–2. Both types of statements are kept short and simple because the detailed costs of goods manufactured or services provided are reported separately.

Cash Budget (Forecast-Actual) (Figure 20–4). As illustrated, this form can be spread over any period of time. Yearly cash budget reports are reported in monthly increments for the upcoming year, then on a yearly basis for the upcoming three to five years. Note that each time period (three months on the sample) allows for the budgeted figure (that which was forecast in advance) and the actual figure (results of real-life efforts).

The cash budget deals with only a portion of the total business operation, namely cash. By forecasting the future cash income and expenditures, you can judge how well you are doing according to plan. If income is below that which you forecast, it gives you an opportunity to take remedial action before a financial crisis develops. This use of the cash budget is discussed in greater detail in Chapter 23.

CHAPTER 21

Your Business and the Tax Collector

Your relationship with the Internal Revenue Service will change greatly as your tax problems change from purely personal exemptions, deductions, and adjustments to the more complex problems of a business. There are tax advantages available to you as an independent contractor, but they are not always obvious. Even when you do find these tax advantages, you are faced with restrictions and limitations. What you need is a general understanding of tax law, of what you can or cannot deduct or charge as a business expense, and what you must account for as personal expenses or personal income.

Your Tax Advisor

Reading will help, but tax law is like reflections from running water; always there, but constantly changing. Unless you are willing to devote full time to tax law, you will be well advised to seek out and pay for the advice and services of a tax advisor, either a CPA or a tax attorney, or both. Your bookkeeper, if you use one, is not likely to have the qualifications required to be a tax advisor. The initial contacts will be frequent, but once your system is established you will be able to operate with only limited contacts, mostly at the end of the tax year or when some new circumstance arises.

How do you select a tax advisor? Much the same way you select a lawyer, as described in Chapter 14. What can the tax advisor do for you? Consider getting answers to the following questions, among others.

- ☐ What are the tax advantages of a sole proprietorship versus a partnership versus a corporation?
- ☐ What are the tax advantages and disadvantages of purchasing versus leasing facilities and equipment?
- ☐ What are the tax regulations and implications of benefits plans?
- ☐ How can I set up a pension plan? A medical plan? An insurance plan?
- ☐ What kind of records must I keep for my business and personal federal, state, and local tax returns?
- ☐ What kinds of records must I keep for my employees?
- ☐ How do I handle payments to other independent contractors I hire to help me in my business?
- ☐ Will the IRS audit me? If they do, what should I do?

Small Business Taxes

Your bible for tax purposes should be IRS Publication 334, *Tax Guide for Small Business*. This 178-page pamphlet covers income, excise, and employment taxes for individuals, partnerships, and corporations. From it you will gain an insight into the areas of importance. You will be able to work more effectively with your tax advisor.

Employer Identification Number

Even with no employees, if you have formed a partnership or a corporation, you will need an EIN (Employer Identification Number) to serve as your company's taxpaying identification number. As a sole proprietor, you will also need an EIN if you pay wages to one or more employees, or if you must file pension or excise tax returns.

To apply for an EIN, request a Form SS-4 from your nearest Social Security office. You will use your EIN when you pay for the services of others, at which time you will make out and file with the IRS a 1099-Misc tax form listing to whom paid, the recipient's Taxpayer Identification Number (either EIN or Social Security Number), and the amount paid.

Tax Recordkeeping

Your tax recordkeeping system comprises the selection of a tax year, an accounting system, and a bookkeeping system.

Your tax year. Your tax year can be the normal calendar year, or an artificial year (for example, April 1 to March 31), called a fiscal year. For most small businesses, the calendar year is the simplest of the two, particularly if your recordkeeping leaves something to be desired. Whatever you choose for your tax year, you must use it consistently from year to year. To change your tax year, you must notify the IRS for permission.

Accounting method. You choose your tax accounting method at the time you file your first business tax return. To change systems, you must work through the IRS. The IRS recognizes the following accounting methods:

1. *Cash method.* This is the simplest method and is the most widely used method for small businesses with no inventory. This method deals only with actual income and expenses.

2. *Accrual method.* The accrual method is more complex than the cash method. If you carry a constantly changing inventory, you will need to use the accrual method. The objective of the accrual method is to match income and expenses in the correct year. Income is recorded when earned, even though actual payment may be in another tax year. Business expenses are deducted or capitalized at the time you become liable for them, even though you may pay them in another tax year.

There are special accounting methods allowed by the IRS, as well as hybrids of several methods. However, the method you choose should show income, and work for you consistently from year to year.

Accounting system. There are two prevailing methods for accounting records (bookkeeping systems). They are single entry and double entry. Single entry is the easiest to handle, particularly if you intend to keep your own books. The double-entry system, however, checks its own accuracy through so-called self-balancing.

In single-entry bookkeeping, you keep track of the flow of income and expenses with daily and monthly summaries of receipts and a monthly summary of disbursements. In double-entry bookkeeping, debit and credit transactions are entered into a journal. Summary totals are entered monthly into ledger accounts, such as income, expense, asset, liability, net worth, and inventory. The sums of the debits must equal the sums of the credits, making the system self-balancing.

Recordkeeping suggestions. Try to keep your personal and your business records in separate bank accounts, both for receipts and for payments. When possible, make disbursements by check. Establish a petty cash fund for small expenditures. These procedures will not only help you follow how well you are adhering to your budget forecast (see

Chapter 8), but will provide documentation if the IRS should demand proof for what you show on your business and personal tax returns. Here are some more suggestions from the IRS:

• When you withdraw income from the business, make a business check payable to yourself.

• Do not write checks to *cash*, but if you do, attach a note or receipt to assist in recordkeeping.

• Support recordkeeping entries with cancelled checks, paid bills, duplicate deposit slips, and such. The IRS does not accept memorandums or sketchy records of approximate income, deductions, or other items affecting your tax liability.

• Classify your accounts by ledgers—for example, income, expenses, assets, liabilities, and equity (net worth). Classify assets as current or fixed and record the date of acquisition, the cost or other original basis, depreciation, depletion, and anything else affecting their bases. (Basis in tax law is the starting point used to calculate present value after allowing for depreciation, modification, etc.)

• Keep books and records available for inspection by the IRS.

• Do not discard or destroy records that will support your reporting of items (both income and expenses) on your tax return until the statute of limitations expires, usually (except for charges of fraud) three years after the date the tax was paid, or your return was due or filed, whichever is later.

• Hold onto records that verify your basis in property as long as you own that property, plus the statute of limitations period. You will use these records to verify your basis for that property at the time you dispose of (or lose or destroy) that property.

• Keep copies of past tax returns.

• If you want to save space by microfilming records, you must meet the specific requirements of IRS Revenue Procedure 81–46.

• If you computerize your records, you must be able to produce legible copies from the system to provide proof of your tax liability.

• Employee tax records (income-tax withholding, Social Security, federal unemployment) must be kept for at least four years after the due date of the return or date the tax is paid, whichever is later.

Small Business Income

The IRS will forgive you if you forget to claim an exemption or deduction, but you had better not forget to list all sources of income. Your challenge will be to differentiate your business income from your personal income.

Business income can be in the form of property, cash, services, or bartering. Business income basically is that which your business receives in return for providing a service or product. Following are some examples of what the IRS recognizes as business income:

- Cash receipts
- Rental income from property
- Prepaid rent with no use restrictions
- Third-party payment of your debt
- Interest on loans
- Dividends
- Capital gains
- Negotiable promissory notes at fair market value
- Debt cancellation to your benefit
- Damages you receive from judicial actions
- Kickbacks you receive
- Recovery of previously deducted items
- Recapture of depreciation for too-rapid value drop

There are more kinds of business income, of course. And each form of income will have its own tax definition, which in some cases may not be obvious to the nonaccountant.

Small Business Deductions

You may deduct certain expenses incurred as you prepare to launch your business, even if you do not go into business. You have the choice of deducting or capitalizing certain capital expenditures. And you can take deductions for the business use of your home, your computer, and your automobile, if you follow certain rules.

Going into Business Expenses

Expenses you may incur as you prepare to launch your business may include travel, market surveys, advertising, legal and other professional fees, and the cost to hire or train employees.

Even if you do not go into business, you are allowed to take specified deductions as capital expenditures losses. If you do go into business, all of the costs incurred getting the business started, including, for example, the legal and filing costs of incorporation, are capital expenditures. These costs then become a part of the basis for your business.

For instance, you can amortize the following costs, deducted as expenses, over a period of sixty months or more: business start-up, corporation or partnership organization, and the cost of acquiring a lease.

Capital Expenditures

A capital expenditure is one that involves obtaining ownership of permanent equipment rather than expendable supplies. Some capital expenditures can be deducted in the year of the expenditure as an expense, or deducted by amortization over a period of time. Those costs for which you can choose deduction or amortization, with varying dollar limits, include:

- Certain carrying charges on property
- Research and experimental costs
- Intangible developmental costs
- Costs of making public facilities more accessible to the elderly and the disabled

An Office in Your Home

There are tax deduction advantages when you use your home as an office or workplace, but the Internal Revenue Service has stringent rules you must follow. For starters:

1. *Gross business income.* The gross income you receive from your business must be at least equal to the tax deductions that you claim. The IRS looks askance on hobbies used to deduct taxes in excess of income.

2. *As an employee.* If you are still an employee and are using a portion of your home to do work for your employer, you must prove that the use of your home is no mere convenience; it must be essential to your job and required by your employer before you can take home-office tax deductions.

3. *Exclusive use.* The area you use for home office or work space must be devoted exclusively to your business activity if you are to be allowed tax deductions.

Even if you do not qualify to deduct expenses for the business use of your home, you may still deduct other expenses created by your business, such as phone calls, postage, and stationery and supplies. An excellent guide to running a business in your home is *Starting and Operating a Home-Based Business,* written by David R. Eyler (New York: John Wiley & Sons, 1990).

Homeowning and home offices. You do not need to be a homeowner to qualify for home-office deductions. The IRS considers any living facility to be a home, including houses, apartments, condominiums, cooperatives, mobile homes, and houseboats. The term *home* includes other structures on your property, such as an unattached garage, studio, barn, or greenhouse.

The IRS use-of-home tests. Unless you pass certain usage tests, the IRS will not allow you to deduct home-office expenses, even if you are self-employed. The burden is on you to prove that the area you are taking deductions for is used both exclusively and regularly for your business: (1) as the principal place of business for any trade or business in which you engage; (2) as a place to meet or deal with your patients, clients, or customers in the normal course of your trade or business; or (3) in connection with your trade or business, if you are using a separate structure that is not attached to your house or residence.

Exclusive means for business purposes alone, and not shared with any personal use. Your work area cannot double as a part-time guest room; it cannot be a desk in the corner of your den, excepting storage of inventory, or use as a day-care facility.

The *regular-use* requirement is in addition to the exclusive-use requirement. You cannot deduct for your attic, for example, if you work only occasionally when the mood strikes, even if you use it for nothing else.

The *principal-place-of-business* test considers the total time you spend in your home office, the facilities you have there with which you work, and the relative amount of your total income received from your work in the home office.

The *meeting-place* test applies to space used regularly and exclusively to meet patients, clients, and customers during the normal course of your business, even though you may also carry on business at another location. An example: an attorney works three days a week in a downtown office; two days a week are devoted to meeting with clients in the home. Home-office deductions are allowed if the other tests are met.

The *separate-structures* test allows tax deductions for the use of a free-standing structure adjacent to the residential home for home-office tax deductions, if it meets the other tests.

The *trade-or-business* test prohibits tax deductions for activities that are not trades or businesses. For example, you cannot take a home-office deduction for an area used exclusively and regularly to read financial periodicals and reports, to clip bond coupons, or for an online computer connection to one's discount broker.

Deduction Allocation. If you survive the exclusive and regular tests, and are engaged in a trade or business, the next step is to allocate the business percentage of your home expenses related to the home office.

To determine the business percentage portion of total home expenses allowable for your home office, you can calculate the space utilized as a percentage of the total space in your home, either on a square-foot basis or on a number-of-rooms basis. For example, 480 square feet in a 2,400 square-foot home is 20 percent; one room in a five-room house is 20 percent.

Using the above example, you will be able to deduct 20 percent of the total expenses related to overall home maintenance, upkeep, and operation, but only when such expenses are required also for the upkeep of your office space. Yard work expense, for instance, is not normally deductible as a home-office expense. As to expenses required exclusively for the home-office area, such as painting, new electrical outlets, and such, 100 percent will be deductible.

What You Can Deduct. Deductions can be for direct expenses and for indirect expenses. Direct expenses are those that apply only to the exclusively allocated home-office space.

Indirect expenses are those which are the office-space allocable proportion of the total house expenses, such as calculated in the previous section. Before such expenses can be deducted, it must be shown that they benefit both the personal and the business part of your home. They include:

- Real estate taxes
- Deductible mortgage interest, both first and second mortgages
- Casualty losses through, for example, fire, storm, flood, if the loss affects the house in general
- Rent, if you do not own your home
- Utilities and services, such as electricity, gas, trash removal, telephone (but not for the first of two or more lines into your home, a "personal" necessity), and cleaning services
- Insurance; homeowner policies can be deducted on a percentage basis; special business related policies are 100 percent deductible
- Repairs required to keep the house in good working order
- Security systems designed to protect the entire home can be deducted on a percentage basis; special business-related security systems are 100 percent deductible.
- Depreciation calculations are too complex to discuss here. Refer to IRS Publication 524 (see Appendix) and use Form 4562, *Depreciation and Amortization*. You will be well advised to consult with a tax accountant or lawyer, at least for the first such filing.

Deduction Limitations. As discussed earlier, your home-office deductions cannot exceed the income generated by your activities using the home office. The depreciation you claim and your business expenses not attributable to the use of your home, such as salaries and supplies, are not allowable home-office deductions.

Reporting Home-Office Deductions. Expenses for the home-office business use of your home are deducted on Schedule C ("Profit or Loss From Business"), which is attached to your Form 1040.

Your Home Computer. If you purchase a computer for exclusive use in your home-office business for less than $10,000, you are allowed to deduct the total expenditure as an expense, or you can amortize (depreciate) it over the allowable period of years.

If your computer is used for both business and personal purposes, more than 50 percent of the time it is used must be for business if you are to qualify for a business deduction. Using your computer for investment calculations does not count as time for business usage.

Automobile Deductions

The rules controlling allowable deductions for the business use of your personal automobile (or the personal use of your business automobile) are similar to those for your personal computer. The important message here, as for the computer, is to keep careful daily records of mileages and purposes for those mileages. See IRS Publication 917, *Business Use of a Car*, listed in the Appendix.

The first requirement is that the business use must exceed 50 percent of the total use. If not, you will be allowed deductions only for the costs of use, not the costs of investment. If you meet the 50 percent requirement, you can calculate your deduction on a mileage allowance basis, or as a business-allocated share of gasoline, oil, tires, repairs, insurance, depreciation, interest, taxes, garage rent, parking fees, tolls, and so forth.

If you select the mileage option to prorate personal versus business expenses, you may deduct $0.24 (in 1989) per mile for the first 15,000 miles driven for business purposes, and $0.11 for all additional business miles. If the vehicle is fully depreciated (over a five-year period), the mileage deduction is only $0.11. If you elect the business allocation approach, you can use relative mileages to prorate the above-listed expenses between personal and business usage.

Other Business Deductions

Following is a list of some of the tax deductions you can claim because of your business activities. Remember, if the activity or usage is partially personal and partially business, you must keep records to show the division, and prorate appropriate amounts for each.

☐ Advertising/promotion expenses
☐ Automobile expenses, unreimbursed

- ☐ Bad debts
- ☐ Business entertainment and meals (80 percent)
- ☐ Business equipment rentals
- ☐ Business gifts (each $25 or less)
- ☐ Business interest expenses
- ☐ Business interruption insurance
- ☐ Business-related accident and theft insurance
- ☐ Business travel (but not commutation)
- ☐ Capital asset depreciation
- ☐ Casualties
- ☐ Charitable contributions
- ☐ Computer time
- ☐ Condemnations
- ☐ Dues and subscriptions
- ☐ Education expenses (with limitations)
- ☐ Employee wages and salaries
- ☐ Fees and services (legal, professional, other)
- ☐ Franchise purchase
- ☐ Insurance (limitations for life insurance)
- ☐ Job interviewee reimbursements
- ☐ Licenses and regulatory fees
- ☐ Lobbying expenses
- ☐ Medical expenses (with limitations)
- ☐ Moving expenses for machinery
- ☐ Office and equipment maintenance and repair
- ☐ Office rent
- ☐ Office supplies
- ☐ Office telephone (but not your personal phone)
- ☐ Office utilities
- ☐ Penalty payments (not fines)
- ☐ Political contributions
- ☐ Property taxes
- ☐ Repayment outgo
- ☐ Supplies and materials
- ☐ Thefts
- ☐ Trademark/tradename purchase

Your Personal Taxes

If this is your first effort at self-employment, you are in for an unpleasant tax shock. Not only will you have to pay your own income and Social Security (FICA) taxes, but you will have to pay your employer (yourself) share of the Social Security tax.

The Self-Employment Tax

The FICA tax and the amount that is subject to the FICA tax is changed from time to time. The current figures can be found on your tax Form 1040 Schedule SE ("Social Security Self-Employment Tax"). You are expected to pay this self-employment tax if you are a non-employee in a trade or business, and you have net self-employment earnings of $400 or more.

Estimated Tax Payments

The second tax shock you will receive is that since you no longer have an employer to withhold taxes and make regular payments to the IRS, you will have to assume the employer's role. You are expected to make quarterly estimated tax payments, and if you do not want the IRS coming after you with penalties and fines, what you pay in during the year had better be at least 90 percent of the tax payment calculated on and submitted with your Form 1040.

CHAPTER 22

Negotiating Contract Terms

There are three basic and compelling reasons why the terms of an agreement as stated in the contract must be explicit and definite:

1. The contract is intended to be a mutually understood and accepted agreement.
2. The written contract is a memorialization and reminder of the terms of the agreement.
3. The contract is a weapon of legal protection and clarification in the event of disagreement or failure to perform.

If there is a disagreement between you and your customer, and all efforts to work out the differences fail, you have the choice of mediation, binding arbitration, or a formal judicial proceeding in a court of law. None of these alternatives can succeed, however, if the terms of the agreement are not clear, explicit, and definite. Before a finding or judgment can be rendered, there must be a factual basis from which a failure to perform can be determined, and from which dollar values of damages can be calculated by the court.

The Negotiating Stance

An essential element of negotiation is *good faith*. Good faith implies the readiness to remain flexible and the willingness to make concessions during the process of negotiation. The key word is *flexible*. Always leave yourself room to maneuver.

Never enter a negotiating session with your final, one-and-only, take-it-or-leave-it offer. Have alternatives ready to present. Start out with options that you can sacrifice (throw-aways, if you wish) to give an aura of cooperation. Protect yourself, but let the other party feel that he or she has some control over the reshaping of your offer.

A truly successful negotiating session is where both parties leave with each feeling that they have been winners.

The Fee Discussion

The problem of how and when to discuss fees is for many independent contractors the most difficult, if not hazardous, question faced during a contract negotiation. Particularly for the newcomer, there is the innate fear that whatever cost is quoted for a job, it will be rejected as too high. The frequent result is to ask for too little. Not only does this mean a loss in profits, perhaps even a loss on the job, but it also diminishes the other party's respect for you.

Of course, it is the other party's responsibility to negotiate the very best deal possible, but not to cheat you or take unfair advantage. Following are some suggestions that will help you during your fee discussions.

1. *Calculate your costs carefully in advance.* Consider everything that will go into the cost of the project, direct and indirect costs, and taxes. Do not forget profit. That is why you are in business. If the job has several steps or aspects, or if there are options that can be picked up or dropped, have cost-figure breakdowns for these also.

2. *Communicate overall and specific details.* If you want to justify your fees in the eyes of the other party, be sure that the other party knows what is involved, including time, labor, equipment, and supplies. Never assume that the other party knows as much about your business as you do.

3. *Take the other party on a job guided tour.* Explain everything carefully. Go through the project step by step. Explain your procedures and the rationale of what you will be doing if you get the job. If you have charts, tables, drawings, flow sheets or models relevant to the work, use them to make points.

4. *Show confidence in yourself.* Show the customer that you have the background, experience, facilities, and backup required to do the work. The customer will want to feel that a good deal has been negotiated. Part of this feeling comes from the assurance that hiring you will be money well spent.

5. *Never admit that a prospective job is easy.* You, as a specialist, may see a job as straightforward and easy, but keep this information to yourself during negotiations. It is perfectly correct to say that you can handle the work, but never give the customer a feeling that you will not have to extend yourself.

Terms for the Contract

Terms that go into your contract will be related to the specific project under consideration, your position relative to your customer, and other considerations. It is essential that the contract terms are clearly and completely stated so that both you and your customer fully understand the working arrangement and contract obligations, and so that there will be a mutual feeling of confidence and trust.

You must understand not only the details of the work to be done, but also the needs and desires of your customer. In turn, your customer must know what to expect from you. Vague terms create doubt; doubt fuels disagreement and distrust.

Following is a checklist of terms that are essential to all well-drafted contracts, regardless of how simple or how complicated.

- ☐ *Statement of parties involved.* All parties with any obligation under the terms of the contract must be fully and clearly designated. Full identification with names, addresses, titles, and affiliations is desirable.
- ☐ *Statement of project.* Make sure that the project is clearly and fully defined. If the project is easily described, the definition can be included directly into the contract document. If it is a complex project, the contract can make reference to another document that describes the work to be accomplished under the contract.
- ☐ *Statement of service scope.* Include a full description of what services you are or are not to provide, what services the customer is or is not to provide, and what services are optional, open to future negotiation.
- ☐ *Statement of work schedule.* When is the work to start? When is it to be completed? If it is a complex project, will there be progress benchmarks? If so, what are they and when are they due?
- ☐ *Statement of who provides what.* Be sure that there is no question remaining about who will order and/or provide (lease, purchase, loan) specific supplies, materials, equipment, and personnel. On what schedule? Who will provide for work-in-progress storage space for equipment, materials, and supplies? Who will transport materials, supplies, and equipment? Who will obtain necessary

permits from local authorities? Who will provide insurance (and of what kind and with what provisions), legal services, and accounting services?

☐ *Statement of who will do what.* Who will be the overall project manager? If the work is to be shared, which party is to do what, and on what schedule related to the work of the other party? How are the specific chores within the overall project to be coordinated between the parties? Who will clean up after the work is completed?

☐ *Statement of how work is to be done.* If there are special requirements because of location, proximity of other structures or equipment, safety, insurance requirements, or equipment and personnel available, be sure that they are specified clearly and in detail.

☐ *Statement of safety provisions.* Who will be responsible for safety inspections and supervision? Who has the authority to enforce safety provisions? Who will provide liaison between the work site and federal, state, or local safety agencies and authorities?

☐ *Definition of reporting hierarchy.* A successful project requires a clear and unambiguous channel for you when reporting to or making requests of the customer. To whom at the customer company will you report?

☐ *Statement of risk of possession.* Which party, you or the customer, bears risk of possession during the work? That is, who must pay in the event of loss by fire or some other calamity, either manmade or natural? Which party is responsible for obtaining loss and liability insurance protection? To what extent is the work to be protected? If the risk is with you and you are providing the insurance protection, be sure that you factor this expense into your costs. Also be sure that there is a statement of when risk of possession will pass to the customer.

☐ *Statement of payment basis.* When and how will you be paid? Monthly invoice? Upon completion of work (and how is completion defined)? With partial or progress payments based on defined and identifiable benchmarks?

☐ *Statement of reimbursement basis.* A large project can tie up a large amount of cash for the purchase of materials and supplies, or for the lease of high-rental construction equipment. Such cash outlays can become severe burdens on your cash-flow status, even though you will be reimbursed eventually. If such a situation will apply to the work under negotiation, be sure that there is a clear and unambiguous provision for when and upon what basis the customer reimburses you for such expenditures.

☐ *Definition of substantial completion.* Many contracts have a clause providing for a shift in responsibility (or risk), as well as specified payments, upon substantial completion of the work. Be sure that there is no question as to what constitutes "substantial completion."

☐ *Provisions for subcontractors.* If the work will require that you hire subcontractors, who holds the authority to approve or disapprove specific subcontractors, or who specifies the provisions you incorporate into your contracts with such subcontractors? Ideally, you should have full control within the limits of your contract with the customer and within legal and regulatory restrictions by government agencies at all levels.

☐ *Statement of creditor status.* Are you named as a primary creditor in the event of insolvency, bankruptcy, or other default of payment by your customer? Or must you wait in line with the also-ran creditors? While this may not be important for small-expense contracts, especially those where the major part of your fee is your own time, it will help protect you from your own creditors for projects that require large cash outlays or commitments, contingent upon reimbursement by the customer.

☐ *Authority to assign rights or duties.* Can you assign your rights to receive payment to another person? Can you assign your duties of work performance to another person? If so, under what conditions? Can your customer assign rights or duties to another party? Under what conditions?

☐ *Duty of indemnification.* Who must indemnify whom for any legal claim arising as a result of failures or negligence in your work? As a result of actions by the customer? It is reasonable for you to indemnify for your own failures or negligence, but not for the customer's. Be sure that you are properly insured or bonded to cover that for which you may be responsible.

☐ *Effects of corporate changes.* What happens to your rights of payment and reimbursement, as well as the right to continue the work defined in the contract, if there is a change in personnel, company objectives, divisional organization, ownership, or other managerial or operational status by the customer? Are you protected? Are terms of protection specific and can values be calculated from these terms?

☐ *Responsibility for delays.* Are you protected from the cost or responsibility for delays caused by the customer? By acts of nature? By legal actions of others? By regulatory or other governmental actions? By intervening impossibility of performance? From the added costs of changes or alterations demanded by the customer? If not, you may find the job spreading out over time, you may find reimbursements delayed, and you may find additional work for which you are not paid.

☐ *Settlement of disputes.* What happens if there is a dispute between you and the customer, one that cannot be reconciled by normal discussions or negotiation? Does your contract have a provision for binding arbitration? For mediation? See Chapter 17 for the handling of "sick" contracts.

☐ *Statement of materials warranties.* Often, customers will specify materials by composition, brand name, or manufacturer, and will insist on a clause where you will warrant that only such materials will be used for the work. Such a clause will prevent you from using generically identical substitutes. If such a clause is in your contract, first be absolutely sure that such materials are available at predictable costs, and that you will be able to obtain them so as to meet the schedules specified in your contract.

☐ *Provisions to terminate the contract.* What if either you or the customer wants to terminate the contract before the work is complete? What are the bases for termination? Mutual consent in writing? With specified notice? If there is termination, what are the payment provisions for work completed, what are the reimbursement provisions for materials and supplies purchased?

☐ *Severability (separability) of clauses.* Does your contract contain a clause stating that if any clause of the contract is declared void, illegal, or otherwise invalid, it can be severed (separated) from the contract without negative effect on the remaining clauses?

☐ *Merger of all agreements.* Does your contract have a clause that merges all prior and all contemporaneous agreements relevant to the project into one new agreement? Such a clause prevents the problems created by the Parol Evidence Rule discussed in Chapter 16.

☐ *Statement of situs of law.* If the unthinkable does come about, and you find it necessary to sue your customer, or if the customer files suit against you, the law of which state will apply? If both you and the customer are local, the law of your local state will apply. But if your customer is multistate or multinational, the law of another jurisdiction may be forced upon you.

☐ *Authority to sign.* Does the representative of the customer have the actual authority to make the commitment embodied in the contract? Authority will be relatively evident in smaller firms, but may not be clear within the hierarchical structure of large firms. If you have doubts, either conduct your own investigation or ask your attorney to do it.

No question, the preceding list is more than a little daunting. Worse yet, there may be other terms to consider under specific situations. But there is a relatively simple solution to this problem: the standard contract.

Your Standard Contract

If you were to discuss each of the above items in detail each time you negotiated a contract, it would not only cost you excessive and unnecessary time, but would most likely discourage your customer. The solution is simple. Based on the type of service you will provide and the type of work involved, have your attorney prepare a standard contract for your use.

Standard clauses in your contract can cover such items as safety provisions, risk of possession, basis for payments and reimbursements, definition of substantial completion, authority for subcontractors, assignment of rights and duties, indemnification, corporate changes, creditor status, delays by customer and impossibility, settling of disputes, provisions for safety, termination provisions, severability, merger, and situs of the law. Spaces will be left to identify the customer.

You then need only to negotiate and present a statement of the project, service scope, work schedule, who provides what and who does what, how the work is to be done, reporting hierarchy, coordination with customer, and materials warranty.

If there are several versions of your service, you may wish to have your attorney prepare a standard contract for each. If some of your projects are small, you may wish to have a simplified, less daunting version. You will have to draft this basic contract only once, unless experience or a change in your services makes it desirable to modify the form.

After the negotiated items are added to the basic standard contract, you can present the final version to the customer who, most likely, will present it to his or her own attorney. The customer will then return with areas of agreement, areas of disagreement, and areas requiring further negotiation.

You will do yourself a favor if you have your standard contract or contracts typeset (not typewritten) and printed on good quality paper. Professional appearances lend credibility; credibility encourages acceptance.

A Customer Standard Contract

Larger firms that contract frequently for outside services will have their own standard contracts with their own desired standard clauses. Even a simple appearing contract can be filled with booby traps and potential liabilities. Be sure that your attorney examines such contracts carefully. Your attorney, not your customer, is the one with your best interests in mind.

If some clauses are unacceptable to you, either request that they be removed or negotiate revisions. If the customer is adamant, refusing to remove or modify a clause that bothers you, you will have to decide, preferably after careful deliberation with your attorney, whether or not to accept the risks. If you find a clause excessively bothersome, you may be well advised to decline the work rather than open yourself to what you may consider unwarranted liability or undesirable working conditions.

Purpose of the Contract

At the risk of repeating an earlier discussion, a main purpose of the written contract is to assure that both parties agree that the written word expresses clearly and accurately the outcome of their verbal give-and-take negotiations. It is often true that when one sees the written version of a verbal discussion, one realizes it does not express the true intentions of both parties. Now, before signing, is the time to make corrections or modifications.

The presigning analysis of a written contract will be helped if the contract is not overly long, and if it is not obfuscated in obscure, often redundant Latinate phrases. A number of states, such as New Jersey, now have plain-English rules for contracts.

Again, the main purpose of a contract is to memorialize areas of agreement. As a last and unpleasant resort, a contract becomes a legal weapon to resolve disagreements. If you know or feel in advance that a customer will not honor the terms of the contract, why bother? A contract is an effective working document only where there is continuing understanding and goodwill between the contracting parties.

CHAPTER 23

Steering The Financial Ship

Cash-Flow Crises

It may come as a surprise, but a business can prosper into bankruptcy. That is what Helen G. and Joel F. did with their independent contractor business. The service they devised was office layout planning. They would plan the office, including furniture, carpeting, lighting, and decorative art, then would provide the furnishings at a price somewhere between the wholesale price they paid and the retail price the customer would have paid. Joel concentrated on the style and ergonomics of the furniture, while Helen had final say in color and decor, including the carpeting, walls, and office-wall art.

They had a dozen customers under contract on the day that they opened for business. Their work was held in high esteem by their customers, and soon, through word of mouth, they had another two-dozen office design contracts. By the end of their first year, they were on top of the world. Midway through the second year, they were out of business, bankrupt.

What happened? They outsmarted themselves. To get the best prices on the office furnishings, they agreed to make payment within 10 days of receipt. Their customers were paying them on a 30-day or 60-day schedule. The more business they developed, the more debt they incurred, until suddenly the whole structure of their business collapsed. They were a marketing success and a cash-flow failure.

Could they have avoided this disaster? Yes, in any of three ways. First, they could have renegotiated their payment agreements with their suppliers. Second, they could have factored (sold) their accounts receivable. Third, if they had taken the time and trouble for cash-flow budgeting, they would have foreseen their cash shortages early enough to obtain and activate a credit line for a loan or revolving series of loans from their bank, pledging their accounts receivable as security.

Cash-flow Budgeting

There is no excuse for not anticipating periods of negative cash flow. Simple spreadsheet analysis of anticipated revenue and corresponding expenses will warn you of impending danger.

There are two types of business cash: working cash and capital cash. *Working cash* is what you draw from to purchase supplies and materials, to pay wages and commissions, and to cover various day-to-day expenses. *Capital cash* is the money you use for additions to or replacements of fixed assets, such as equipment, tools, and other tax-depreciable items.

It is important to recognize the differences between working cash and capital cash. Your financial tool for this purpose is your budget (current and forecast). It is your budget forecast, however, that will help you anticipate temporary or cyclic shortages of cash in time to take remedial action.

Your starting point in preparing your cash-flow analysis is to estimate *sales revenue*. While it will not be exact, use your best judgment. To be safe, err on the low side. If your business is cyclical or seasonal, try to anticipate how your revenue will vary month by month. Step two is to estimate *working cash* and *capital cash* needs on a month-by-month basis, a combination of direct and indirect costs, as discussed in Chapter 20 on budgeting.

Place these figures on a 12-month spreadsheet in monthly sequence and you will immediately see which months show a net profit and which show a net deficit. Where the net profit carryover from one month compensates for the net deficit of the following month, there is no problem. Or you may be able to prevent a cash-flow shortage by deferring a capital cash outlay. Where the deficit is not covered, you can now anticipate and prepare to handle a cash-flow shortage.

Profit for Survival

The single biggest cause of business failure is the inability to price one's service so as to produce a profit. Sometimes an entrepreneur will believe that a bid will create a profit, when it does not even cover basic expenses.

There are three major dollar elements that must be covered in every project bid or cost estimate: direct costs, indirect costs (or overhead), and profit.

Profit = Revenue – (Direct Costs + Overhead Costs)

As discussed earlier, direct costs are those that are related directly and solely to the project at hand. Indirect costs are those that are related to keeping your doors open for business, even if you have no revenue. We all know what profit is, or at least we think we do.

If you know your business, you should have no trouble calculating direct costs for a specific project. Overhead, however, is more difficult to determine. If, for example, it costs you $3,000 a month just to keep your doors open, that totals $36,000 a year. If direct costs for a typical job will be $1,000 and you anticipate 36 jobs per year, then what must you charge per job for breakeven?

Profit (zero for breakeven) = $36y - (36 \times 1,000 + 36,000)$
Where y = dollar charge for a job
$y = (36,000 + 36,000)/36 = \$2,000$ per job

Assume that your profit objective is $36,000 a year. Then the number of $2,000 jobs you would need is:

$36,000 = 2,000x - (1,000x \times 36,000)$
Where x = number of jobs per year
$x = (36,000 + 36,000)/1000 = 72$ jobs per year

What if you feel that you can only win 54 jobs yearly, but still want the $36,000 profit? What must you charge for your work?

$36,000 = 54y - (54 \times 1000 + 36,000)$
Where y = charge per job
$y = (36,000 + 36,000 + 54,000)/54 = \$2,333.33/$job

Now you know how to bid. Each job you win as a contract must carry with it an average of $1,333.33 combined indirect cost and profit if your 54 jobs per year are to produce $36,000 of annual profit. But not all jobs will be for $2,333.33. Some will be for $500, some for $5,000. Do you want to burden a $500 job with an extra $1,333.33 for overhead and profit? Of course not.

Enter the *overhead ratio* and the *profit ratio*. Of the $2,333.33 per job, $1,000 is for direct costs. The remaining $1,333.33 is half overhead, namely $666.67. The other half is profit. Allowing for a combined overhead/profit ratio factor, multiply the estimated direct costs by a factor of 2.4 ($1,333.33 + $1,000 = $2,333.33) for your bid price.

What if the bidding is very competitive? You will lose the bid if you do not shave your bid. How far down can you go? At the very least, you should cover overhead. The lowest you can go and still meet breakeven is 1.7 times estimated direct cost.

But, you say, while 54 jobs a year is what I expect after I've been in business two or so years, I'll be lucky to sign up a half dozen jobs the first year and maybe thirty or so the second year. How does this affect the overhead and profit ratios? Not at all for overhead charges. You will not raise overhead so that six jobs will defray a $36,000 annual overhead. You would never get any business. As to your profit objectives, hold steady there too. It is bad practice to lower your prices too much. Your customers will learn to expect the bargain rates. Where does this leave you?

Year 1 Profit = $6 \times 2,333.33 - (6 \times 1,000 + 36,000) = -\$28,000$
Year 2 Profit = $30 \times 2,333.33 - (30 \times 1,000 + 36,000) = +\$4,000$

This, then, becomes the basis for your projection of what financial backing you will require to keep you in business until you achieve a breakeven operation. (See Chapter 6 for money sources, Chapter 8 for your Business Plan, and Chapter 20 for budgeting.)

CHAPTER 24

Secrets of
Business Success

It is said that 70 percent of all new businesses fail within one year of being started. The odds for survival improve greatly for those still in business the second year and are very good for those who continue into and through the third year.

Why Businesses Fail

Should you be discouraged? No. There are reasons for these dreary figures. There is no excuse for the hopefuls who plunge into self-employment without knowing what needs to be done, or even more, without knowing the difference between offering a skill and running a business.

What are the survival risks that all too often cause the death of a dream?

1. *Start-up undercapitalization.* It will take time for your business to become profitable. During the start-up period, you will need financial resources (your own or from others) to keep you going (see Chapters 6, 20, and 23).

2. *Too few customers.* Sounds obvious, yet people will gamble their self-employment future by starting without a Marketing Plan (see Chapter 7). They are too full of themselves and their skill or experience to

analyze the demand for their service and the impact of competition.

3. *Failure to control expenses.* Another obvious one. Failure through spending too much too soon on frills or nonessentials; failure to keep financial records; and failure to create an operating and forecast budget and adhering to it (see Chapter 20).

4. *Defective bid calculations.* If one is to make bids that will develop into profitable contracts, one must understand the true cost of doing business (see Chapters 8, 20, and 23).

5. *Lack of determination.* Starting a business is neither simple nor easy. If you recognize within yourself the tendency to be easily discouraged, think carefully before you start.

There are other reasons for business failure. They include overpricing the service, failure to listen to customers' needs, inability to get along with people, a word-of-mouth reputation for poor quality work, and poor planning and scheduling.

The Secrets of Success

There is no magic to business success, only good planning, hard work, and bulldog determination. Topping all reasons for success in self-employment as an independent contractor are a stubborn refusal to admit defeat and the flexibility to meet and overcome obstacles. Your chances for success will be excellent if you are a person who turns mistakes into lessons, who has the sensitivity to learn and respond to the problems and needs of others, and who creates a positive image of confidence, quality, and capability.

In addition to your personal qualities, here are a few of the basic laws of business success:

- Recognize that Murphy is your navigator.
- Control costs. Control costs. Control costs.
- Keep track of your financial and cash-flow statuses.
- Avoid long-term financial obligations.
- Prepare standby alternatives and options.
- Be flexible, willing to negotiate and cooperate.
- Never refuse a legitimate and profitable project.
- Always have time to market and sell.
- Do not let the clock control your workday.
- Never overestimate your essentiality to your customers.
- Set reasonable, competitive fees and stick to them.
- Be totally ethical; respect all confidences.
- Always give full service and a little more.

- Never poormouth the competition.
- Never overpromise nor underperform.
- Avoid overextending yourself.

Ethics in Business

Don't fluff off this section with the offhand statement, "Of course, I'm ethical." In business, there are ethical subtleties that do not often arise in personal relationships. Being ethical is more than merely being honest.

Top on the list of business ethics is the question of confidentiality. Confidences are to be kept, not broadcast. Merely because a customer fails to tell you that the details of your contract are confidential does not give you carte blanche to share these details with other customers, particularly those who may be competitive with the earlier customer.

What, then, is a confidence? It is anything you learn from a person or customer that, if told to others, could be harmful to that person or customer. Even apparently harmless gossip can be harmful. Share information only on a need-to-know basis.

Equally important in the business ethics arena is financial integrity. Padded bills and under-the-table rebates may be common among your competitors, but they can backfire. As one old-time politician said, "If you take money under the table, you're a bum. And every bum in town knows you're a bum." The same applies to business.

Security in Supplies

Do you need special supplies, materials, or equipment for the performance of your service? How many sources have you identified from which you can get what you need when you need it, and for a price you can afford? Only one? What if they go out of business, have a major fire, or are closed down by labor trouble? Better start looking for alternative sources.

Here are some points to check as you identify potential suppliers:

☐ Reputation for prompt deliveries
☐ Ability to meet your quality specifications
☐ Policy of replacement for defective items
☐ Fair pricing
☐ Supplier credit extended
☐ Large inventory; ready for immediate delivery

Good Daily Management

By now you must realize that to operate a financially successful business, even a one-person independent contractor service business, you must either have or develop a number of business-oriented skills. You will be a scheduler and expediter; a cost estimator and analyzer; a manager of finances and time; a communicator and motivator; and a marketer and salesperson.

Equally important will be the attention to daily details that will be required by your business. Business and customer records are essential, as is the finding of and selling to new customers. You must avoid legal complications, and you must be able to negotiate with profit-generating bids. You must see that supplies and materials arrive on time to meet promised completion schedules. Most important of all, you must keep a wary eye out for Murphy, your unpredictable navigator.

Learn, Learn, Learn

A successful businessperson never stops learning. Each negotiation, each contract, each daily event carries with it a lesson. There are other sources of learning, too.

SCORE (Service Corps of Retired Executives) provides no-charge advice to small businesses, both proposed and operating. SCORE, formed in 1964 with encouragement from the United States Small Business Administration (SBA), is an independent voluntary nonprofit association chartered under the laws of the District of Columbia. The organization has more than 13,000 volunteers operating out of more than 750 locations throughout the 50 states, the District of Columbia, Puerto Rico, the Virgin Islands, and the United States Trust Territories.

Through SCORE, you can benefit by counseling from retired, successful business executives. SCORE also offers broadly focused specialized classes, seminars, and conferences on such subjects as organization, site selection, trade promotion, marketing, taxation, financing, and more. SCORE provides books, publications, and other forms of information on utilizing the services and facilities of lawyers, accountants, bankers, advertising agencies, and federal agencies.

To contact SCORE, check your local telephone directory under United States Government, Small Business Administration. Or call the national SCORE office by dialing 1–800–368–5855. You can write to SCORE at 655 15th Street, N.W., Suite 901, Washington, DC 20005–5742. The local phone number is 1–202–653–6279.

The Small Business Administration is another source of learning assistance for small businesspersons. *Small,* by the way, means your annual receipts do not exceed $3.5 million. The SBA Management Assistance Program comprises a network of community-based, small-business-oriented resources that provide a full range of business management services covering training, counseling, and information. SBA Resource Program counseling covers marketing, buying, producing, selling, recordkeeping, financial management, financing, and administration. Specialists are also available in SBA field offices.

As mentioned, one of the SBA resources is SCORE. The counterpart of SCORE, also an SBA resource, is ACE (Active Corps of Executives), organized in 1969 to supplement SCORE. The SBA's SBI (Small Business Institute) program, started in 1972, is a three-way cooperative effort between more than 500 collegiate schools of business administration, the SBA, and members of the nation's small business community. Supervised seniors and graduate students in business administration work directly with owners of small firms to provide on-site volunteer management counseling.

SBA pre-business training, created for all prospective business owners as well as uninformed new owners, provides basic information on how to start a business the *right way.* Topics include needed personality traits, management skills, success and failure factors, market analysis, legal aspects, recordkeeping, financial factors, sources of capital, regulations, taxes, and insurance. The pre-business follow-up program provides more advanced information on marketing plans, financial plans, and the operational/administrative control plan. There are sessions on management basics, as well as workshops on special topics.

The SBA publishes a number of free management assistance publications (contact SBA, PO Box 15434, Fort Worth, TX 76119) plus a large selection of for-sale publications (contact Superintendent of Documents, U.S. Government Printing Office, Washington, DC 20402). Management assistance topics include financial management and analysis, planning, general management and administration, marketing, organization and personnel, legal and government affairs, and additional miscellaneous subjects. In addition, there are small business bibliographies and a starting-out series for various types of businesses.

SBA for-sale publications include several series (small business management, starting and managing, and 23 business basics booklets), plus nonseries publications for such topics as exporting, managing profits, and buying and selling a small business.

To contact the SBA, look for the nearest local office in your telephone directory, listed under United States Government, or call the Washington, DC, office at 1–202–653–7794.

CHAPTER 25

Decision Time

You have been through the entire procedure now, from self-analysis to Marketing Plan to Business Plan and more. Now is the moment of decision.

- ☐ Is self-employment right for me?
- ☐ Do I have marketable skills and experience?
- ☐ Should I do it alone, or with others?
- ☐ Am I willing to put in long, hard hours?
- ☐ Do I have the backing and encouragement of my family?
- ☐ Am I pleased with my Marketing and Business Plans?
- ☐ Can I swing it financially?

Now Is the Time

It would be criminal to squander your hard-earned experience. Why cling to a dead-end job? Why spend your days struggling with unsatisfying, unrewarding work, when you can invest your efforts to build a business of your own?

Once again, are you ready? If so, what are you waiting for? Welcome to the ranks of the self-employed.

APPENDIX

Helpful Reading

Following is a list of publications that you will find valuable both as you prepare to establish your own independent contracting activity and, later, as you look for ways to improve an ongoing operation.

The listing is presented in three sections:

1. Commercial and association publications
2. Federal government publications
3. Internal Revenue Service publications

Commercial and Association Publications

Building Your Business Plan, by Harold J. McLaughlin; 6×9 in., hardbound, 297 pp., 1985; a Roland Press Publication, John Wiley & Sons, Inc., 605 Third Avenue, New York, NY 10158–0012. Step-by-step approach to creating a solid business plan. Covers organizational design, market analysis and planning, revenue distribution, income-outgo allocation, sources for competitive data, success-failure examples, and financial reports.

The Consultant's Guide to Proposal Writing, 2d ed., by Herman Holtz; 6×9 in., hardbound, 294 pp., 1990; John Wiley & Sons, Inc., 605 Third Avenue, New York, NY 10158–0012. Information aimed at all independent contractors who must rely on the preparation and presentation of proposals to obtain service contracts. Covers writing, strategies, persuasion, gathering market intelligence, graphics, the executive summary, and more.

The Consultant's Problem-Solving Workbook, by Ron Tepper; 8.5×11 in., hardbound, 323 pp., 1987; John Wiley & Sons, Inc., 605 Third Avenue, New York, NY 10158–0012. Practical day-to-day guide for handling problems that face not only the consultant, but all other levels of independent contractor activities. Covers agreements and client contracts, fee setting and billing, brochures, proposals, free publicity, promotional tools, advertising, direct mail, newsletters, audiovisuals, letters and telephone calls, credit, collections, accounting, and more. Contains numerous samples and examples.

Contract Documents; 8.5×11 in., softbound, 195 pp., 1987; American Specialty Contractors, Inc., 7315 Wisconsin Avenue, Bethesda, MD 20814–3299; phone 301–657–3110. Excellent presentation of contractual problems faced by subcontractors in the construction industry. Includes suggested contract clauses for bidding, collections, payments, agreement improvement, legal precedents, national joint guidelines, subcontract forms, federal contracts, and arbitration and mediation rules for the construction industry.

Financial Management for Small Business, by Edward N. Rausch; 6×9 in., softbound, 184 pp., 1979; AMACOM (Div. of American Management Associations), 135 West 50th Street, New York, NY 10020); phone 212–586–8100. Basic book written in easy-to-follow style. Covers profit planning for start-up or growth, sources of money, comparing fiscal results with profit plans, building a personal estate from your business, surviving bankruptcy, making your business more profitable.

Getting New Clients, by Richard A. Connor, Jr., and Jeffrey P. Davidson; 6×9 in., hardbound, 305 pp., 1987; John Wiley & Sons, Inc., 605 Third Avenue, New York, NY 10158–0012. Particularly helpful advice for finding business clients. While emphasis is on consultants, the techniques apply equally well to all levels of independent contractor activities. Includes how to find and target niche markets, promote one's services, meet with clients, handle group discussions, write winning proposals.

Good-Bye Job, Hello Me, by Myer Waxler and Robert L. Wolf; 6×9 in., hardbound, 287 pp., 1987; Scott Foresman & Co., 1900 East Lake Avenue, Glenview, IL 60025. Two psychologists focus on the emotional and psychological aspects of leaving or losing a job, of getting acquainted with one's self, of charting a course of action and getting started, and of selling one's self.

How to Start and Manage Your Own Business, by Gardinaer G. Greene; 5.5×6 in., hardbound, 243 pp., 1975; McGraw-Hill Book Co., 1221 Avenue of the Americas, New York, NY 10022. Basic book for small businesses. Includes how to pick the service to offer, sources of capital, how to deal with bankers, lawyers, and accountants, the purchasing of materials and services, insurance programs, developing managerial skills, choosing advertising agencies, when to start the business, when to avoid government contracts, and making money with franchises.

How to Succeed as an Independent Consultant, 2d ed., by Herman Holtz; 6×9 in., hardbound, 406 pp., 1988; John Wiley & Sons, Inc., 605 Third Avenue, New York, NY 10158–0012. Written for consultants, but with much information that applies to any type of entrepreneurial service business. Covers reasons for failure and how to avoid them. Includes advice regarding marketing and sales, promotion, meetings with clients, proposals, negotiations, presentations, fees and collections, and business ethics.

Marketing Your Consulting and Professional Services, by Robert A. Connor, Jr., and Jeffrey P. Davidson; 6×9 in., hardbound, 219 pp., 1985; John Wiley & Sons, Inc., 605 Third Avenue, New York, NY 10158–0012. Another consultant's book with valuable information relevant to all levels of independent contracting. Covers the use of "leverage" for marketing results, or how to place your greatest concentration on the smallest practical number of business prospects to produce the greatest amount of profitable revenue. Includes client-oriented marketing, personal promotion, nonpersonal promotion, strategic focus, and the Marketing Plan.

Quit Your Job!, by Jay Levinson; 5×8 in., softbound, 216 pp., 1987; Dodd, Mead & Co., New York, NY. Inspirational guide for those who are about to make the decision to leave a job. How to make the break and how to make it work. Discusses life without a job, the best ways to quit, what to do after you quit, how to be your own boss, enjoying your life. Includes information that helps you get started.

The Salesperson's Legal Guide, by Stephen Mitchell Sack and Howard Jay Seinberg; 6×9 in., hardbound, 133 pp., 1981; Prentice-Hall, Englewood Cliffs, NJ 07632, or c/o *The Sales Rep's Advisor*, 1133 Broadway, Ste. 1407, New York, NY 10010; phone 212–206–7979. Thoughtful guide for salespersons, both independent and employee, covering the legal and contractual aspects of being a salesperson. Covers employment terms, commission sales, competing with your company, changing the contractual relationship, remedies for breach of contract, legal options for the salesperson, protection from exploitation, tax tips.

Successful Consulting for Engineers and Data Processing Professionals, by Steven P. Tomczak; 8.5×11 in., hardbound, 337 pp., 1982; John Wiley & Sons, Inc., 605 Third Avenue, New York, NY 10158–0012 (1985). Although aimed at the high-tech professional consultant, here is another book with a wealth of information of value to all levels of independent contracting. Includes promotion, presentations, fee structuring, negotiation, contract basics, tax savings, financial planning, organizational forms, and sample contracts.

Total Business Planning, by E. James Burton and W. Blan McBride; 8.5×11 in., hardbound, 205 pp., 1988; John Wiley & Sons, Inc., 605 Third Avenue, New York, NY 10158–0012. Basic book covering construction of Business Plans, with scenarios for small start-up businesses, small ongoing single-product businesses, and a variety of larger businesses. Presents the six levels of the planning process: philosophy and mission, strategic plan, corporate objectives, planning unit goals, tactics and projections, and coordination. Includes a number of forms ready for use by photocopying.

Federal Government Publications

Most of the following federal government publications relating to small businesses are available from the Small Business Administration (SBA). All federal government publications are available from the Superintendent of Documents, U.S. Government Printing Office, Washington, DC 20402-9325. For information on current prices, write to the above address, or telephone 202-783-3238. Orders can be placed by mail, but you may eliminate as much as six weeks waiting time with a telephoned credit-card order (VISA or MasterCard).

A Handbook of Small Business Finance, by Jack Zwick; 6×9 in., softbound, 55 pp., 1987; SBA Small Business Management Series No. 15; order number S/N 045-000-00242-0. Excellent starting point for owners and managers of small businesses who wish to sharpen their financial management skills. Covers the major areas of financial management, describing a few of the many techniques that can help the small-business person to understand the results of past decisions and apply this understanding when making decisions for the future. Includes definition of financial management, financial statements, ratio analysis of financial statements, different types of financing, and secured and unsecured borrowing for working capital.

Buying and Selling a Small Business, 2d ed., by Vern A. Bunn; 6×9 in., softbound, 122 pp., 1979; SBA Office of Business Development; order number S/N 045-000-00164-4. What you need to know before you purchase (or sell) an existing small business of any type. Tells where to find information about the business, how to correlate and interpret the data, using financial statements, and how to apply the data to a negotiated buy-sell transaction.

Financial Management: How to Make a Go of Your Business, by Linda Hawarth Mackay; 6×9 in., softbound, 73 pp., 1986; SBA Small Business Management Series No. 44; order number S/N 045-000-00233-1. Written to acquaint the small business owner-manager with the basic tools of sound financial management. Covers the need for financial planning, understanding financial statements, a health checkup for your business, financial ratio analysis, forecasting profits, cash-flow management, budgeting and controlling costs, pricing policies, forecasting and obtaining capital, financial management planning.

Franchise Index/Profile, by C. R. Stigelman; 6×9 in., softbound, 55 pp., 1986; SBA Small Business Management Series No. 35; order number S/N 045-000-00231-4. A questionnaire approach to help prospective franchisees to determine if a specific franchise is right for them and to evaluate chances for monetary returns. Questions include: "Is the product or service considered reputable?" "Is the franchise local, regional, national, or international?" "Why have franchises failed?" "Is the franchise exclusive or nonexclusive?" And more. From the answers, a franchise profile is created. Includes appendix information about the Federal Trade Commission disclosure documents required, about the International Franchise Association, and about the Small Business Administration.

Franchise Opportunities Handbook, 21st ed., compiled by Andrew Kostecka; 8.5×11 in., softbound, 303 pp., 1988; International Trade Association, Department of Commerce, and the Minority Business Development Agency; order number S/N 003-009-00528-1. Directory that lists more than 1,700 franchisers from AAMCO Transmissions to ZM Video Rental. Each listed franchise includes addresses, description of operations, number of franchisees, equity capital needed, training provided, managerial assistance, and more. Introduction discusses franchising, investing in a franchise, code of ethics, government assistance programs, nongovernment assistance and information, and sources of franchising information. Also includes a checklist with which to evaluate a franchise.

Handbook for Small Business, A Survey of Small Business Programs of the Federal Government, 5th ed., Committee on Small Business, United States Senate; 8.5 × 11 in., softbound, 228 pp., 1984; Senate Document No. 98–33; order number S/N 052–071–00680–0. Brief descriptions of selected federal programs that are designed to assist small businesses. Departmental and agency listings include: Agriculture, Commerce, Defense, Education, Energy, Environmental Protection Agency, Export-Import Bank, Federal Trade Commission, General Accounting Office, General Services Administration, Health and Human Services, Housing and Urban Development, Interior, Interstate Commerce Commission, Justice, Labor, National Aeronautics and Space Administration, Securities and Exchange Commission, Small Business Administration, State and AID, Tennessee Valley Authority, Transportation, Treasury, United States Trade Representative, and Veterans Administration.

How to Buy or Sell a Business, by John A. Johansen; 8.5 × 11 in., softbound, 12 pp., 1988; SBA Management Aids No. 2.029; order number S/N 045–000–00251–9. An outline of buying and selling factors, and of the procedures involved in structuring transactions, negotiations, and settlements. Contains discussions of making the decision to buy or sell a business, preparing the business for sale, finding buyers and sellers, evaluating the business, financing the purchase, pricing the business, the role of advisors, structuring the transaction, negotiation, making and evaluating offers, closing the transaction.

Researching Your Market, by J. Ford Laumer, Jr., James R. Harris, Hugh J. Guffey, Jr., and Robert C. Erffmeyer; 8.5 × 11 in., softbound, 8 pp., 1988; SBA; order number S/N 045–000–00245–4. Description of what market research is and how it is accomplished. Presents inexpensive techniques that small business owner-managers can use to gather facts about their customers and prospective customers. Includes what marketing research is, why it is needed, how to do it, defining the problem, assessing available information, gathering additional information, going outside for marketing research data, and what you can do. Contains a bibliography of helpful government and nongovernment publications.

Starting and Managing a Small Business of Your Own, by Oliver Galbraith III; 6 × 9 in., softbound, 76 pp., 1982; SBA Starting and Managing Series, vol. 1; order number S/N 045–000–00212–8. One of the most popular books ever offered for sale by the Superintendent of Documents. Beginning with the chapter "So You Are Thinking of Going into Business," the book includes chapters on starting the new business, buying a going business, investing in a franchise, managing your business, looking into special requirements and needs, women and minority owners, and "Decision Time."

Starting and Managing a Small Service Business, by Robert A. Schaefer; 6 × 9 in., softbound, 57 pp., 1986; SBA Starting and Managing Series, vol. 101; order number S/N 045–000–00238. A start-up aid for those who plan to establish their own service business. Includes advice on how to get experience, buying procedures, bookkeeping, and more. Covers selecting the right business for you, skills needed, need for the service, capital needed, preparing for the opening, building the business, keeping track of the business.

Internal Revenue Service Publications

A number of Internal Revenue Service (IRS) publications apply directly and specifically to small businesses, others have either indirect application or apply to personal finances and tax laws. While you should rely on the professional advice of an accountant or tax attorney regarding your tax records, you will be well advised to obtain and study copies of the IRS publications described below.

Local libraries often have copies of most or all of these publications. Your accountant or tax attorney are other sources. Or you can obtain your own copies at no cost from the IRS Distribution Center for your state, as follows:

- Rancho Cordova, CA 95743–0001: For Alaska, Arizona, California, Colorado, Hawaii, Idaho, Montana, Nevada, New Mexico, Oregon, Utah, Washington, Wyoming.
- PO Box 9903, Bloomington, IL 61799: For Alabama, Arkansas, Illinois, Indiana; Iowa, Kansas, Kentucky, Louisiana, Michigan, Minnesota, Mississippi, Missouri, Nebraska, North Dakota, Ohio, Oklahoma, South Dakota, Tennessee, Texas, Wisconsin.
- PO Box 25866, Richmond, VA 23289: For Connecticut, Delaware, District of Columbia, Florida, Georgia, Maine, Maryland, Massachusetts, New Hampshire, New Jersey, New York, North Carolina, Pennsylvania, Rhode Island, South Carolina, Vermont, Virginia, West Virginia.
- Forms Distribution Center, PO Box 25866, Richmond, VA 23289: For Puerto Rico.
- V.I. Bureau of Internal Revenue, Lockharts Garden, No. 1A, Charlotte Amalie, St. Thomas, VI 00802: For Virgin Islands.

Your Rights as a Taxpayer, Publication 1. Four pages listing your rights as a taxpayer, including free information and help preparing returns, privacy and confidentiality, appeals of examination findings, income-tax appeal procedure, cancellation of penalties, special help to resolve problems, and a list of Taxpayer Assistance Numbers.

Tax Guide for Small Business, Publication 334. 181 pages covering income, excise, and employment taxes for individuals, sole proprietorships, partnerships, corporations, and S corporations. Includes business organization considerations, books and records, accounting periods and methods, capital expenditures and business assets, how to figure gross profit, how to figure net income or loss, disposing of business assets, credits, other taxes, and information returns. Sample filled-in tax forms for sole proprietorships, partnerships, S corporations, and regular corporations (long and short forms).

Travel, Entertainment, and Gift Expenses, Publication 463. 20 pages regarding business-related expenses that you can deduct on your income tax returns.

Covers rules for the self-employed person, as well as for employees and employers. Includes travel expenses, mean and entertainment expenses, business gift expenses, how to report these expenses. Contains examples.

Tax Withholding and Estimated Tax, Publication 505. 36 pages with information on tax withholding and estimated tax, covering salaries and wages, tips, fringe benefits, sick pay, pensions and annuities, gambling winnings, backup withholding, and advance earned income credit. For estimated tax, covers who must make estimated tax payments, how to figure the payments, how much estimated tax to pay, and how to pay it. Also discusses rules regarding penalties for underpayment of taxes.

Taxable and Nontaxable Income, Publication 525. 30 pages covering types of income and whether or not they are exempt from taxation. Covers all types of employee compensation (fringe, disability, stock-option, miscellaneous), special rules (for clergy, foreign employer, military, veterans, volunteers), miscellaneous taxable income (bartering, below-market loans, partnership income, S corporation income, recoveries, repayments, royalties, unemployment compensation), and income that is not taxed (life insurance proceeds, welfare and public assistance payments). Has standard deduction table and worksheets for refunds of itemized deductions.

Self-Employment Tax, Publication 533. 8 pages covering who must pay self-employment taxes, the distinction between self-employment income and other types of income, and how to figure the amount of self-employment tax. Covers the Short and Long Schedules SE, the Farm and Nonfarm Optional Methods, and an example of Schedule SE.

Depreciation, Publication 534. 111 pages covering depreciation and the Section-179 deduction for recovery of cost of business or income-producing property used for more than one tax year. Covers what can be depreciated, when to claim depreciation, recapture of the Section-179 deduction, MACRS (assets placed in service after 1986), ACRS (assets placed in service after 1980 and before 1987), passenger automobiles, partial business use and associated records, depreciation recovery, figuring depreciation, example Form 4562, and related tables.

Business Expenses, Publication 535. 39 pages regarding common business expenses that are and are not deductible. Covers employee pay and fringe benefits, rent, interest, taxes, insurance, amortization, depletion, costs you can either deduct or capitalize, and other expenses.

Net Operating Losses, Publication 536. 12 pages covering NOL (net operating loss), which results when deductions for the year exceed income for the year. Covers NOL steps, how to figure NOL, when to use NOL, how to use NOL, how to take a NOL deduction. Includes partnerships, regular and S corporations, and a NOL worksheet.

Accounting Periods and Methods, Publication 538. 20 pages of rules for accounting periods and methods for partnerships and S and personal service corporations. Covers calendar and fiscal tax years, the 52–53 week and the short tax year, changing the accounting period, an improper tax year, excise tax periods, employment tax periods, and Section 444 election. Also covers cash or accrual accounting methods, inventory evaluation and cost identification, uniform capitalization rules, and user fees.

Tax Information on Corporations, Publication 542. 31 pages primarily concerned with ordinary domestic corporations subject to the general tax laws. Includes filing forms 1120 and 1120–A, amending returns, where and when to file, forming a corporation (stock issuance, start-up expenses, organizational expenses), special provisions (below-market loan, stock transfer, golden parachute payments, adjustments-tax preferences, dividends, reduction in stock basis, charitable contributions, capital losses, related taxpayers), net income or loss, figuring the tax, the alternative minimum tax, the minimum tax credit, the estimated income tax, capital contributions and retained earnings, reconciliation statements, distributions, liquidations and stock redemptions, sample returns, and fees for rulings, determinations, and opinions.

Basis of Assets, Publication 551. 8 pages on "basis" when measuring your investment in property for tax purposes, with adjustments for depreciation, amortization, depletion, and casualty losses. Covers cost basis, other basis, and adjusted basis.

Self-Employed Retirement Plans, Publication 560. 24 pages regarding retirement plans for self-employed persons, including certain partners in partnerships; includes Keogh (H.R. 10) plans. Covers types of plans, Keogh plan tax benefits, deductions for contributions (employer, voluntary, profit-sharing plan, money purchase pension plan, elective deferrals, when contributions are considered made), tax on distributions (rollovers, premature and excess distributions, loans treated as distributions, withholding and estimated tax), prohibited transactions, investing-plan assets, reporting requirements, plan qualification rules, definitions, form 5500EZ example.

Business Use of Your Home, Publication 587. 7 pages with rules and tests for deduction of an office in your home. Includes use tests (exclusive, exceptions to exclusive use test, regular use, principal place of business, place to meet patients (or clients, separate structures, trade or business use), figuring the business percentage of your home, what to deduct, recordkeeping, deduction limitation, day-care facility, sale or exchange of home, and a Schedule C example and worksheet instructions.

Tax Information on S Corporations, Publication 589. 23 pages covering all aspects of the S corporation. Includes becoming an S corporation (requirements, tax year, electing S status, filing form 2553), filing form 11205, S corporation taxes, income, expenses, and distributions to shareholders, terminating S corporation status, and a sample return.

Information Returns, Publication 916. 16 pages discussing those forms you must file when you have made a payment, as to an independent contractor, where you are not required to withhold taxes. Covers forms for acquisition or abandonment of acquired property, proceeds from broker and barter-exchange transactions, distributions of dividends, recipients of certain government payments, recipients of interest income, miscellaneous income, and more.

Business Use of a Car, Publication 917. 20 pages regarding expenses that can be deducted on your income tax form for business use of your car. Discusses commuting expenses, standard mileage rates, deduction of actual expenses, leasing a car, car provided by employer for combined business/personal use, recordkeeping, how to report car expenses, examples.

Explanation of the Tax Reform Act of 1986 for Business, Publication 921. 36 pages providing an overview of the major provisions of the law and how they differ from the previous law; also, which old-law provisions were repealed. Covers gross income, business expenses, depreciation, tax credits, corporation taxes, employee benefit plans, penalties, accounting periods and methods, excise taxes, miscellaneous provisions, and more.

Index